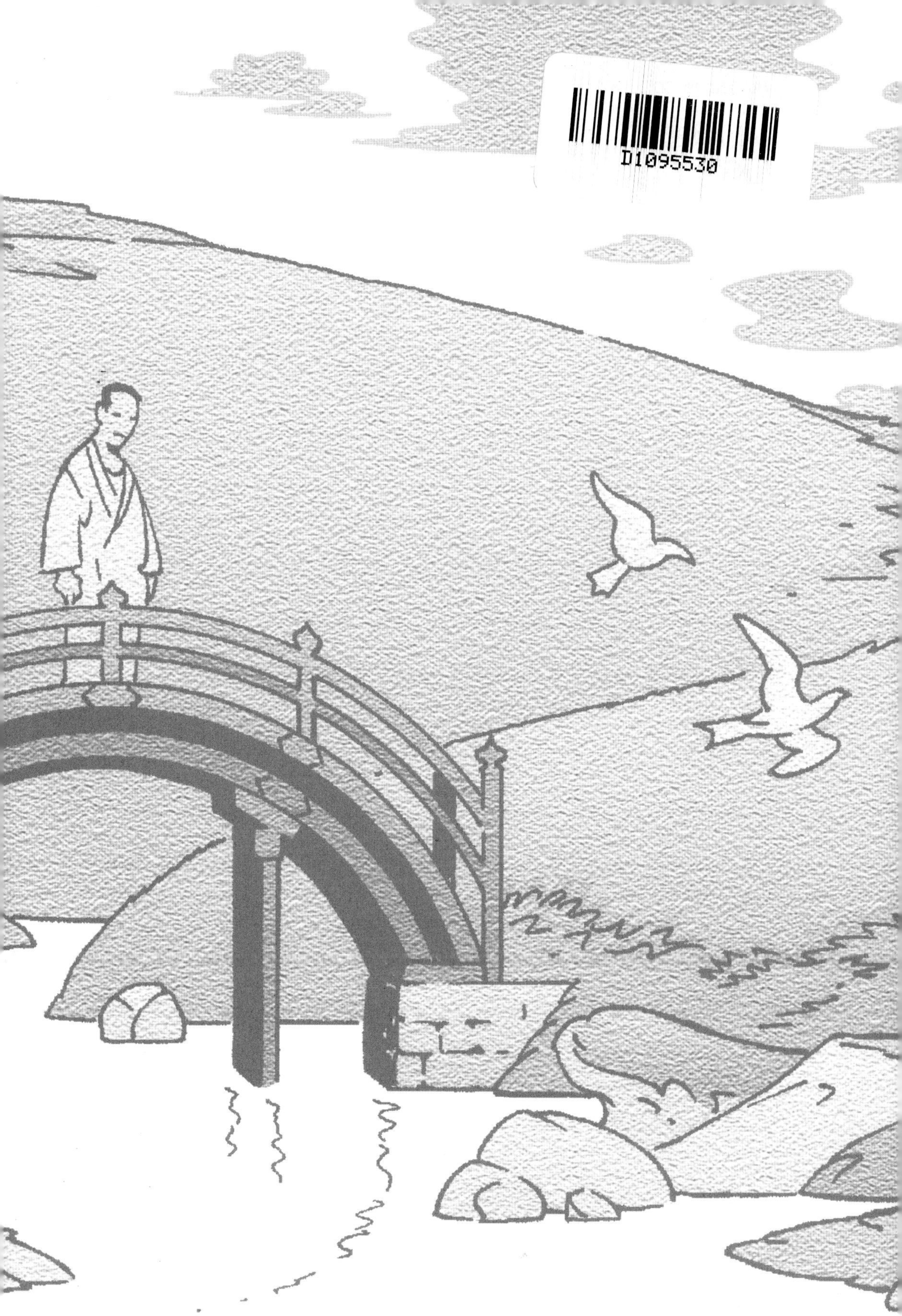

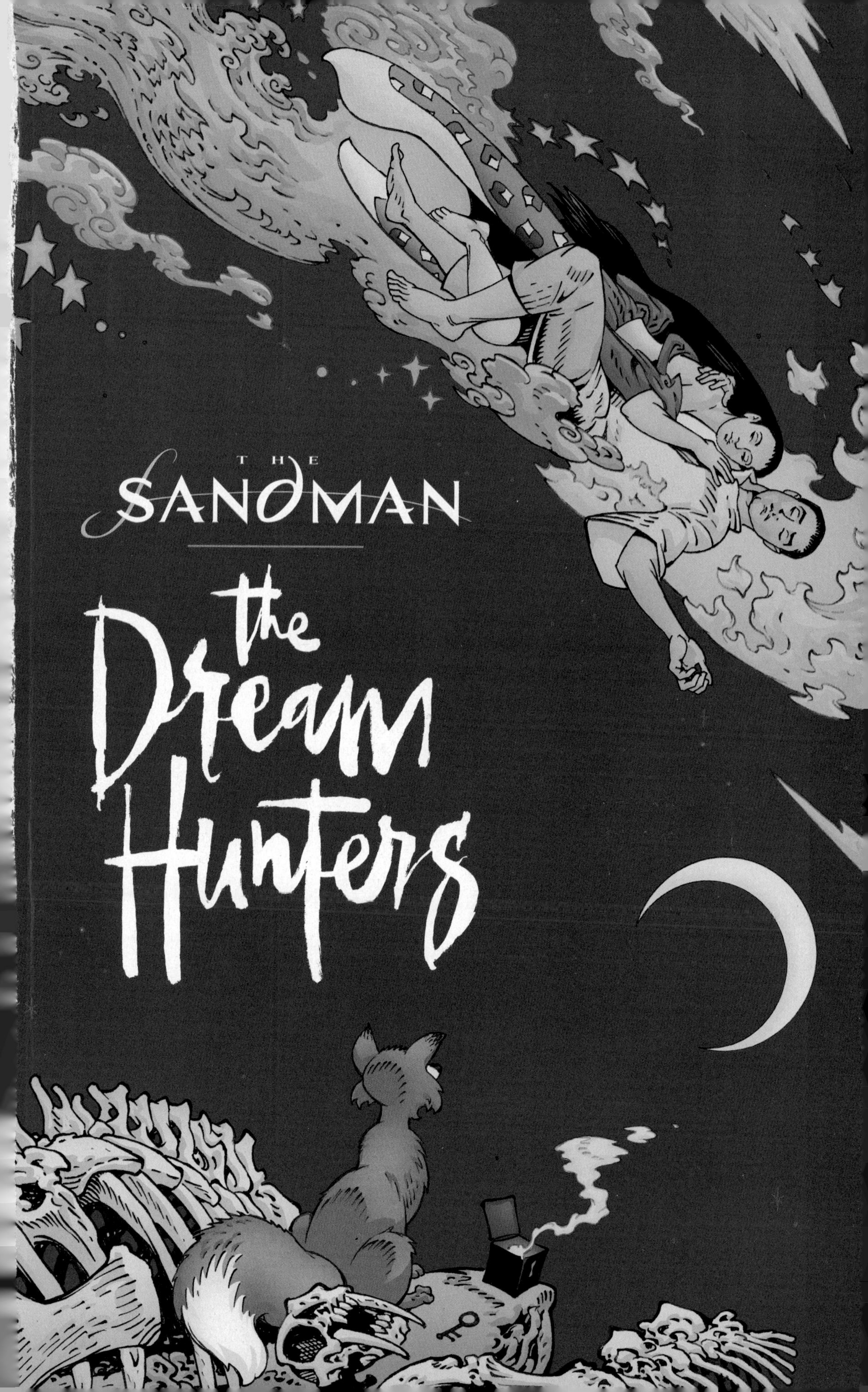
THE SANDMAN
the Dream Hunters

the Dream

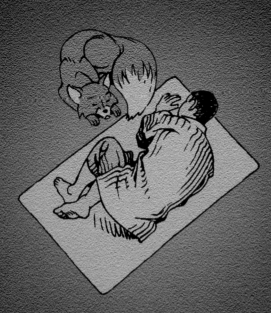

THE SANDMAN

Hunters

Original words by **Neil Gaiman**

Graphicplay and art by **P. Craig Russell**

Coloring by **Lovern Kindzierski**

Lettering by **Todd Klein**

Sandman characters created by **Gaiman, Kieth and Dringenberg**

Ise Monogatari translation by **Sheldon Drzka**

Adapted by P. Craig Russell from the multi-award-winning illustrated novella
THE SANDMAN: THE DREAM HUNTERS by Neil Gaiman and Yoshitaka Amano

Cover by P. Craig Russell. | Cover color by Lovern Kindzierski. | THE DREAM HUNTERS logo by Nancy Ogami.

THE SANDMAN: THE DREAM HUNTERS

Published by DC Comics. Cover, text and compilation Copyright © 2009 DC Comics. All Rights Reserved.

Originally published as THE SANDMAN: THE DREAM HUNTERS 1 - 4. Copyright © 2009 DC Comics.

All Rights Reserved. Vertigo, Sandman and all characters, their distinctive likenesses and related elements featured in this publication are trademarks of DC Comics. The stories, characters and incidents featured in this publication are entirely fictional. DC Comics does not read or accept unsolicited submissions of ideas, stories or artwork.

DC Comics
1700 Broadway, New York, NY 10019.
A Warner Bros. Entertainment Company.

Printed in the USA. First Printing.
HC ISBN: 978-1-4012-2424-0
SC ISBN: 978-1-4012-2428-8

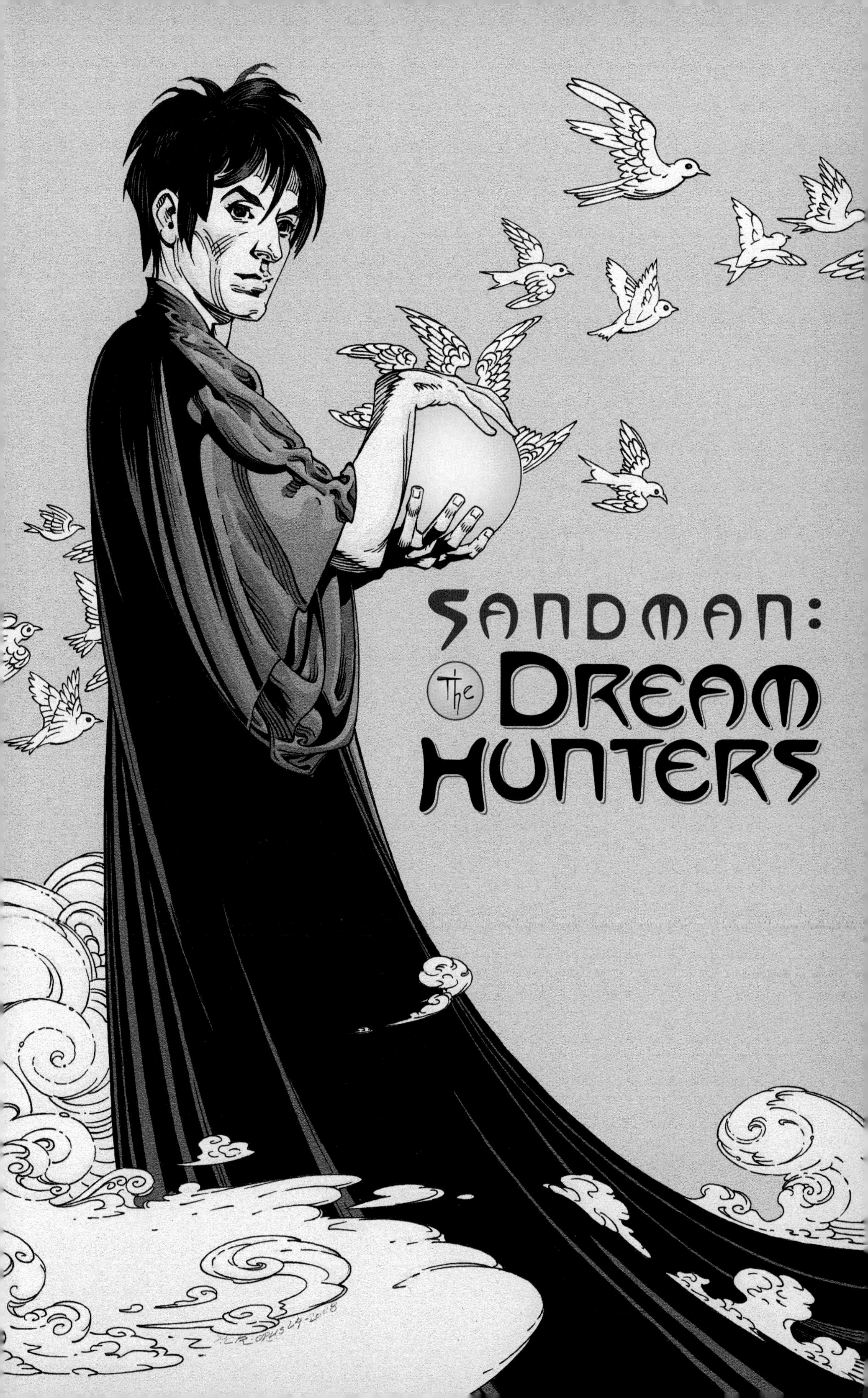
SANDMAN:
The DREAM HUNTERS

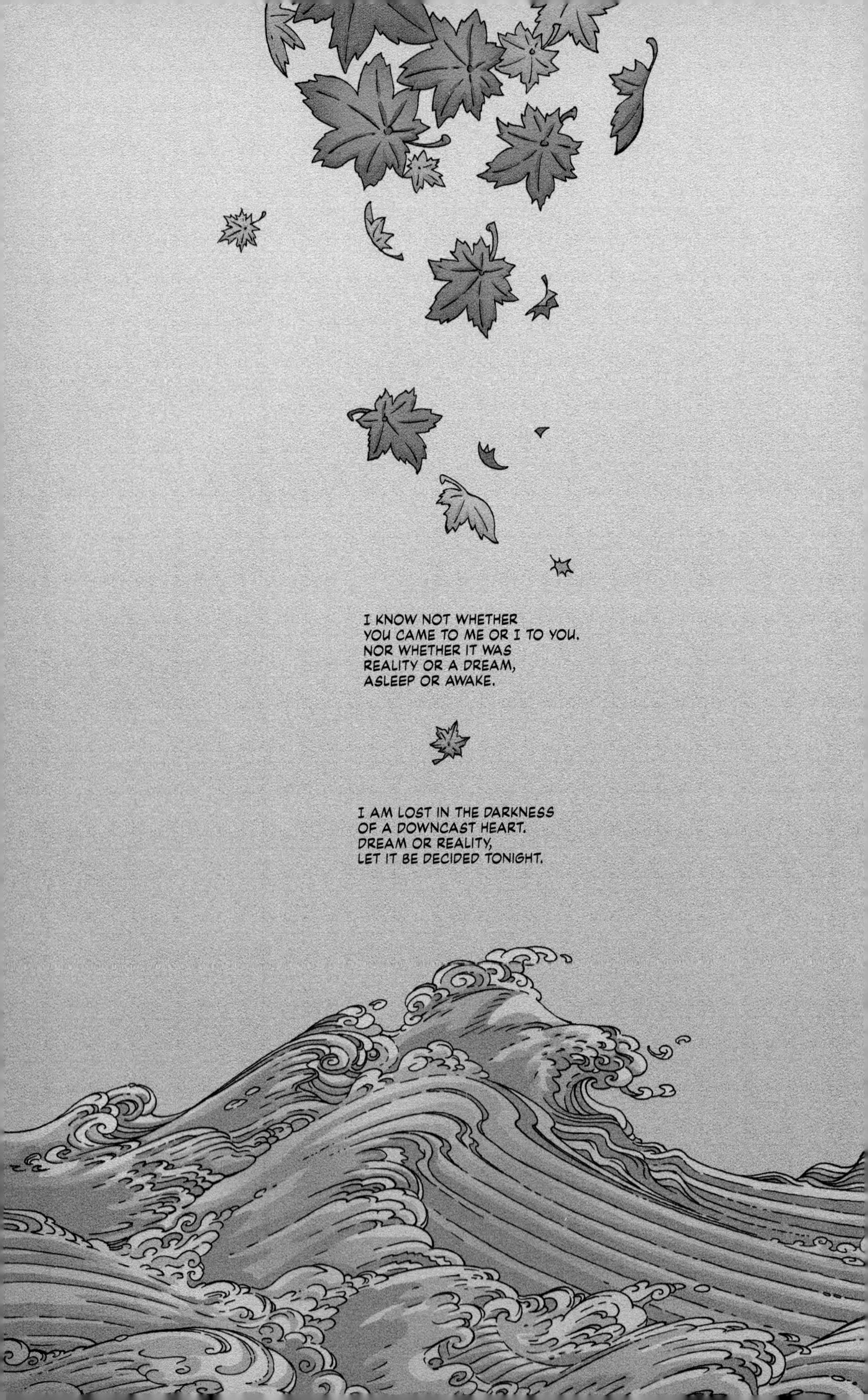
I KNOW NOT WHETHER
YOU CAME TO ME OR I TO YOU.
NOR WHETHER IT WAS
REALITY OR A DREAM,
ASLEEP OR AWAKE.
I AM LOST IN THE DARKNESS
OF A DOWNCAST HEART.
DREAM OR REALITY,
LET IT BE DECIDED TONIGHT.

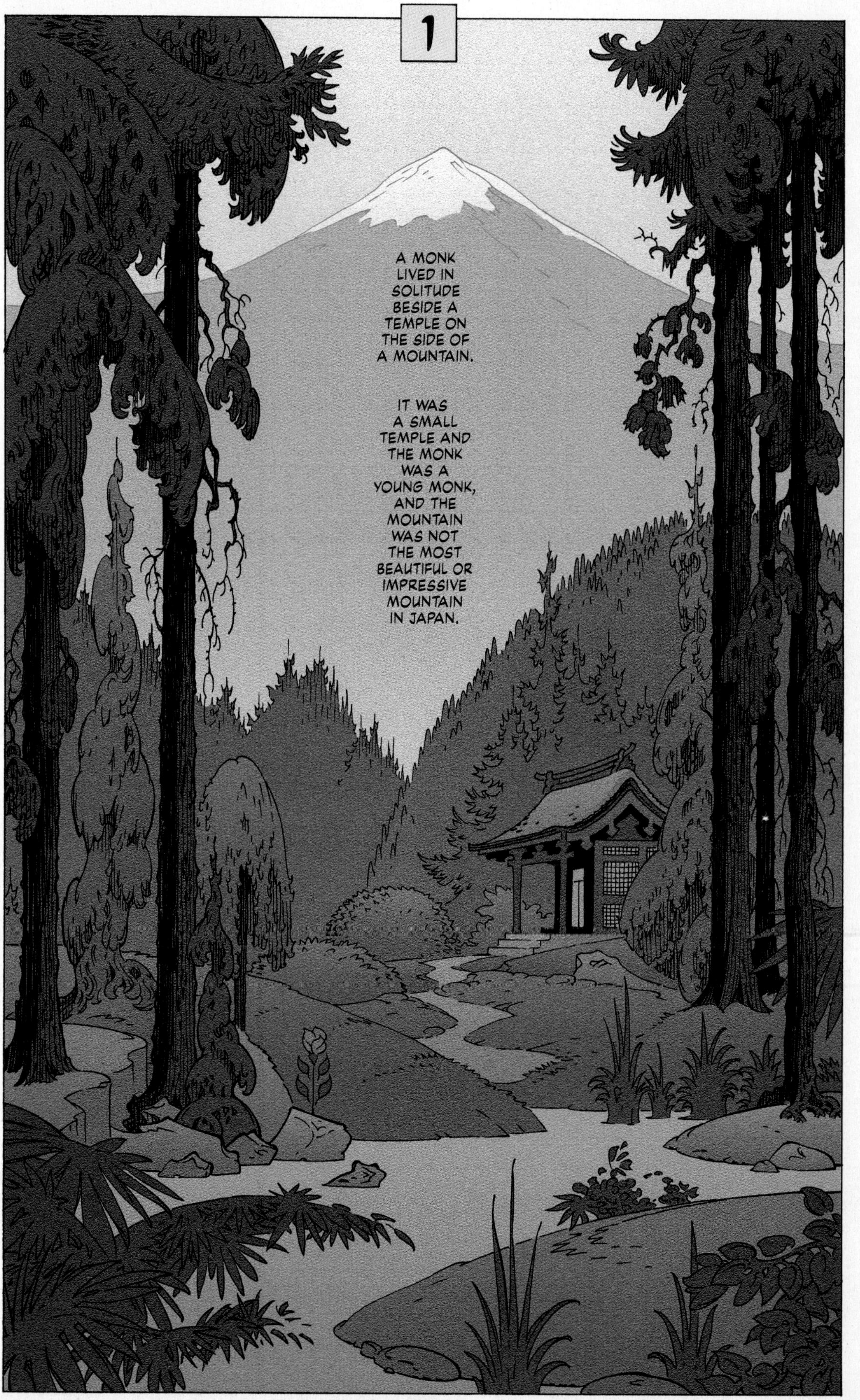
1
A MONK LIVED IN SOLITUDE BESIDE A TEMPLE ON THE SIDE OF A MOUNTAIN.
IT WAS A SMALL TEMPLE AND THE MONK WAS A YOUNG MONK, AND THE MOUNTAIN WAS NOT THE MOST BEAUTIFUL OR IMPRESSIVE MOUNTAIN IN JAPAN.

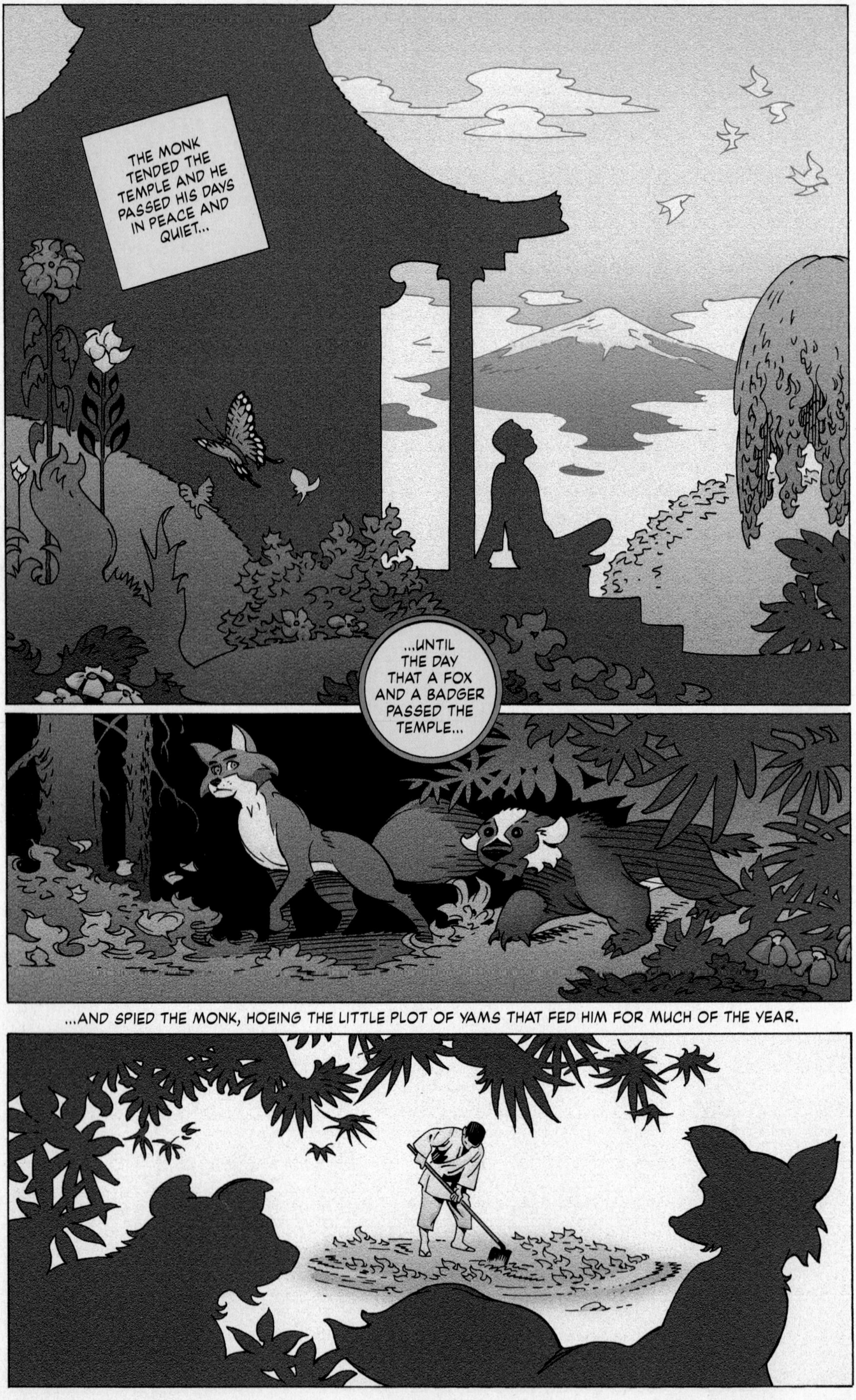
THE MONK TENDED THE TEMPLE AND HE PASSED HIS DAYS IN PEACE AND QUIET...
...UNTIL THE DAY THAT A FOX AND A BADGER PASSED THE TEMPLE...
...AND SPIED THE MONK, HOEING THE LITTLE PLOT OF YAMS THAT FED HIM FOR MUCH OF THE YEAR.

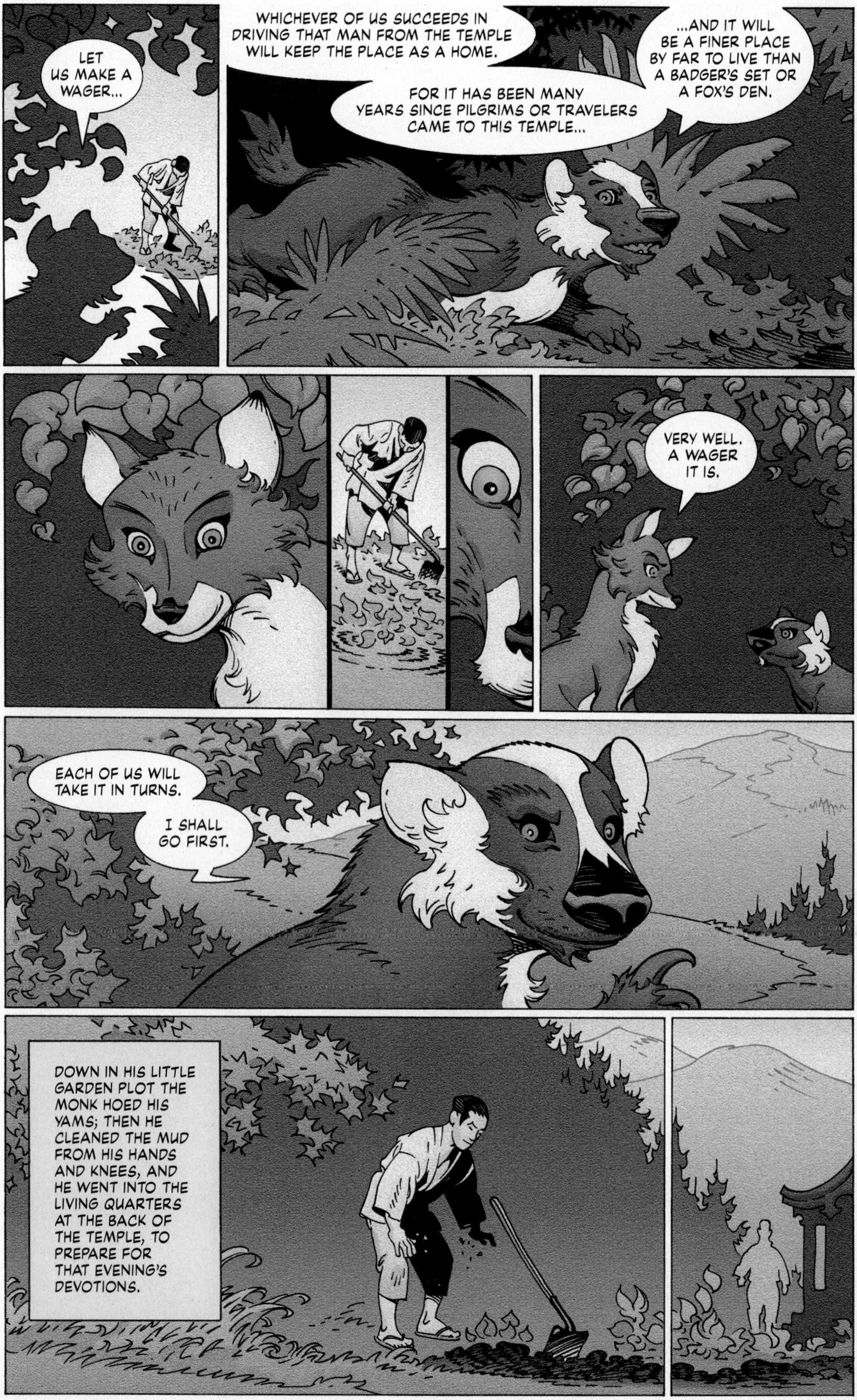
LET US MAKE A WAGER...
WHICHEVER OF US SUCCEEDS IN DRIVING THAT MAN FROM THE TEMPLE WILL KEEP THE PLACE AS A HOME.
FOR IT HAS BEEN MANY YEARS SINCE PILGRIMS OR TRAVELERS CAME TO THIS TEMPLE...
...AND IT WILL BE A FINER PLACE BY FAR TO LIVE THAN A BADGER'S SET OR A FOX'S DEN.
VERY WELL. A WAGER IT IS.
EACH OF US WILL TAKE IT IN TURNS.
I SHALL GO FIRST.
DOWN IN HIS LITTLE GARDEN PLOT THE MONK HOED HIS YAMS; THEN HE CLEANED THE MUD FROM HIS HANDS AND KNEES, AND HE WENT INTO THE LIVING QUARTERS AT THE BACK OF THE TEMPLE, TO PREPARE FOR THAT EVENING'S DEVOTIONS.

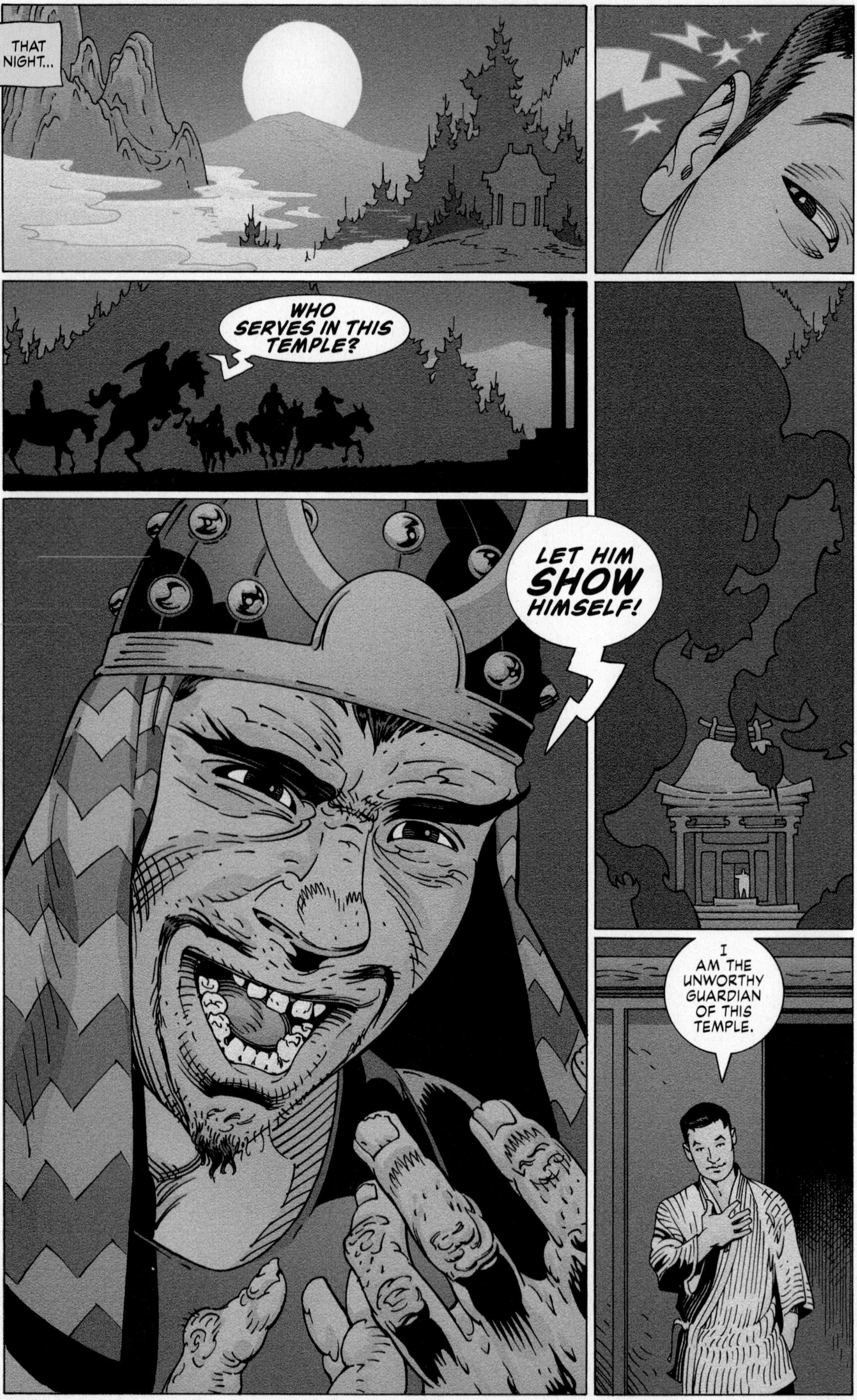
THAT NIGHT...
WHO SERVES IN THIS TEMPLE?
LET HIM SHOW HIMSELF!
I AM THE UNWORTHY GUARDIAN OF THIS TEMPLE.

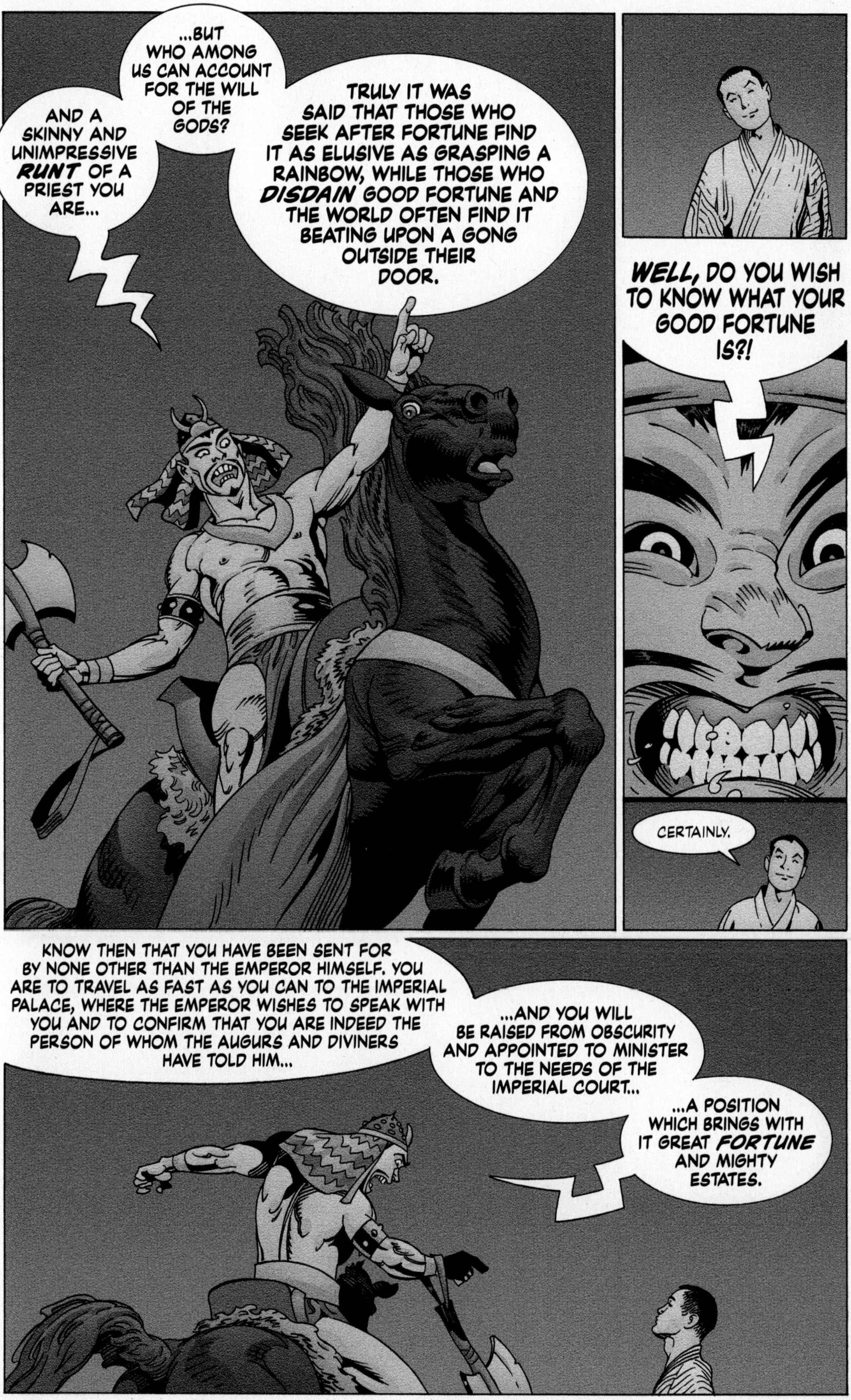
AND A SKINNY AND UNIMPRESSIVE RUNT OF A PRIEST YOU ARE...
...BUT WHO AMONG US CAN ACCOUNT FOR THE WILL OF THE GODS?
TRULY IT WAS SAID THAT THOSE WHO SEEK AFTER FORTUNE FIND IT AS ELUSIVE AS GRASPING A RAINBOW, WHILE THOSE WHO DISDAIN GOOD FORTUNE AND THE WORLD OFTEN FIND IT BEATING UPON A GONG OUTSIDE THEIR DOOR.
WELL, DO YOU WISH TO KNOW WHAT YOUR GOOD FORTUNE IS?!
CERTAINLY.
KNOW THEN THAT YOU HAVE BEEN SENT FOR BY NONE OTHER THAN THE EMPEROR HIMSELF. YOU ARE TO TRAVEL AS FAST AS YOU CAN TO THE IMPERIAL PALACE, WHERE THE EMPEROR WISHES TO SPEAK WITH YOU AND TO CONFIRM THAT YOU ARE INDEED THE PERSON OF WHOM THE AUGURS AND DIVINERS HAVE TOLD HIM...
...AND YOU WILL BE RAISED FROM OBSCURITY AND APPOINTED TO MINISTER TO THE NEEDS OF THE IMPERIAL COURT...
...A POSITION WHICH BRINGS WITH IT GREAT FORTUNE AND MIGHTY ESTATES.

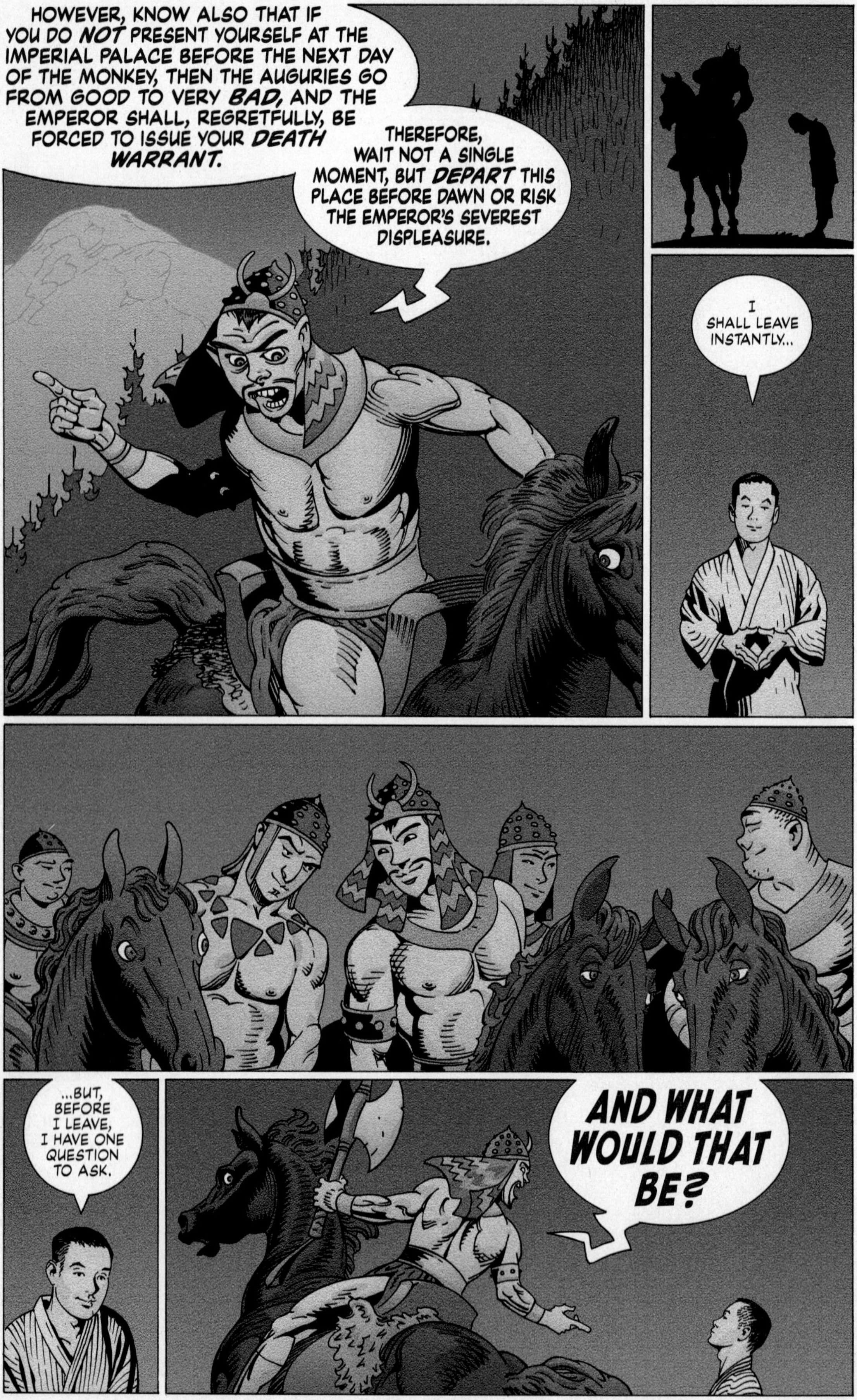
HOWEVER, KNOW ALSO THAT IF YOU DO NOT PRESENT YOURSELF AT THE IMPERIAL PALACE BEFORE THE NEXT DAY OF THE MONKEY, THEN THE AUGURIES GO FROM GOOD TO VERY BAD, AND THE EMPEROR SHALL, REGRETFULLY, BE FORCED TO ISSUE YOUR DEATH WARRANT.
THEREFORE, WAIT NOT A SINGLE MOMENT, BUT DEPART THIS PLACE BEFORE DAWN OR RISK THE EMPEROR'S SEVEREST DISPLEASURE.
I SHALL LEAVE INSTANTLY...
...BUT, BEFORE I LEAVE, I HAVE ONE QUESTION TO ASK.
AND WHAT WOULD THAT BE?

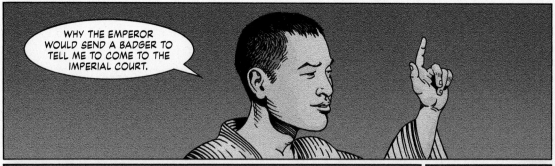

WHY THE EMPEROR WOULD SEND A BADGER TO TELL ME TO COME TO THE IMPERIAL COURT.

THE MONK HAD OBSERVED THAT WHILE THE FIRST FOUR HORSES HAD THE TAILS OF HORSES, THE LAST HORSE HAD THE TAIL OF A BADGER.

!

HA! HA! HA!

YIP! YIP! YIP!

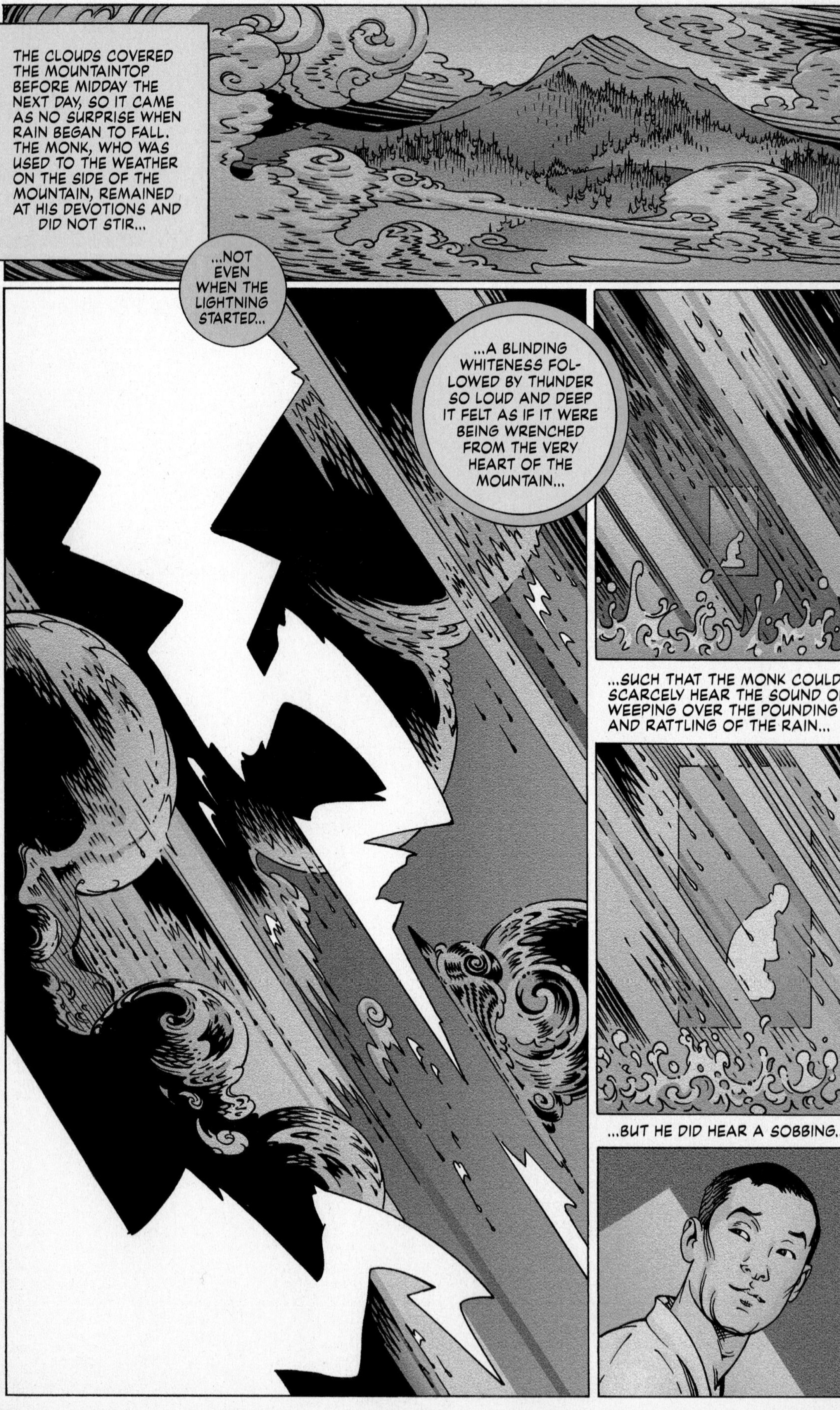
THE CLOUDS COVERED THE MOUNTAINTOP BEFORE MIDDAY THE NEXT DAY, SO IT CAME AS NO SURPRISE WHEN RAIN BEGAN TO FALL. THE MONK, WHO WAS USED TO THE WEATHER ON THE SIDE OF THE MOUNTAIN, REMAINED AT HIS DEVOTIONS AND DID NOT STIR...
...NOT EVEN WHEN THE LIGHTNING STARTED...
...A BLINDING WHITENESS FOL-LOWED BY THUNDER SO LOUD AND DEEP IT FELT AS IF IT WERE BEING WRENCHED FROM THE VERY HEART OF THE MOUNTAIN...
...SUCH THAT THE MONK COULD SCARCELY HEAR THE SOUND OF WEEPING OVER THE POUNDING AND RATTLING OF THE RAIN...
...BUT HE DID HEAR A SOBBING...

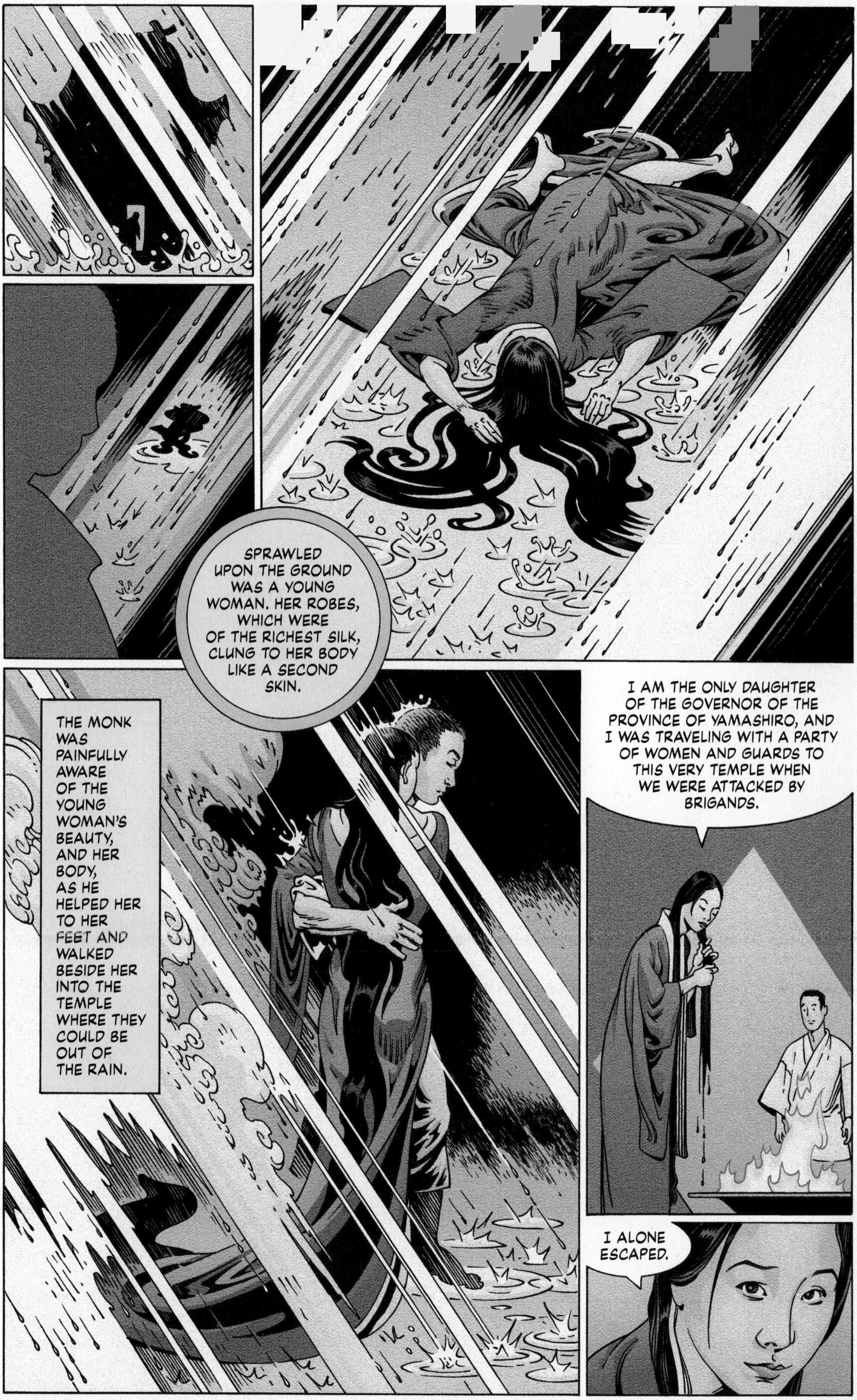
SPRAWLED UPON THE GROUND WAS A YOUNG WOMAN. HER ROBES, WHICH WERE OF THE RICHEST SILK, CLUNG TO HER BODY LIKE A SECOND SKIN.
THE MONK WAS PAINFULLY AWARE OF THE YOUNG WOMAN'S BEAUTY, AND HER BODY, AS HE HELPED HER TO HER FEET AND WALKED BESIDE HER INTO THE TEMPLE WHERE THEY COULD BE OUT OF THE RAIN.
I AM THE ONLY DAUGHTER OF THE GOVERNOR OF THE PROVINCE OF YAMASHIRO, AND I WAS TRAVELING WITH A PARTY OF WOMEN AND GUARDS TO THIS VERY TEMPLE WHEN WE WERE ATTACKED BY BRIGANDS.
I ALONE ESCAPED.

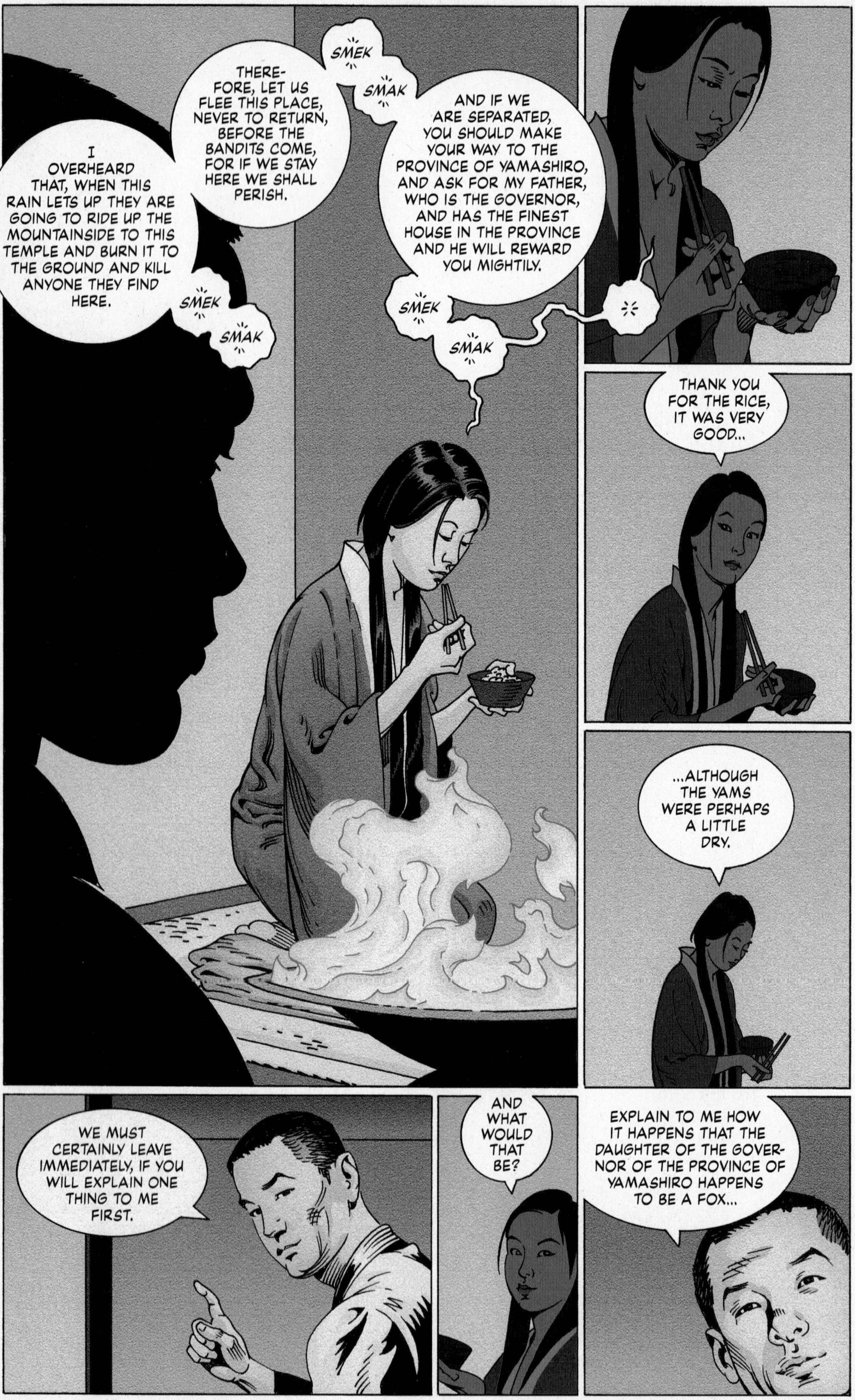
I OVERHEARD THAT, WHEN THIS RAIN LETS UP THEY ARE GOING TO RIDE UP THE MOUNTAINSIDE TO THIS TEMPLE AND BURN IT TO THE GROUND AND KILL ANYONE THEY FIND HERE.
SMEK
SMAK
THEREFORE, LET US FLEE THIS PLACE, NEVER TO RETURN, BEFORE THE BANDITS COME, FOR IF WE STAY HERE WE SHALL PERISH.
SMEK
SMAK
AND IF WE ARE SEPARATED, YOU SHOULD MAKE YOUR WAY TO THE PROVINCE OF YAMASHIRO, AND ASK FOR MY FATHER, WHO IS THE GOVERNOR, AND HAS THE FINEST HOUSE IN THE PROVINCE AND HE WILL REWARD YOU MIGHTILY.
SMEK
SMAK
THANK YOU FOR THE RICE, IT WAS VERY GOOD...
...ALTHOUGH THE YAMS WERE PERHAPS A LITTLE DRY.
WE MUST CERTAINLY LEAVE IMMEDIATELY, IF YOU WILL EXPLAIN ONE THING TO ME FIRST.
AND WHAT WOULD THAT BE?
EXPLAIN TO ME HOW IT HAPPENS THAT THE DAUGHTER OF THE GOVERNOR OF THE PROVINCE OF YAMASHIRO HAPPENS TO BE A FOX...

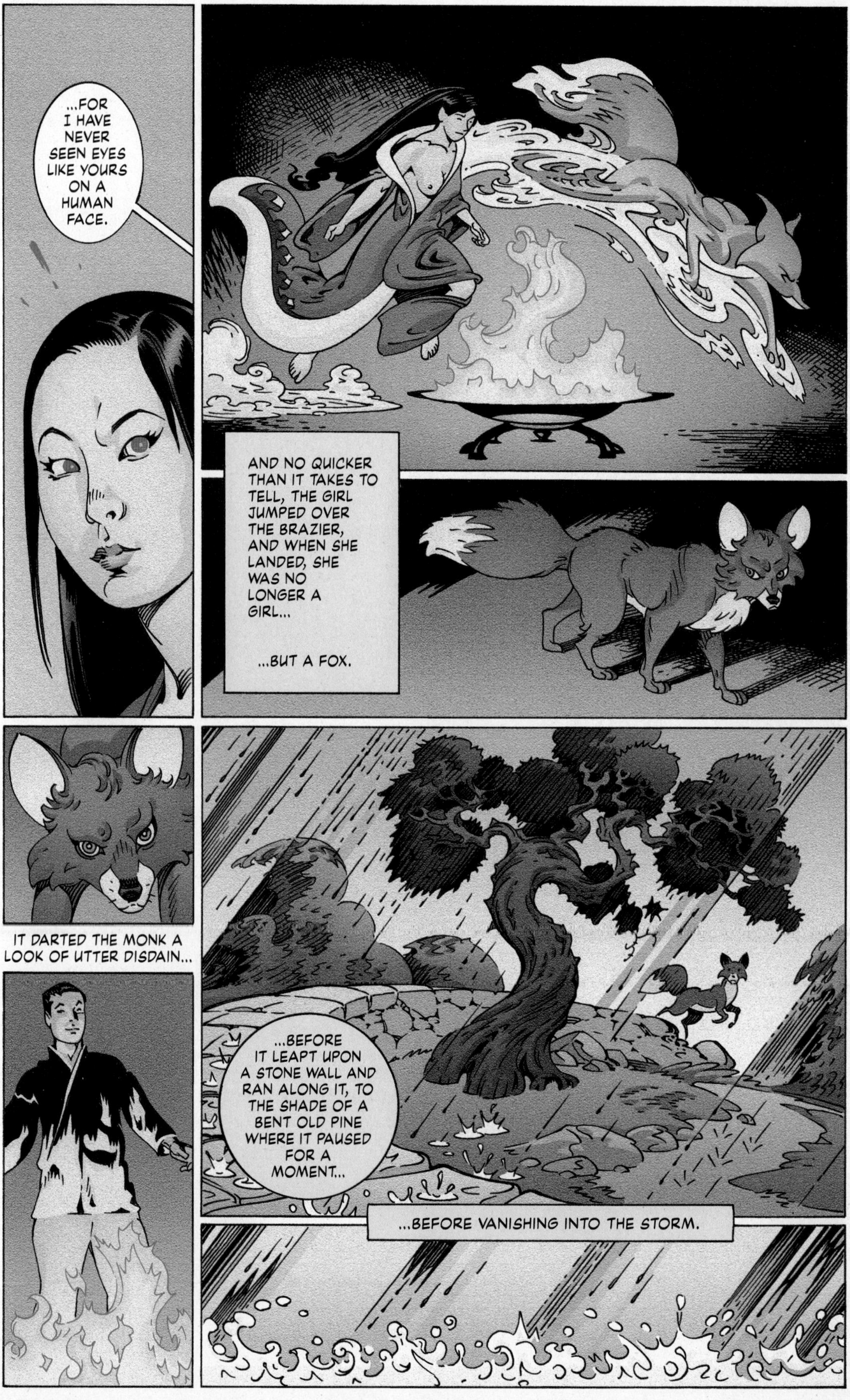
...FOR I HAVE NEVER SEEN EYES LIKE YOURS ON A HUMAN FACE.
AND NO QUICKER THAN IT TAKES TO TELL, THE GIRL JUMPED OVER THE BRAZIER, AND WHEN SHE LANDED, SHE WAS NO LONGER A GIRL...
...BUT A FOX.
IT DARTED THE MONK A LOOK OF UTTER DISDAIN...
...BEFORE IT LEAPT UPON A STONE WALL AND RAN ALONG IT, TO THE SHADE OF A BENT OLD PINE WHERE IT PAUSED FOR A MOMENT...
...BEFORE VANISHING INTO THE STORM.

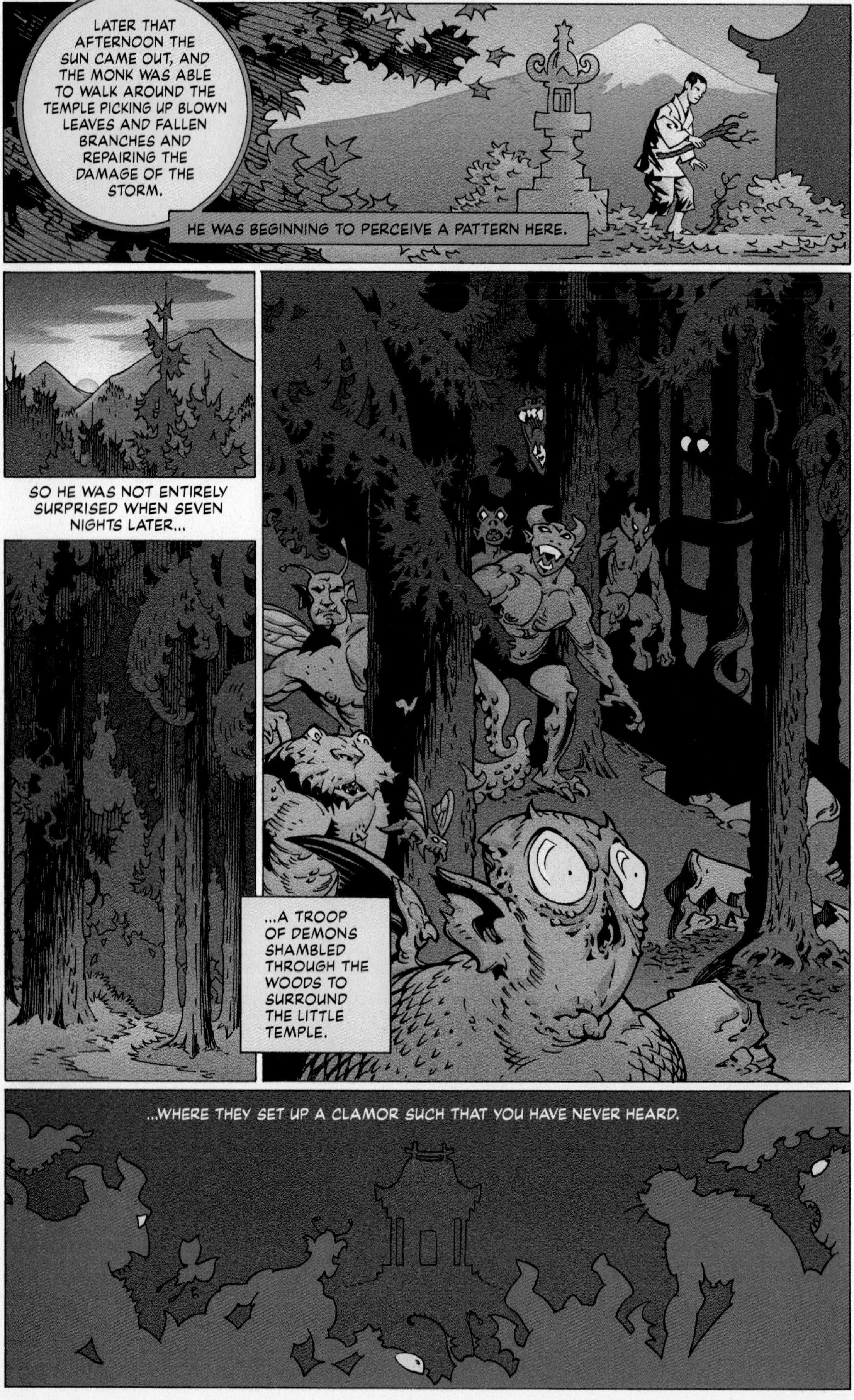
LATER THAT AFTERNOON THE SUN CAME OUT, AND THE MONK WAS ABLE TO WALK AROUND THE TEMPLE PICKING UP BLOWN LEAVES AND FALLEN BRANCHES AND REPAIRING THE DAMAGE OF THE STORM.
HE WAS BEGINNING TO PERCEIVE A PATTERN HERE.
SO HE WAS NOT ENTIRELY SURPRISED WHEN SEVEN NIGHTS LATER...
...A TROOP OF DEMONS SHAMBLED THROUGH THE WOODS TO SURROUND THE LITTLE TEMPLE.
...WHERE THEY SET UP A CLAMOR SUCH THAT YOU HAVE NEVER HEARD.

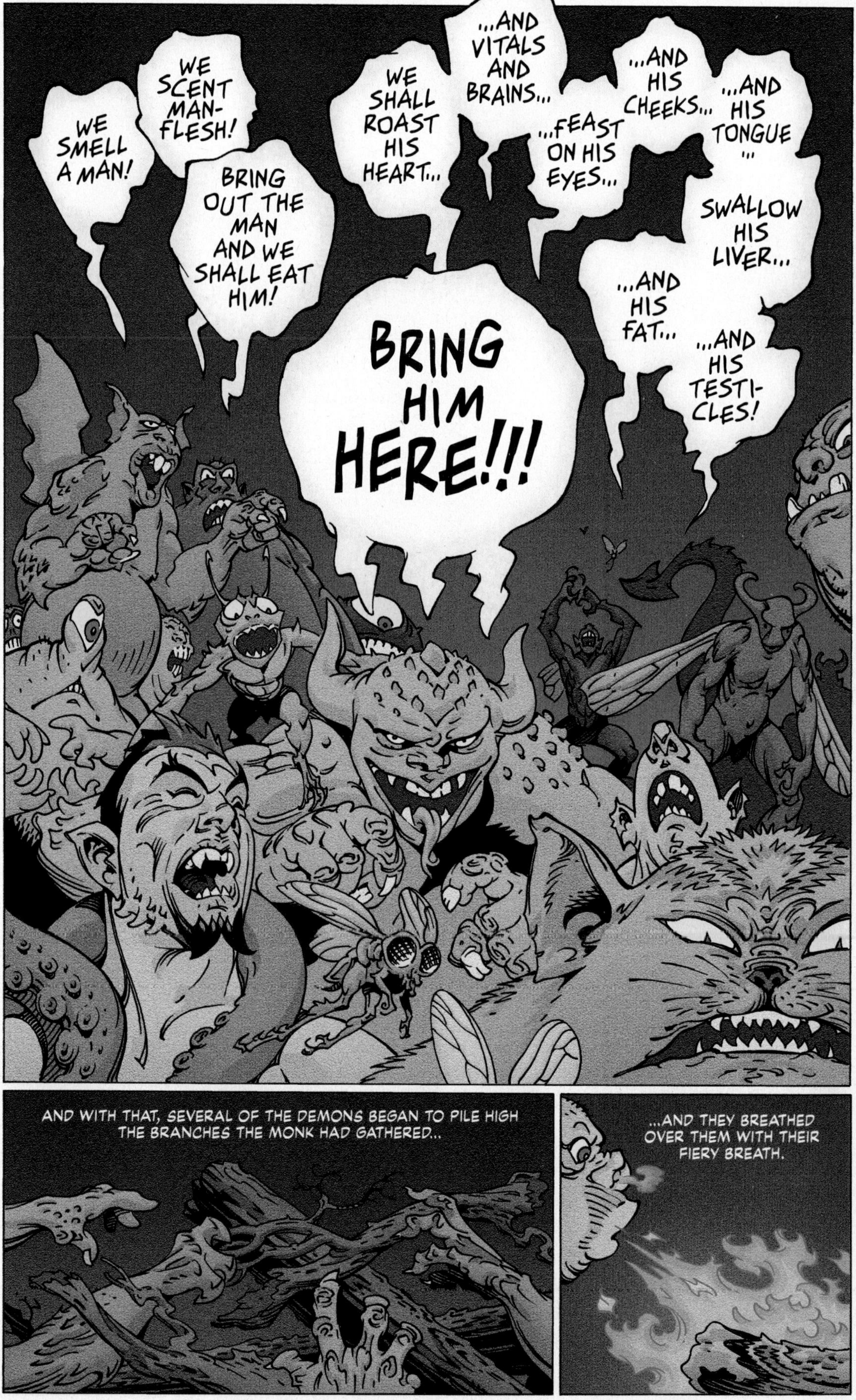
WE SMELL A MAN!
WE SCENT MAN-FLESH!
BRING OUT THE MAN AND WE SHALL EAT HIM!
WE SHALL ROAST HIS HEART...
...AND VITALS AND BRAINS...
...FEAST ON HIS EYES...
...AND HIS CHEEKS...
...AND HIS TONGUE...
SWALLOW HIS LIVER...
...AND HIS FAT...
...AND HIS TESTICLES!
BRING HIM HERE!!!
AND WITH THAT, SEVERAL OF THE DEMONS BEGAN TO PILE HIGH THE BRANCHES THE MONK HAD GATHERED...
...AND THEY BREATHED OVER THEM WITH THEIR FIERY BREATH.

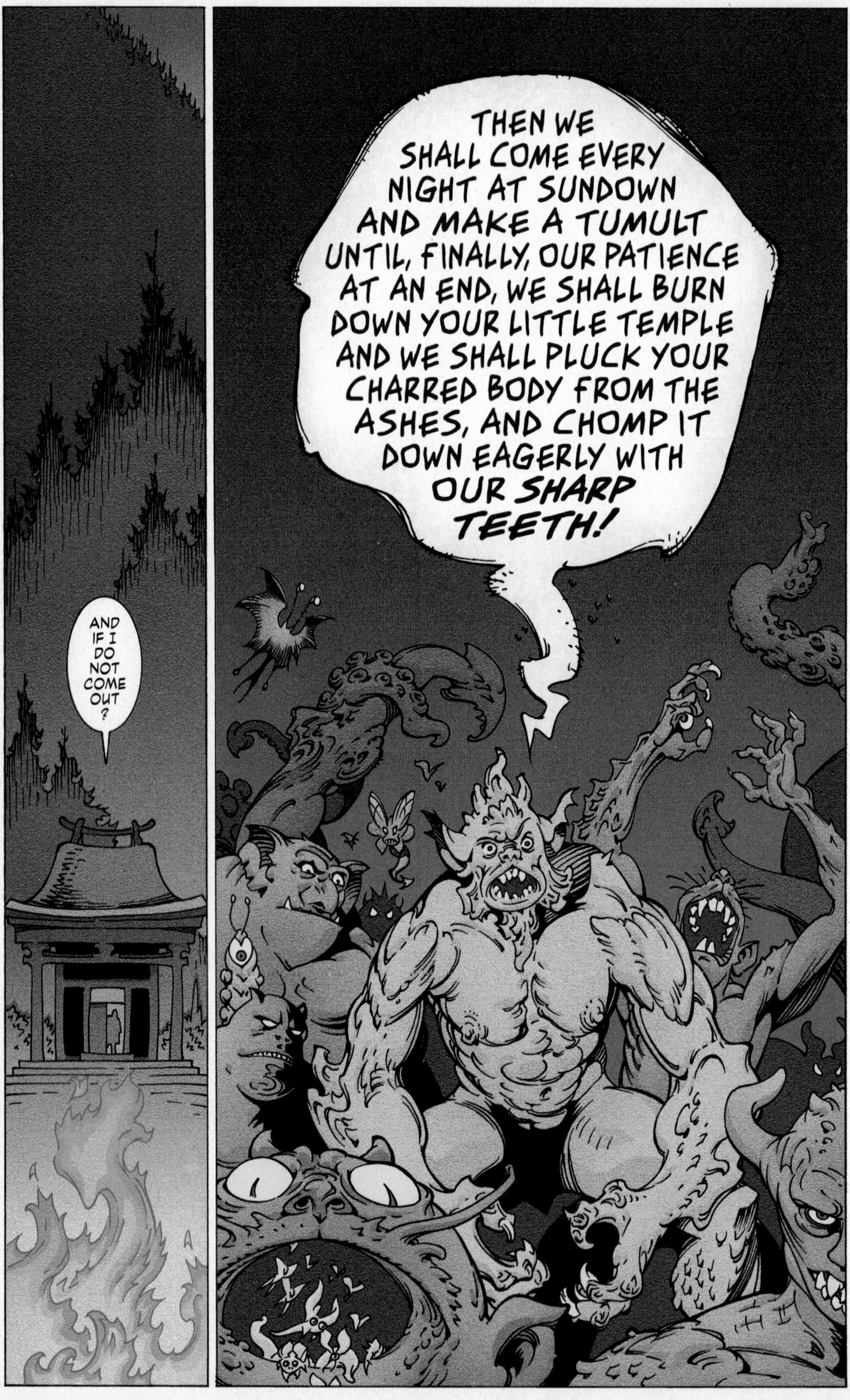
AND IF I DO NOT COME OUT?
THEN WE SHALL COME EVERY NIGHT AT SUNDOWN AND MAKE A TUMULT UNTIL, FINALLY, OUR PATIENCE AT AN END, WE SHALL BURN DOWN YOUR LITTLE TEMPLE AND WE SHALL PLUCK YOUR CHARRED BODY FROM THE ASHES, AND CHOMP IT DOWN EAGERLY WITH OUR SHARP TEETH!

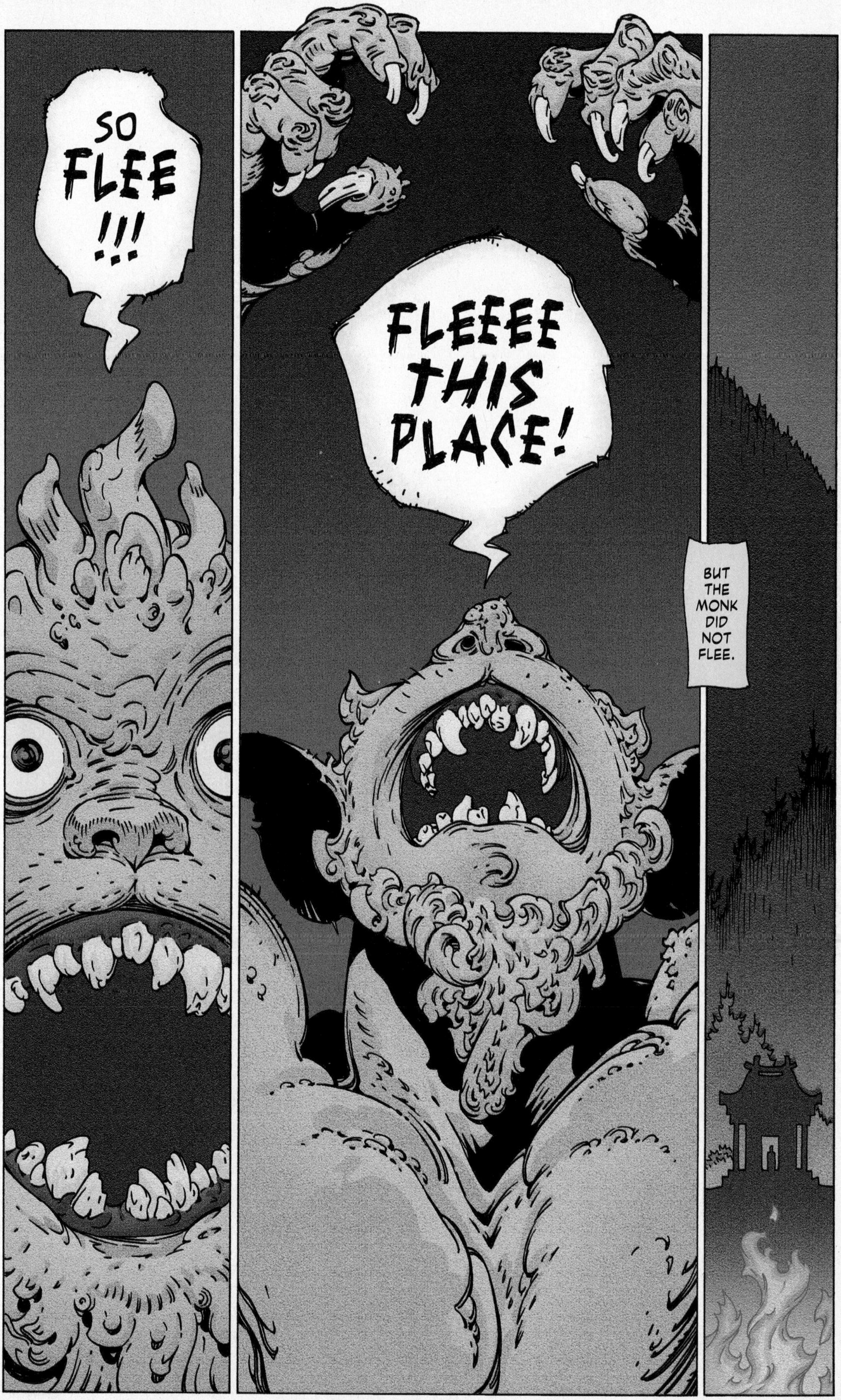
SO FLEE !!!
FLEEEE THIS PLACE!
BUT THE MONK DID NOT FLEE.

I WILL NOT LEAVE THIS PLACE...

...AND I AM TIRED OF THESE PERFORMANCES.

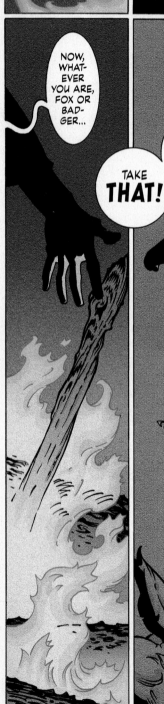

NOW, WHAT-EVER YOU ARE, FOX OR BADGER...

TAKE THAT!

AND THAT!

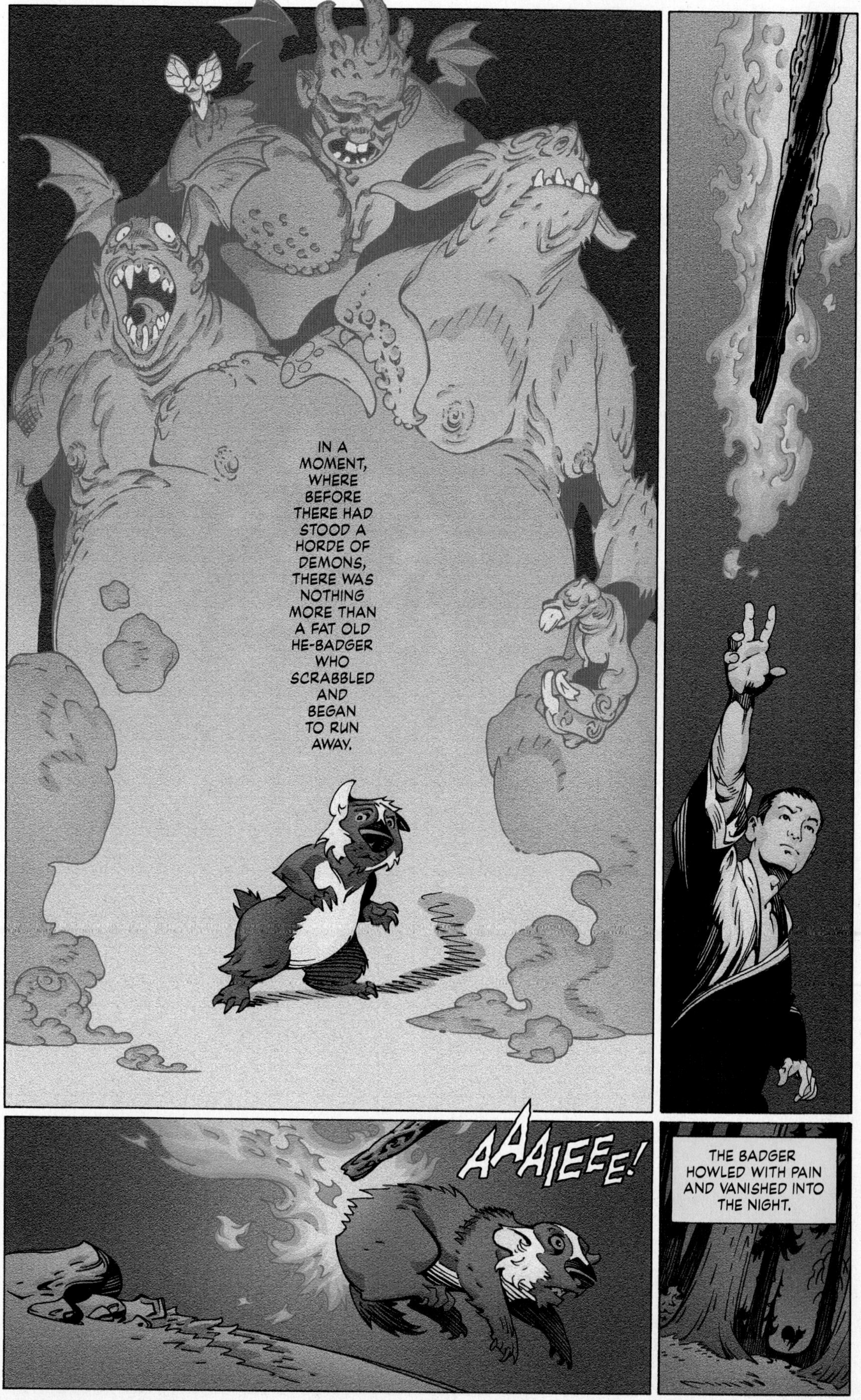

IN A MOMENT, WHERE BEFORE THERE HAD STOOD A HORDE OF DEMONS, THERE WAS NOTHING MORE THAN A FAT OLD HE-BADGER WHO SCRABBLED AND BEGAN TO RUN AWAY.
AAAIEEEE!
THE BADGER HOWLED WITH PAIN AND VANISHED INTO THE NIGHT.

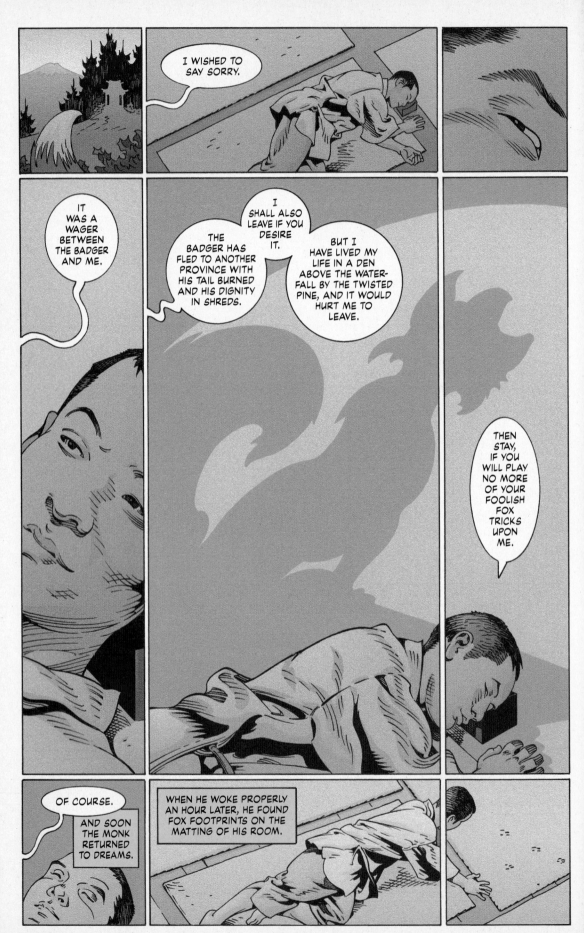

I WISHED TO SAY SORRY.

IT WAS A WAGER BETWEEN THE BADGER AND ME.

THE BADGER HAS FLED TO ANOTHER PROVINCE WITH HIS TAIL BURNED AND HIS DIGNITY IN SHREDS.

I SHALL ALSO LEAVE IF YOU DESIRE IT.

BUT I HAVE LIVED MY LIFE IN A DEN ABOVE THE WATERFALL BY THE TWISTED PINE, AND IT WOULD HURT ME TO LEAVE.

THEN STAY, IF YOU WILL PLAY NO MORE OF YOUR FOOLISH FOX TRICKS UPON ME.

OF COURSE.

AND SOON THE MONK RETURNED TO DREAMS.

WHEN HE WOKE PROPERLY AN HOUR LATER, HE FOUND FOX FOOTPRINTS ON THE MATTING OF HIS ROOM.

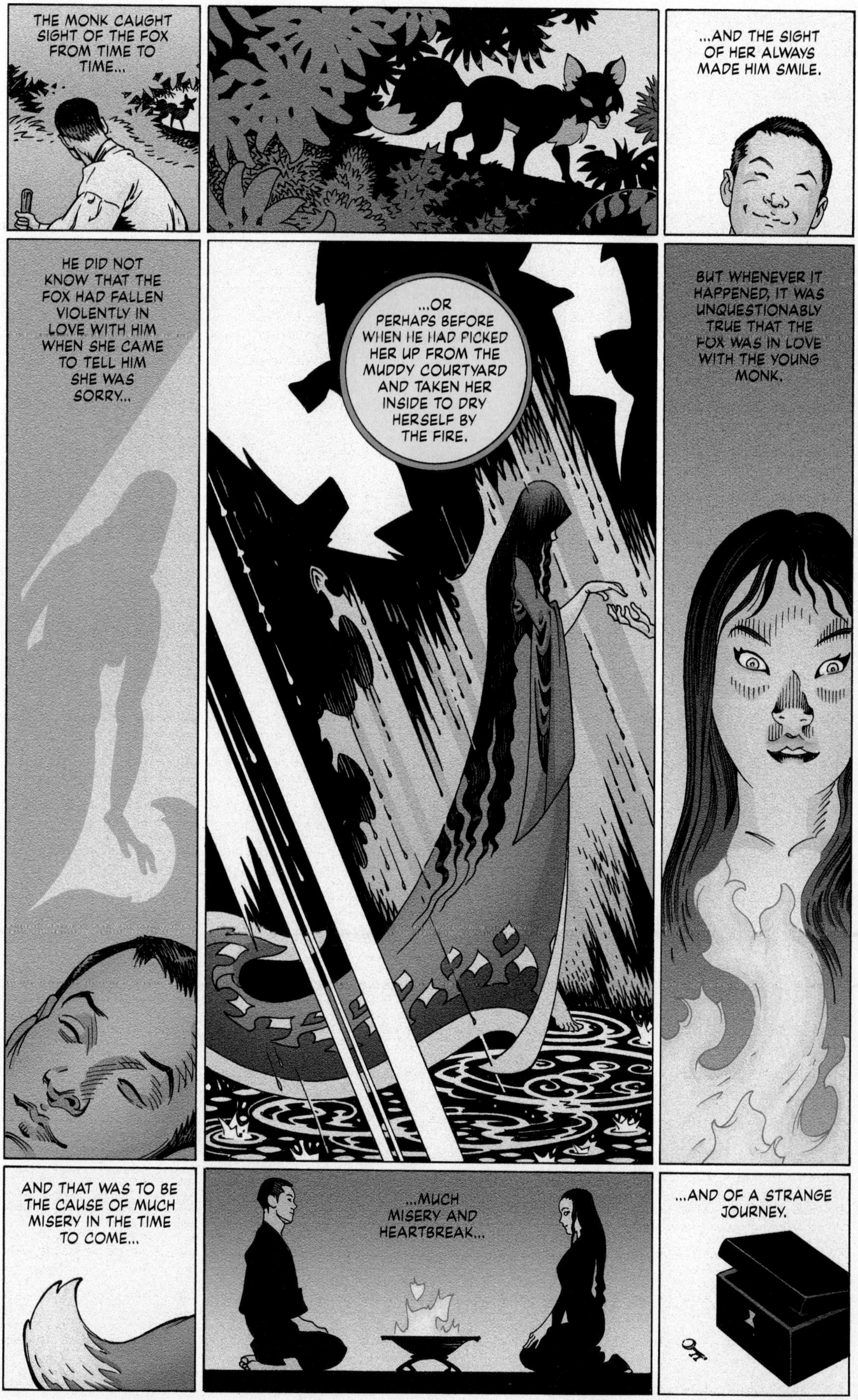
THE MONK CAUGHT SIGHT OF THE FOX FROM TIME TO TIME...
...AND THE SIGHT OF HER ALWAYS MADE HIM SMILE.
HE DID NOT KNOW THAT THE FOX HAD FALLEN VIOLENTLY IN LOVE WITH HIM WHEN SHE CAME TO TELL HIM SHE WAS SORRY...
...OR PERHAPS BEFORE WHEN HE HAD PICKED HER UP FROM THE MUDDY COURTYARD AND TAKEN HER INSIDE TO DRY HERSELF BY THE FIRE.
BUT WHENEVER IT HAPPENED, IT WAS UNQUESTIONABLY TRUE THAT THE FOX WAS IN LOVE WITH THE YOUNG MONK.
AND THAT WAS TO BE THE CAUSE OF MUCH MISERY IN THE TIME TO COME...
...MUCH MISERY AND HEARTBREAK...
...AND OF A STRANGE JOURNEY.

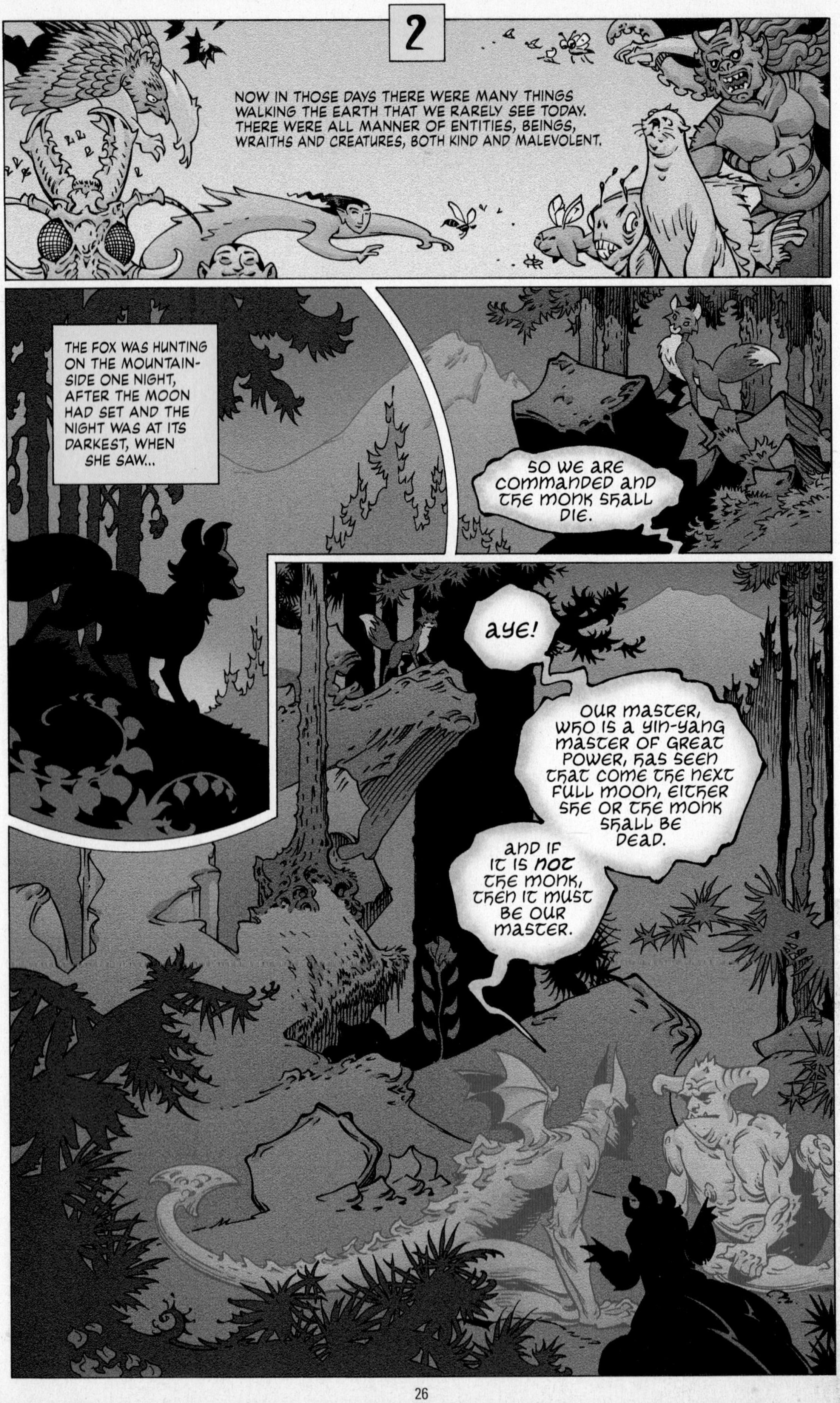
2
NOW IN THOSE DAYS THERE WERE MANY THINGS WALKING THE EARTH THAT WE RARELY SEE TODAY. THERE WERE ALL MANNER OF ENTITIES, BEINGS, WRAITHS AND CREATURES, BOTH KIND AND MALEVOLENT.
THE FOX WAS HUNTING ON THE MOUNTAIN-SIDE ONE NIGHT, AFTER THE MOON HAD SET AND THE NIGHT WAS AT ITS DARKEST, WHEN SHE SAW...
SO WE ARE COMMANDED AND THE MONK SHALL DIE.
AYE!
OUR MASTER, WHO IS A YIN-YANG MASTER OF GREAT POWER, HAS SEEN THAT COME THE NEXT FULL MOON, EITHER SHE OR THE MONK SHALL BE DEAD.
AND IF IT IS NOT THE MONK, THEN IT MUST BE OUR MASTER.

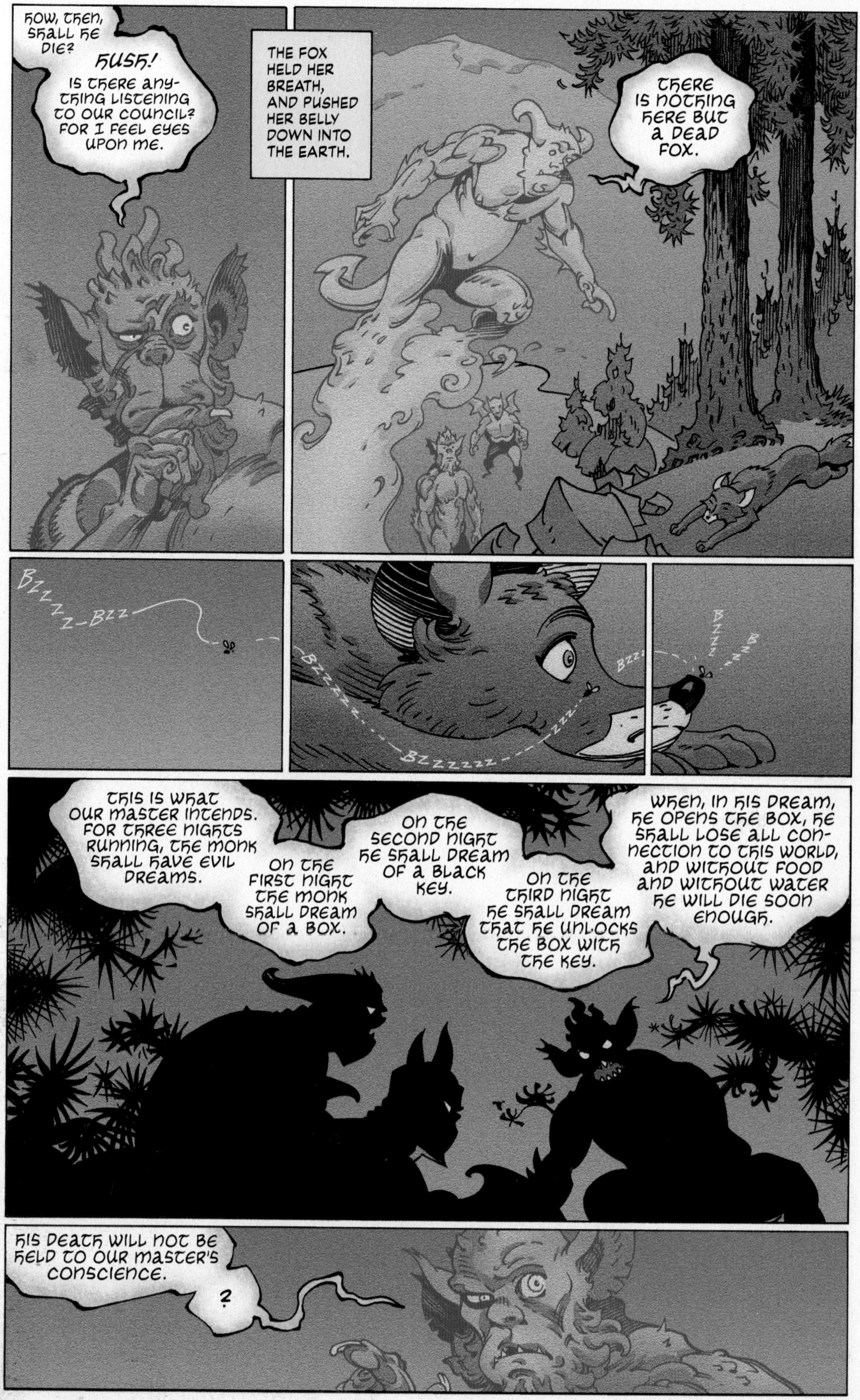
HOW, THEN, SHALL HE DIE?
HUSH!
IS THERE ANYTHING LISTENING TO OUR COUNCIL? FOR I FEEL EYES UPON ME.
THE FOX HELD HER BREATH, AND PUSHED HER BELLY DOWN INTO THE EARTH.
THERE IS NOTHING HERE BUT A DEAD FOX.
BZZZZ-BZZ
BZZZZZZZ
BZZZZZZ
BZZZ
BZZZ
BZZ
THIS IS WHAT OUR MASTER INTENDS. FOR THREE NIGHTS RUNNING, THE MONK SHALL HAVE EVIL DREAMS.
ON THE FIRST NIGHT THE MONK SHALL DREAM OF A BOX.
ON THE SECOND NIGHT HE SHALL DREAM OF A BLACK KEY.
ON THE THIRD NIGHT HE SHALL DREAM THAT HE UNLOCKS THE BOX WITH THE KEY.
WHEN, IN HIS DREAM, HE OPENS THE BOX, HE SHALL LOSE ALL CONNECTION TO THIS WORLD, AND WITHOUT FOOD AND WITHOUT WATER HE WILL DIE SOON ENOUGH.
HIS DEATH WILL NOT BE HELD TO OUR MASTER'S CONSCIENCE.
?

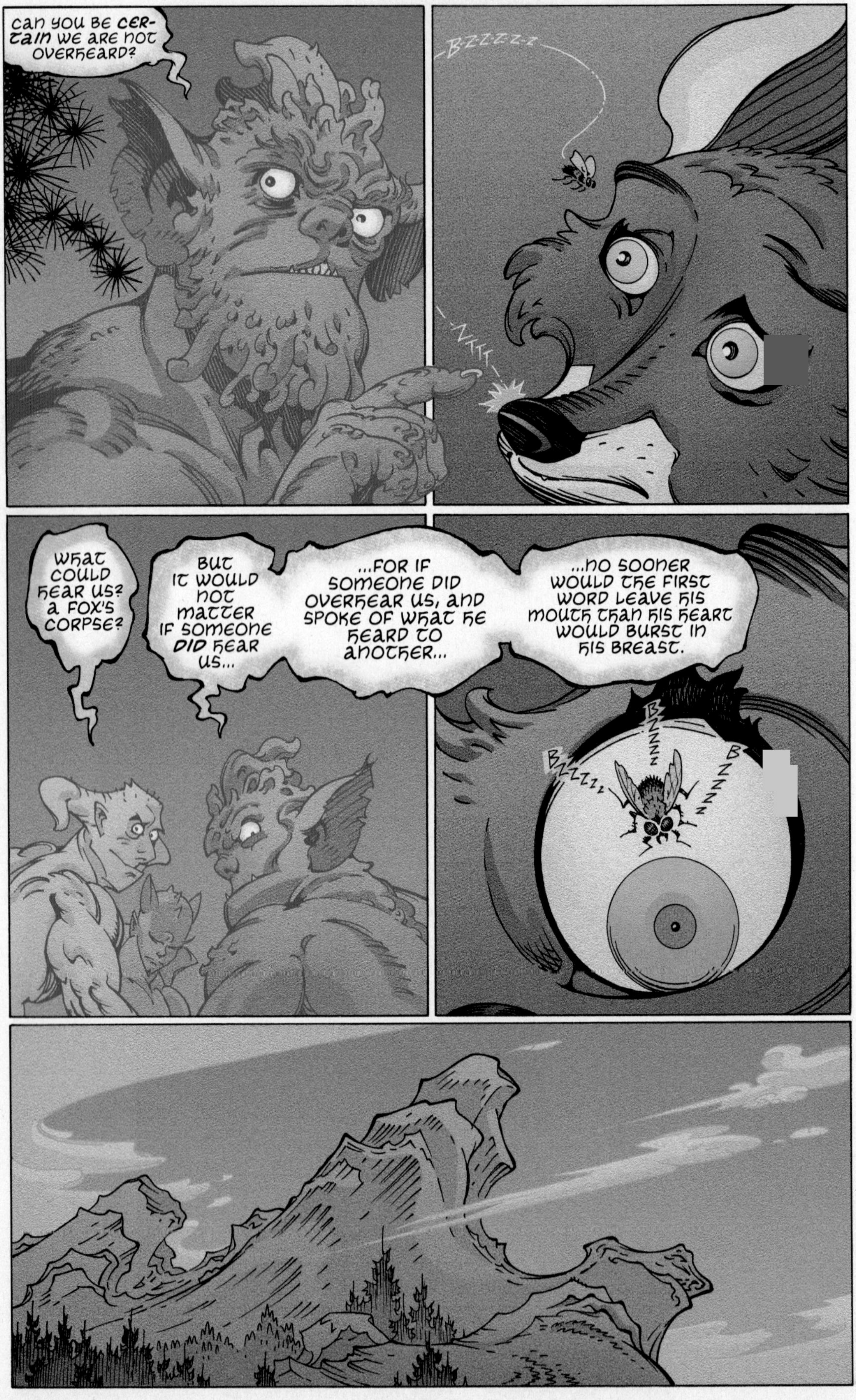
CAN YOU BE CERTAIN WE ARE NOT OVERHEARD?
-B-Z-Z-Z-Z-Z
ZTTT
WHAT COULD HEAR US? A FOX'S CORPSE?
BUT IT WOULD NOT MATTER IF SOMEONE DID HEAR US...
...FOR IF SOMEONE DID OVERHEAR US, AND SPOKE OF WHAT HE HEARD TO ANOTHER...
...NO SOONER WOULD THE FIRST WORD LEAVE HIS MOUTH THAN HIS HEART WOULD BURST IN HIS BREAST.
BZZZZ
BZZZZZ
BZZZZZ

BUT THERE IS NO WAY THE MONK CAN ESCAPE HIS FATE?

ONLY ONE WAY...

BZZZZ---

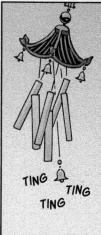

TING
TING
TING

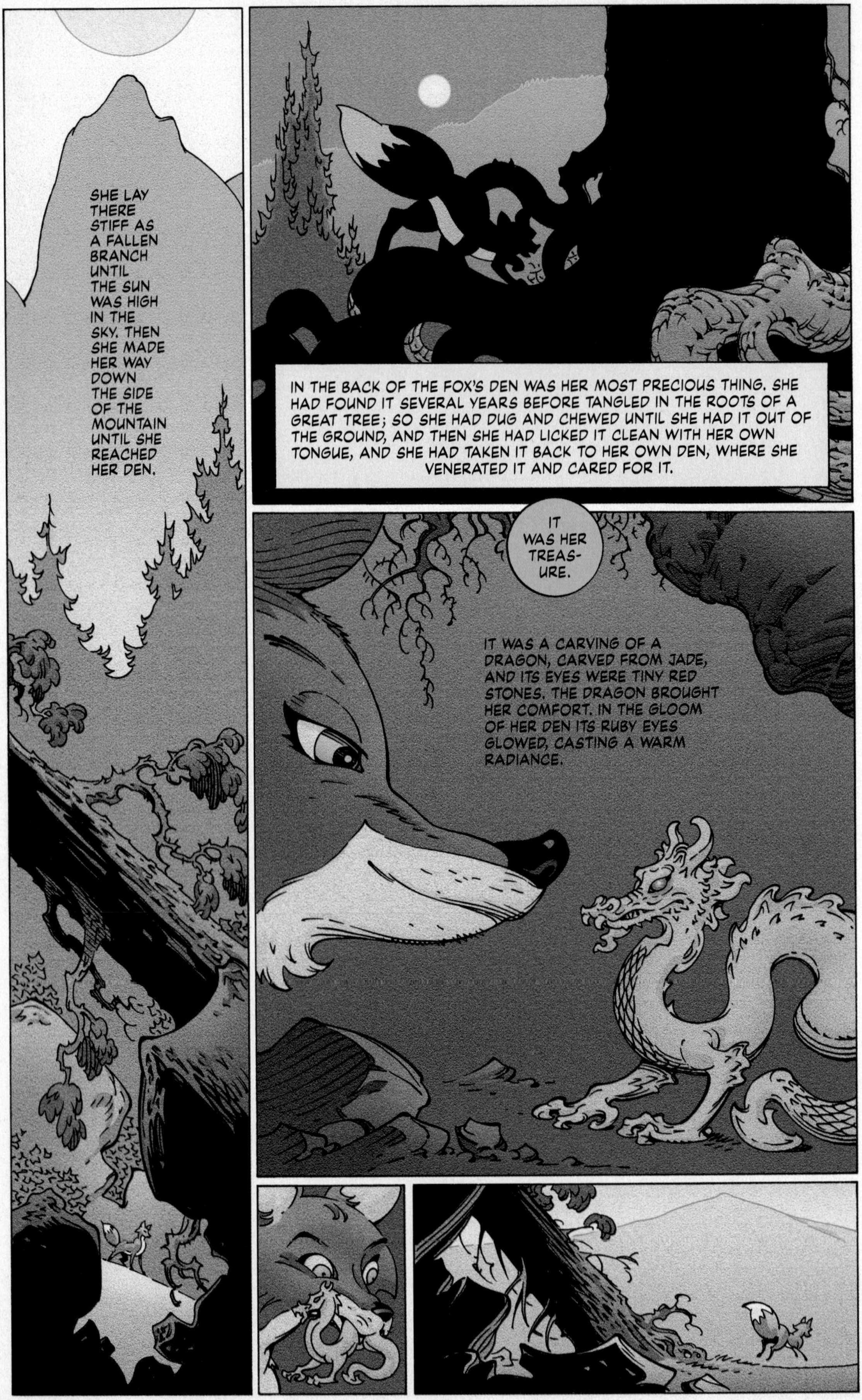
SHE LAY THERE STIFF AS A FALLEN BRANCH UNTIL THE SUN WAS HIGH IN THE SKY. THEN SHE MADE HER WAY DOWN THE SIDE OF THE MOUNTAIN UNTIL SHE REACHED HER DEN.
IN THE BACK OF THE FOX'S DEN WAS HER MOST PRECIOUS THING. SHE HAD FOUND IT SEVERAL YEARS BEFORE TANGLED IN THE ROOTS OF A GREAT TREE; SO SHE HAD DUG AND CHEWED UNTIL SHE HAD IT OUT OF THE GROUND, AND THEN SHE HAD LICKED IT CLEAN WITH HER OWN TONGUE, AND SHE HAD TAKEN IT BACK TO HER OWN DEN, WHERE SHE VENERATED IT AND CARED FOR IT.
IT WAS HER TREASURE.
IT WAS A CARVING OF A DRAGON, CARVED FROM JADE, AND ITS EYES WERE TINY RED STONES. THE DRAGON BROUGHT HER COMFORT. IN THE GLOOM OF HER DEN ITS RUBY EYES GLOWED, CASTING A WARM RADIANCE.

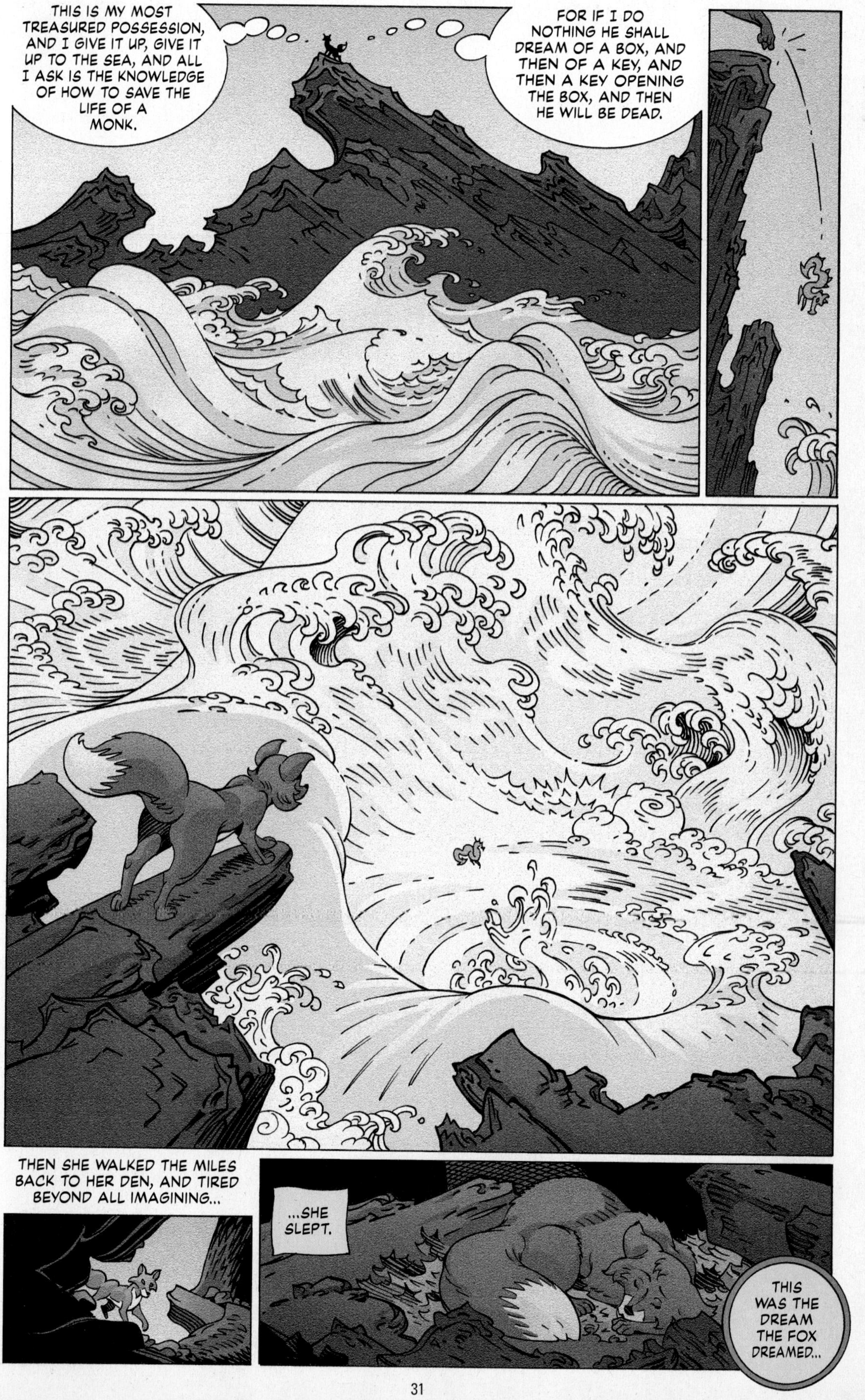
THIS IS MY MOST TREASURED POSSESSION, AND I GIVE IT UP, GIVE IT UP TO THE SEA, AND ALL I ASK IS THE KNOWLEDGE OF HOW TO SAVE THE LIFE OF A MONK.
FOR IF I DO NOTHING HE SHALL DREAM OF A BOX, AND THEN OF A KEY, AND THEN A KEY OPENING THE BOX, AND THEN HE WILL BE DEAD.
THEN SHE WALKED THE MILES BACK TO HER DEN, AND TIRED BEYOND ALL IMAGINING...
...SHE SLEPT.
THIS WAS THE DREAM THE FOX DREAMED...

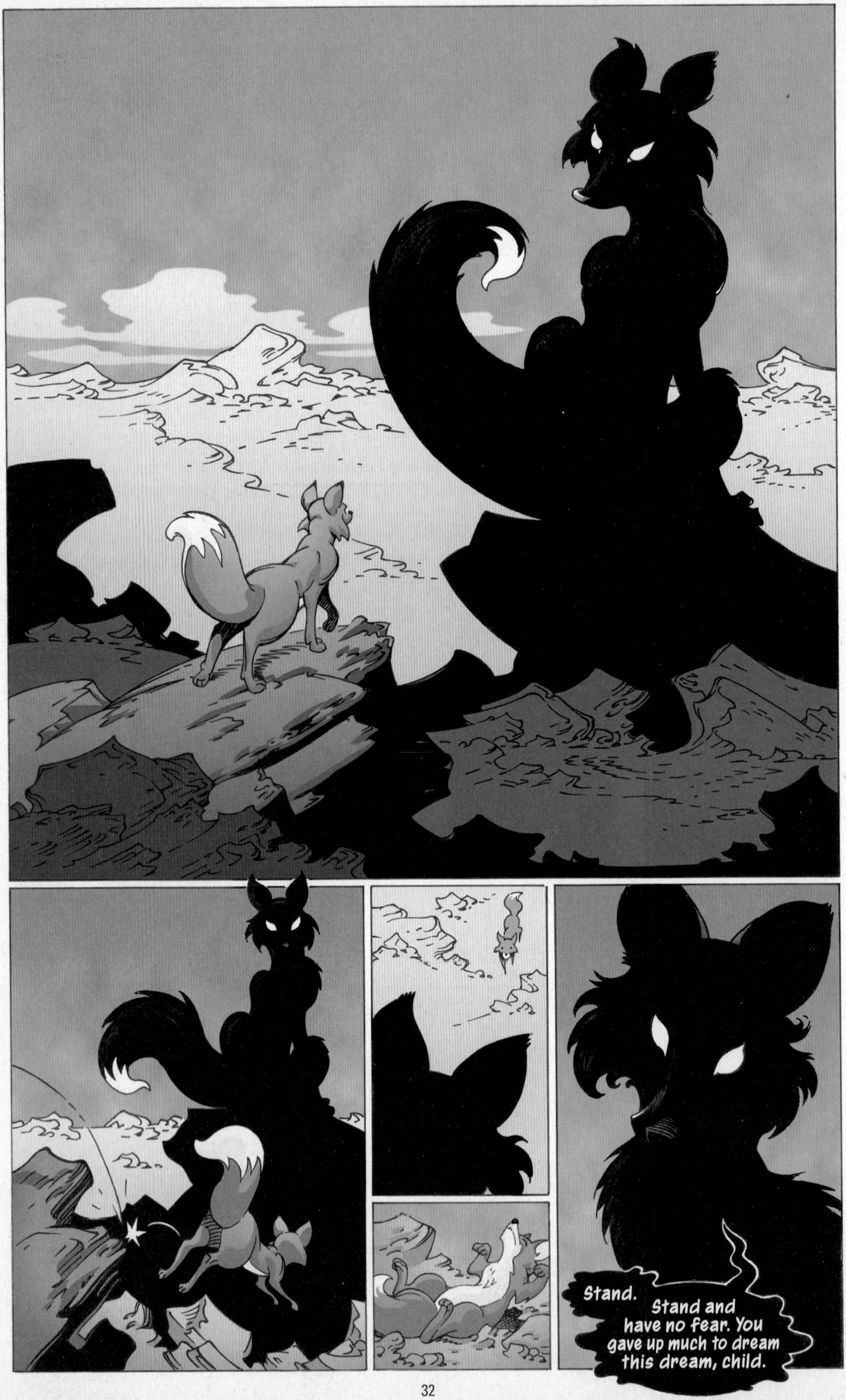
Stand.
Stand and have no fear. You gave up much to dream this dream, child.

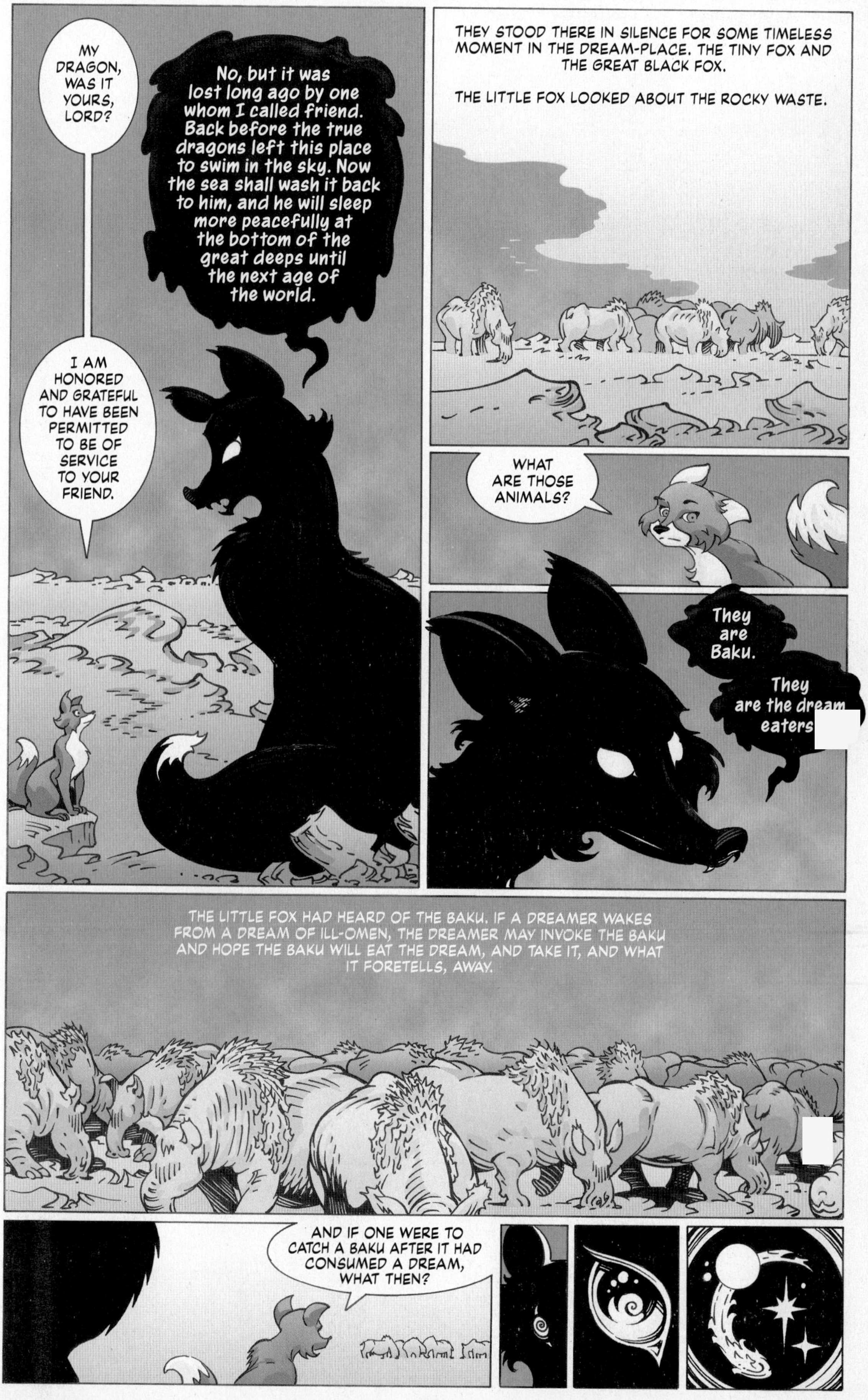
MY DRAGON, WAS IT YOURS, LORD?
No, but it was lost long ago by one whom I called friend. Back before the true dragons left this place to swim in the sky. Now the sea shall wash it back to him, and he will sleep more peacefully at the bottom of the great deeps until the next age of the world.
I AM HONORED AND GRATEFUL TO HAVE BEEN PERMITTED TO BE OF SERVICE TO YOUR FRIEND.
THEY STOOD THERE IN SILENCE FOR SOME TIMELESS MOMENT IN THE DREAM-PLACE. THE TINY FOX AND THE GREAT BLACK FOX.
THE LITTLE FOX LOOKED ABOUT THE ROCKY WASTE.
WHAT ARE THOSE ANIMALS?
They are Baku.
They are the dream eaters
THE LITTLE FOX HAD HEARD OF THE BAKU. IF A DREAMER WAKES FROM A DREAM OF ILL-OMEN, THE DREAMER MAY INVOKE THE BAKU AND HOPE THE BAKU WILL EAT THE DREAM, AND TAKE IT, AND WHAT IT FORETELLS, AWAY.
AND IF ONE WERE TO CATCH A BAKU AFTER IT HAD CONSUMED A DREAM, WHAT THEN?

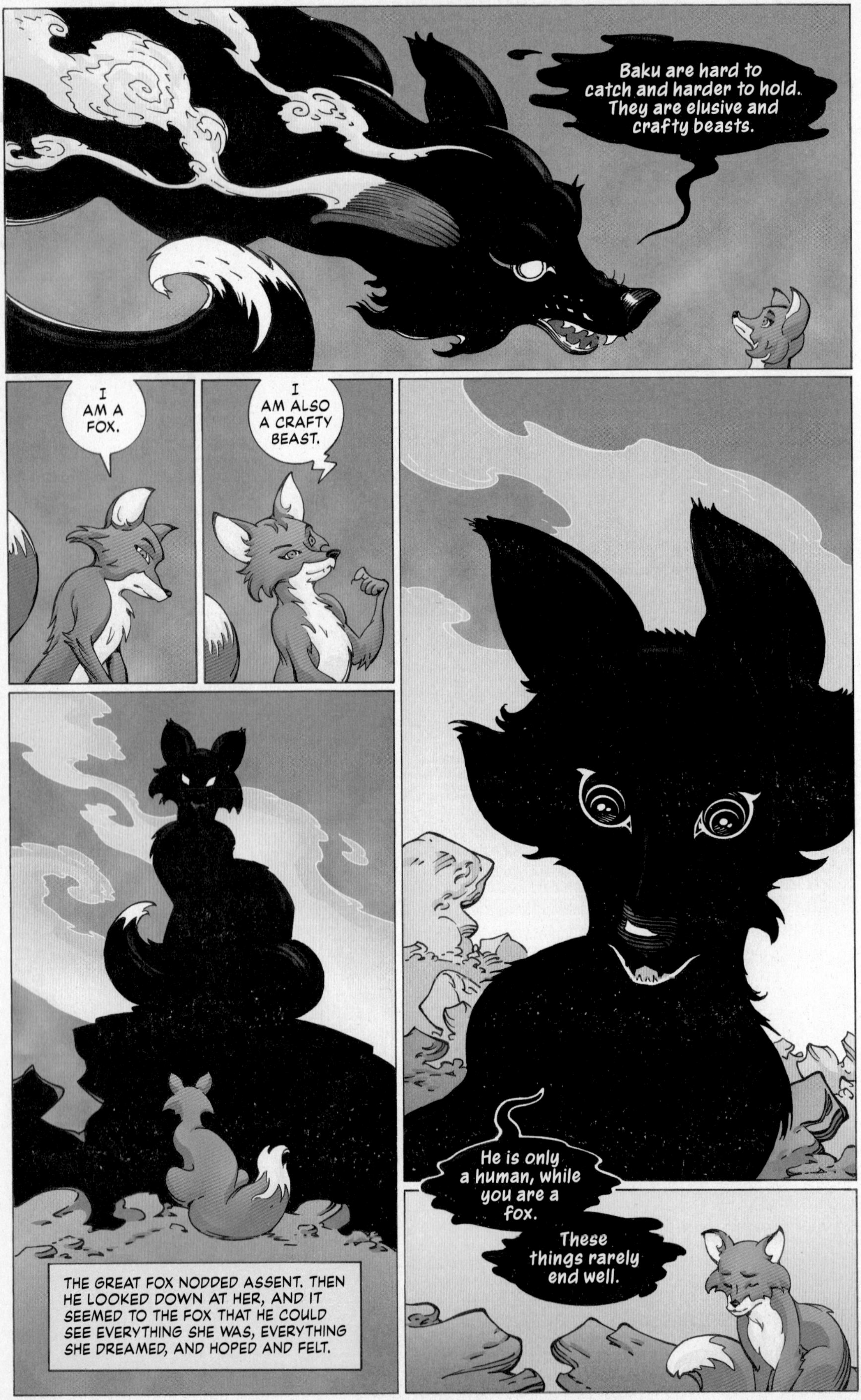

Baku are hard to catch and harder to hold. They are elusive and crafty beasts.
I AM A FOX.
I AM ALSO A CRAFTY BEAST.
THE GREAT FOX NODDED ASSENT. THEN HE LOOKED DOWN AT HER, AND IT SEEMED TO THE FOX THAT HE COULD SEE EVERYTHING SHE WAS, EVERYTHING SHE DREAMED, AND HOPED AND FELT.
He is only a human, while you are a fox.
These things rarely end well.

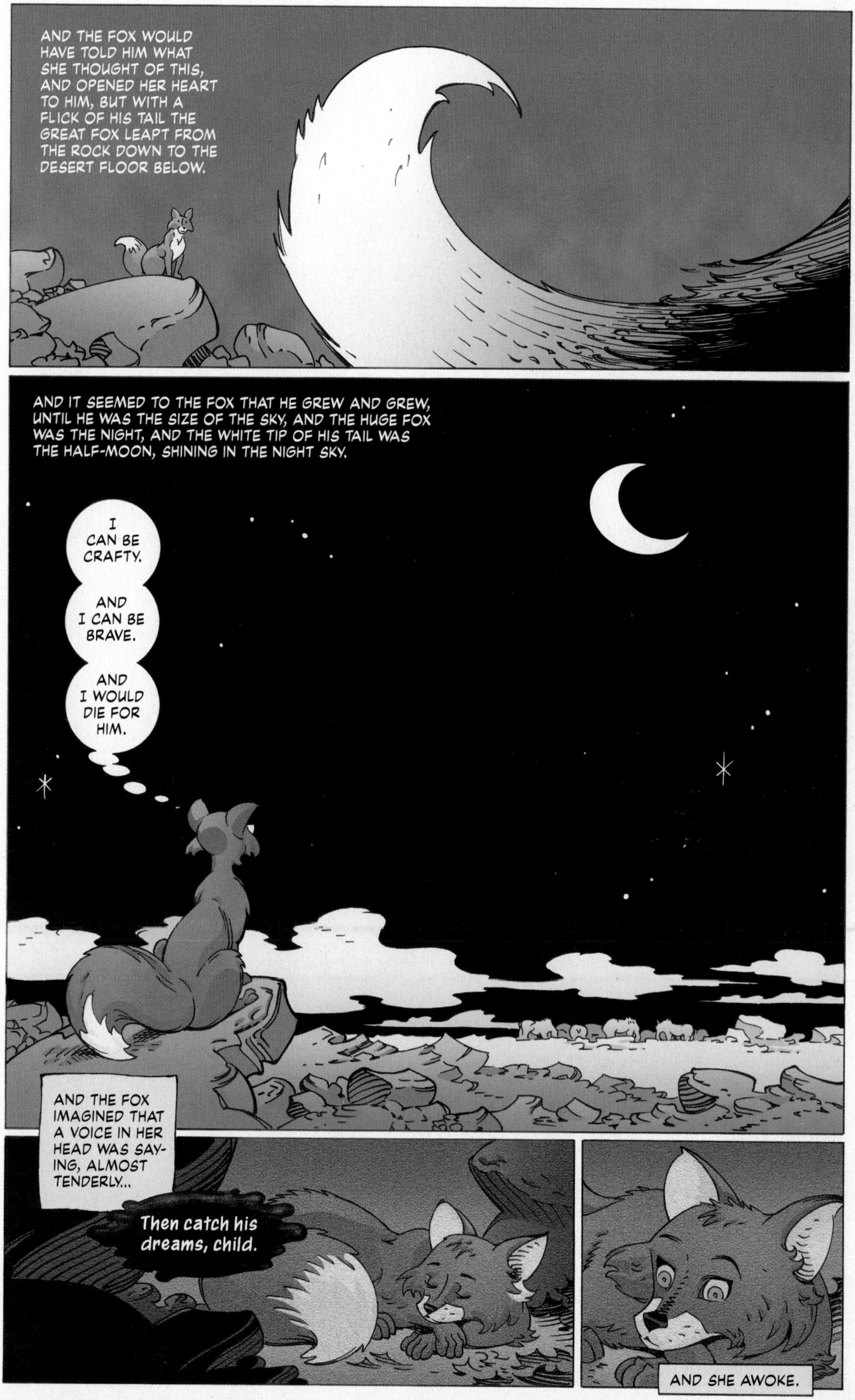
AND THE FOX WOULD HAVE TOLD HIM WHAT SHE THOUGHT OF THIS, AND OPENED HER HEART TO HIM, BUT WITH A FLICK OF HIS TAIL THE GREAT FOX LEAPT FROM THE ROCK DOWN TO THE DESERT FLOOR BELOW.
AND IT SEEMED TO THE FOX THAT HE GREW AND GREW, UNTIL HE WAS THE SIZE OF THE SKY, AND THE HUGE FOX WAS THE NIGHT, AND THE WHITE TIP OF HIS TAIL WAS THE HALF-MOON, SHINING IN THE NIGHT SKY.
I CAN BE CRAFTY.
AND I CAN BE BRAVE.
AND I WOULD DIE FOR HIM.
AND THE FOX IMAGINED THAT A VOICE IN HER HEAD WAS SAYING, ALMOST TENDERLY...
Then catch his dreams, child.
AND SHE AWOKE.

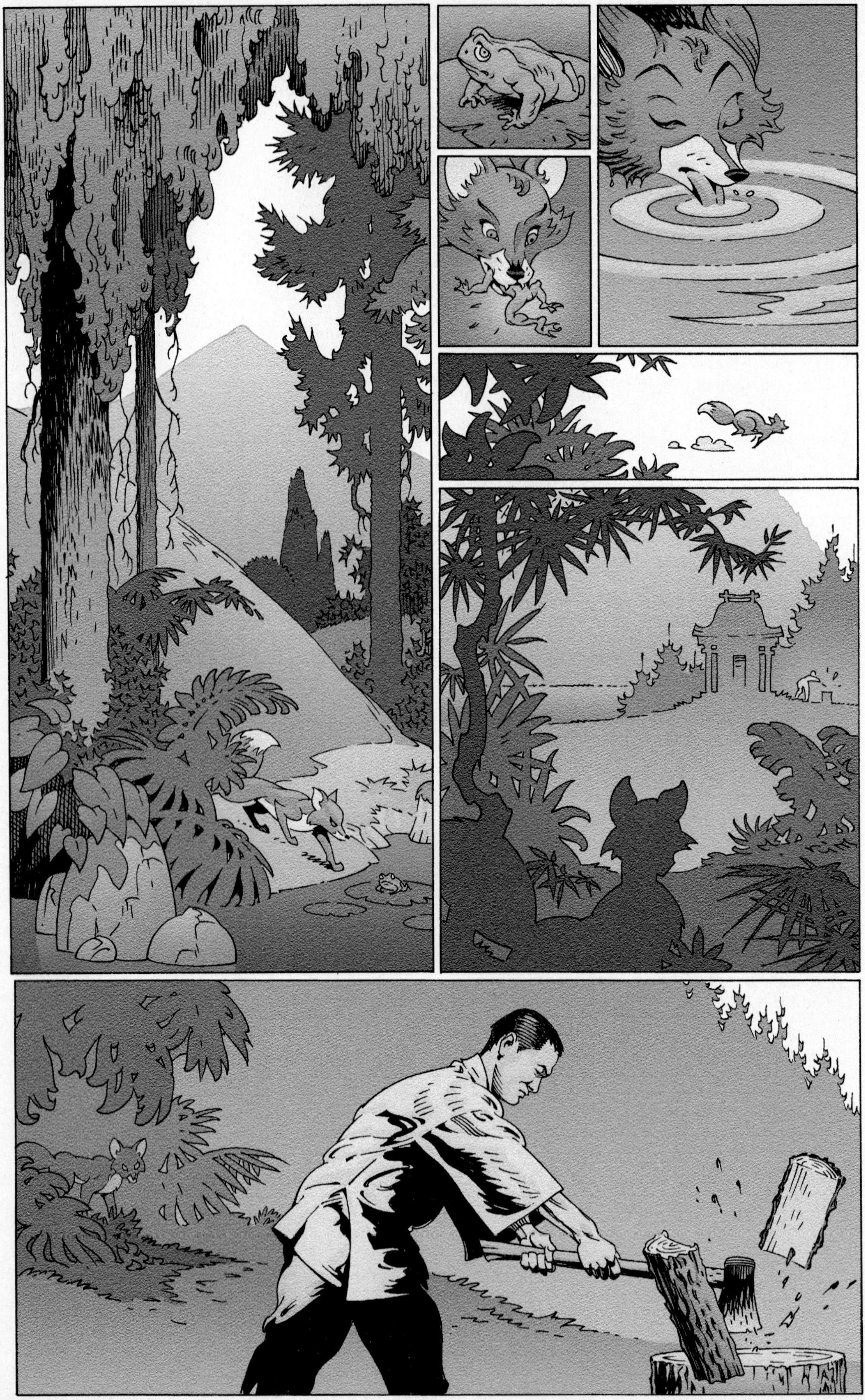

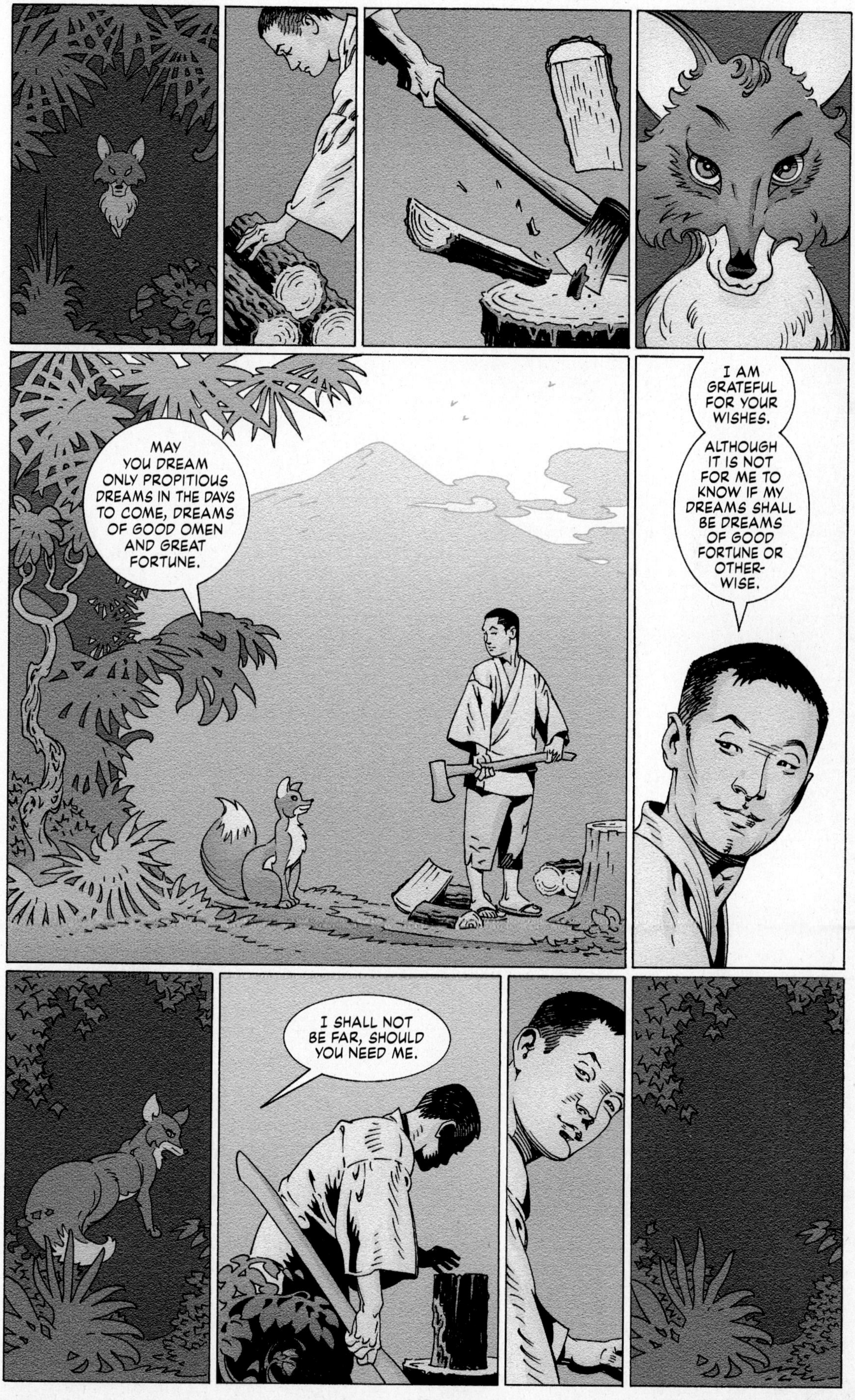
MAY YOU DREAM ONLY PROPITIOUS DREAMS IN THE DAYS TO COME, DREAMS OF GOOD OMEN AND GREAT FORTUNE.
I AM GRATEFUL FOR YOUR WISHES.
ALTHOUGH IT IS NOT FOR ME TO KNOW IF MY DREAMS SHALL BE DREAMS OF GOOD FORTUNE OR OTHER-WISE.
I SHALL NOT BE FAR, SHOULD YOU NEED ME.

3

FAR TO THE SOUTH AND THE WEST, IN HIS HOUSE IN KYOTO...

...THE MASTER OF YIN-YANG, THE ONMYOJI, BURNED A LAMP AT A SMALL TABLE, UPON WHICH HE HAD PLACED A SQUARE OF PAINTED SILK, AND UPON IT A LACQUER CHEST AND A BLACK WOODEN KEY.

ARRANGED ACCORDING TO THE FIVE CARDINAL POINTS OF THE COMPASS WERE FIVE SMALL PORCELAIN PLATES, UPON THREE OF WHICH WERE POWDERED MATTER...

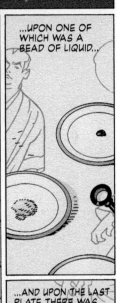

...UPON ONE OF WHICH WAS A BEAD OF LIQUID...

...AND UPON THE LAST PLATE THERE WAS NOTHING AT ALL.

THE ONMYOJI WAS A RICH MAN, A HIGH OFFICIAL IN THE BOARD OF DIVINATION, AND MANY SOUGHT HIS ADVICE AND FAVORS.

BUT HE WAS NOT A HAPPY MAN.

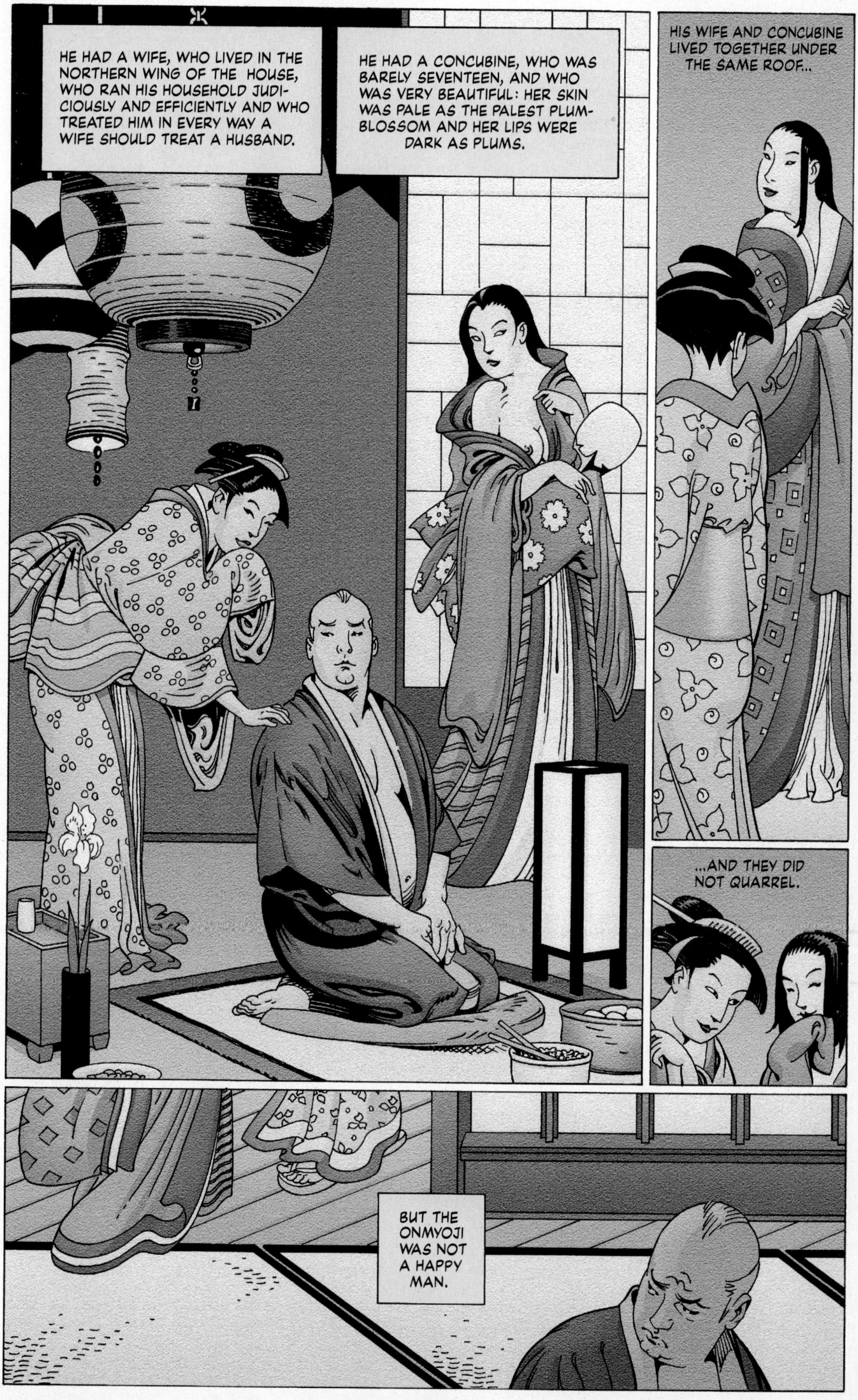
HE HAD A WIFE, WHO LIVED IN THE NORTHERN WING OF THE HOUSE, WHO RAN HIS HOUSEHOLD JUDICIOUSLY AND EFFICIENTLY AND WHO TREATED HIM IN EVERY WAY A WIFE SHOULD TREAT A HUSBAND.
HE HAD A CONCUBINE, WHO WAS BARELY SEVENTEEN, AND WHO WAS VERY BEAUTIFUL: HER SKIN WAS PALE AS THE PALEST PLUM-BLOSSOM AND HER LIPS WERE DARK AS PLUMS.
HIS WIFE AND CONCUBINE LIVED TOGETHER UNDER THE SAME ROOF...
...AND THEY DID NOT QUARREL.
BUT THE ONMYOJI WAS NOT A HAPPY MAN.

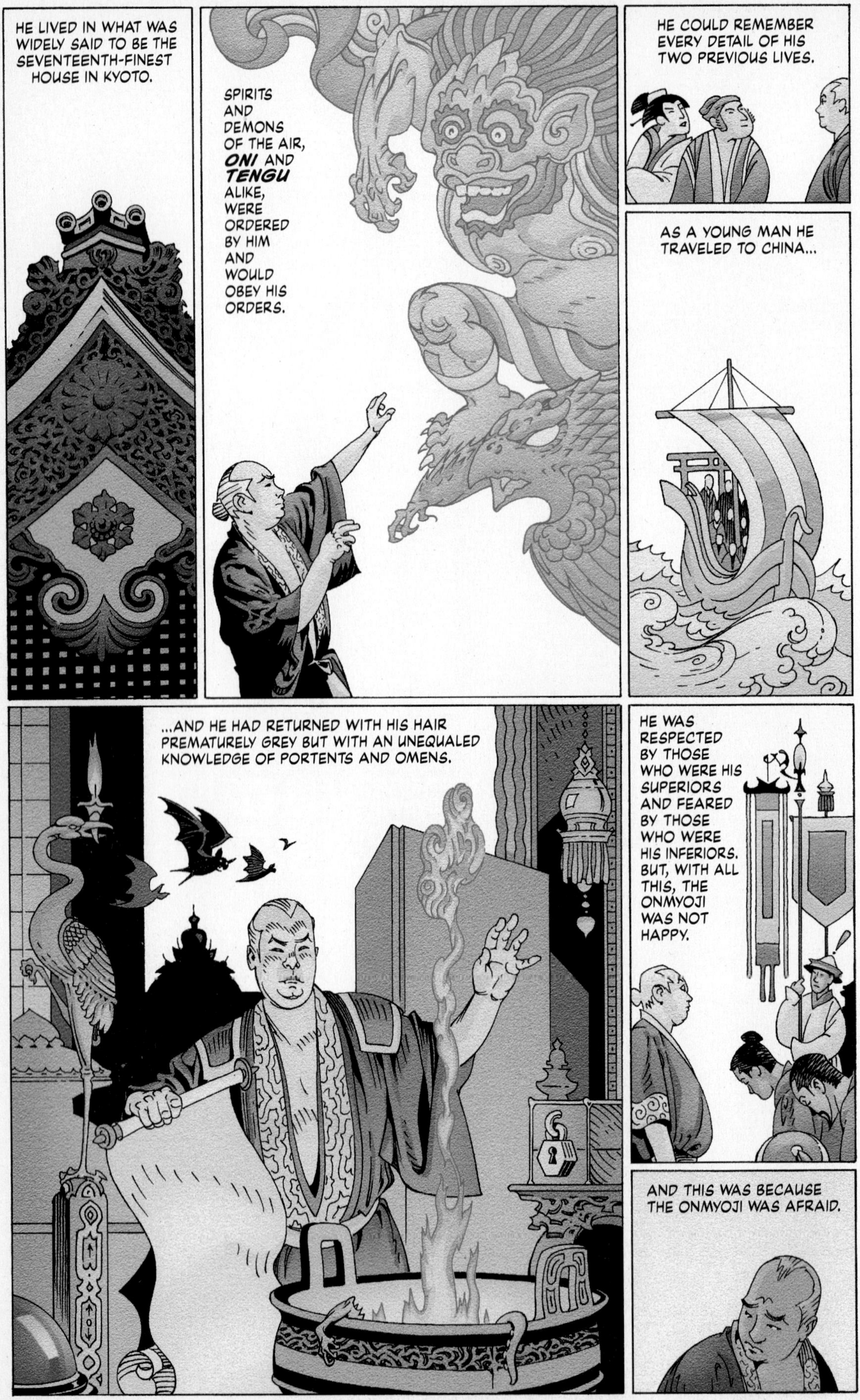
HE LIVED IN WHAT WAS WIDELY SAID TO BE THE SEVENTEENTH-FINEST HOUSE IN KYOTO.
SPIRITS AND DEMONS OF THE AIR, ONI AND TENGU ALIKE, WERE ORDERED BY HIM AND WOULD OBEY HIS ORDERS.
HE COULD REMEMBER EVERY DETAIL OF HIS TWO PREVIOUS LIVES.
AS A YOUNG MAN HE TRAVELED TO CHINA...
...AND HE HAD RETURNED WITH HIS HAIR PREMATURELY GREY BUT WITH AN UNEQUALED KNOWLEDGE OF PORTENTS AND OMENS.
HE WAS RESPECTED BY THOSE WHO WERE HIS SUPERIORS AND FEARED BY THOSE WHO WERE HIS INFERIORS. BUT, WITH ALL THIS, THE ONMYOJI WAS NOT HAPPY.
AND THIS WAS BECAUSE THE ONMYOJI WAS AFRAID.

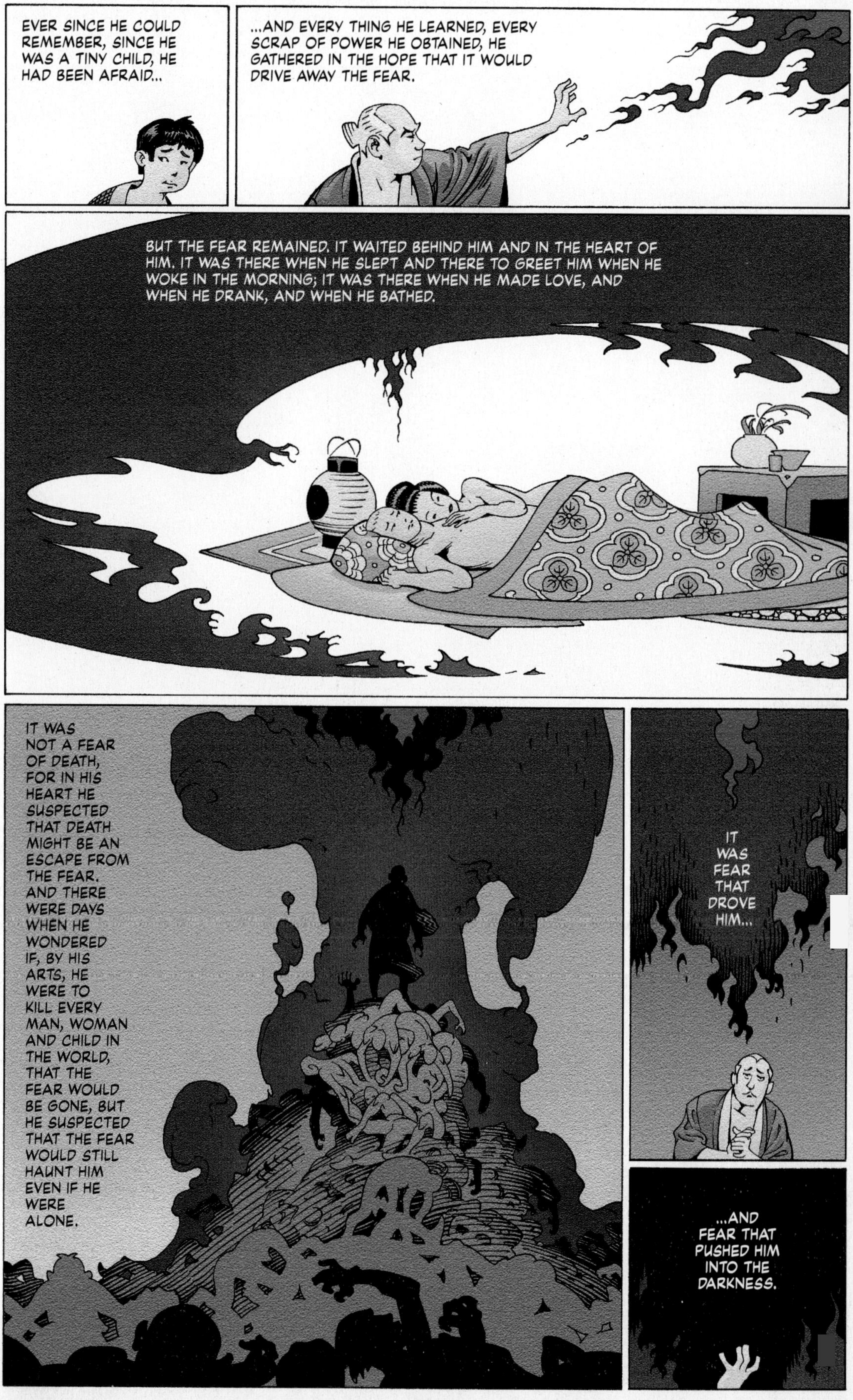
EVER SINCE HE COULD REMEMBER, SINCE HE WAS A TINY CHILD, HE HAD BEEN AFRAID...
...AND EVERY THING HE LEARNED, EVERY SCRAP OF POWER HE OBTAINED, HE GATHERED IN THE HOPE THAT IT WOULD DRIVE AWAY THE FEAR.
BUT THE FEAR REMAINED. IT WAITED BEHIND HIM AND IN THE HEART OF HIM. IT WAS THERE WHEN HE SLEPT AND THERE TO GREET HIM WHEN HE WOKE IN THE MORNING; IT WAS THERE WHEN HE MADE LOVE, AND WHEN HE DRANK, AND WHEN HE BATHED.
IT WAS NOT A FEAR OF DEATH, FOR IN HIS HEART HE SUSPECTED THAT DEATH MIGHT BE AN ESCAPE FROM THE FEAR. AND THERE WERE DAYS WHEN HE WONDERED IF, BY HIS ARTS, HE WERE TO KILL EVERY MAN, WOMAN AND CHILD IN THE WORLD, THAT THE FEAR WOULD BE GONE, BUT HE SUSPECTED THAT THE FEAR WOULD STILL HAUNT HIM EVEN IF HE WERE ALONE.
IT WAS FEAR THAT DROVE HIM...
...AND FEAR THAT PUSHED HIM INTO THE DARKNESS.

THE MASTER OF YIN-YANG SOUGHT KNOWLEDGE OF THE DEFILERS OF GRAVES. HE MET WITH MISSHAPEN CREATURES IN THE TWILIGHT, AND HE DANCED THEIR DANCES, AND HE PARTOOK OF THEIR FEASTS.

ON THE OUTSKIRTS OF THE CITY, HE KEPT A DILAPIDATED HOUSE, AND IN THAT HOUSE THERE WERE THREE WOMEN...

...ONE OLD, ONE YOUNG, AND ONE WHO WAS NEITHER YOUNG NOR OLD. THE WOMEN SOLD HERBS AND REMEDIES TO WOMEN WHO FOUND THEMSELVES IN UNFORTUNATE SITUATIONS.

IT WAS WHISPERED THAT UNWARY TRAVELERS WHO STOPPED IN THAT HOUSE WERE NEVER SEEN AGAIN.

BE THAT AS IT MAY, NO MAN KNEW OF THE ONMYOJI'S INVOLVEMENT WITH THE THREE WOMEN, NOR OF HIS VISITS TO THE HOUSE ON THOSE NIGHTS WHEN THE MOON WAS DARK.

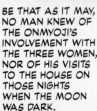

IN HIS HEAD, AND IN HIS HEART, HE WAS NOT AN EVIL MAN. HE WAS FRIGHTENED.

42

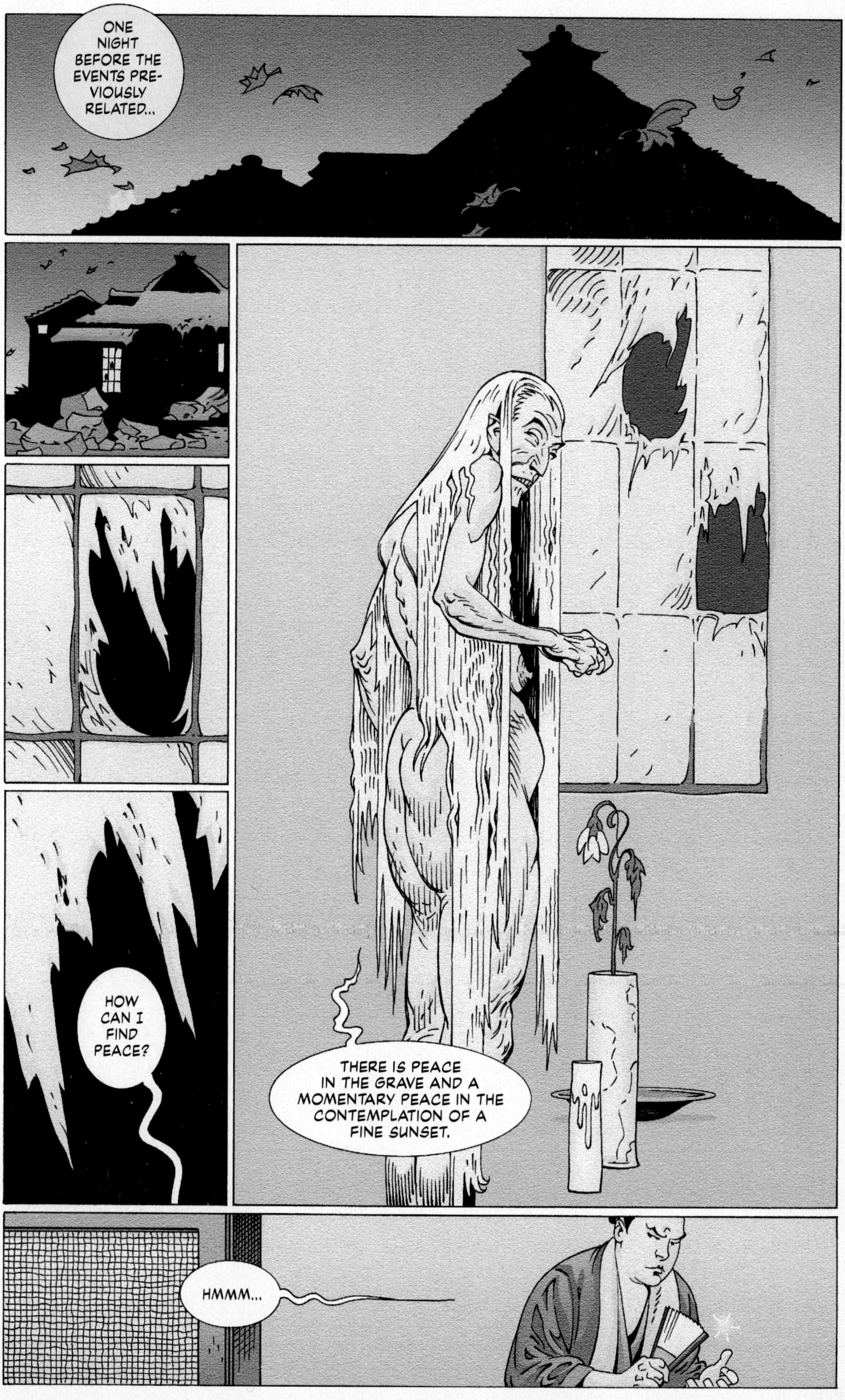
ONE NIGHT BEFORE THE EVENTS PRE-VIOUSLY RELATED...
HOW CAN I FIND PEACE?
THERE IS PEACE IN THE GRAVE AND A MOMENTARY PEACE IN THE CONTEMPLATION OF A FINE SUNSET.
HMMM...

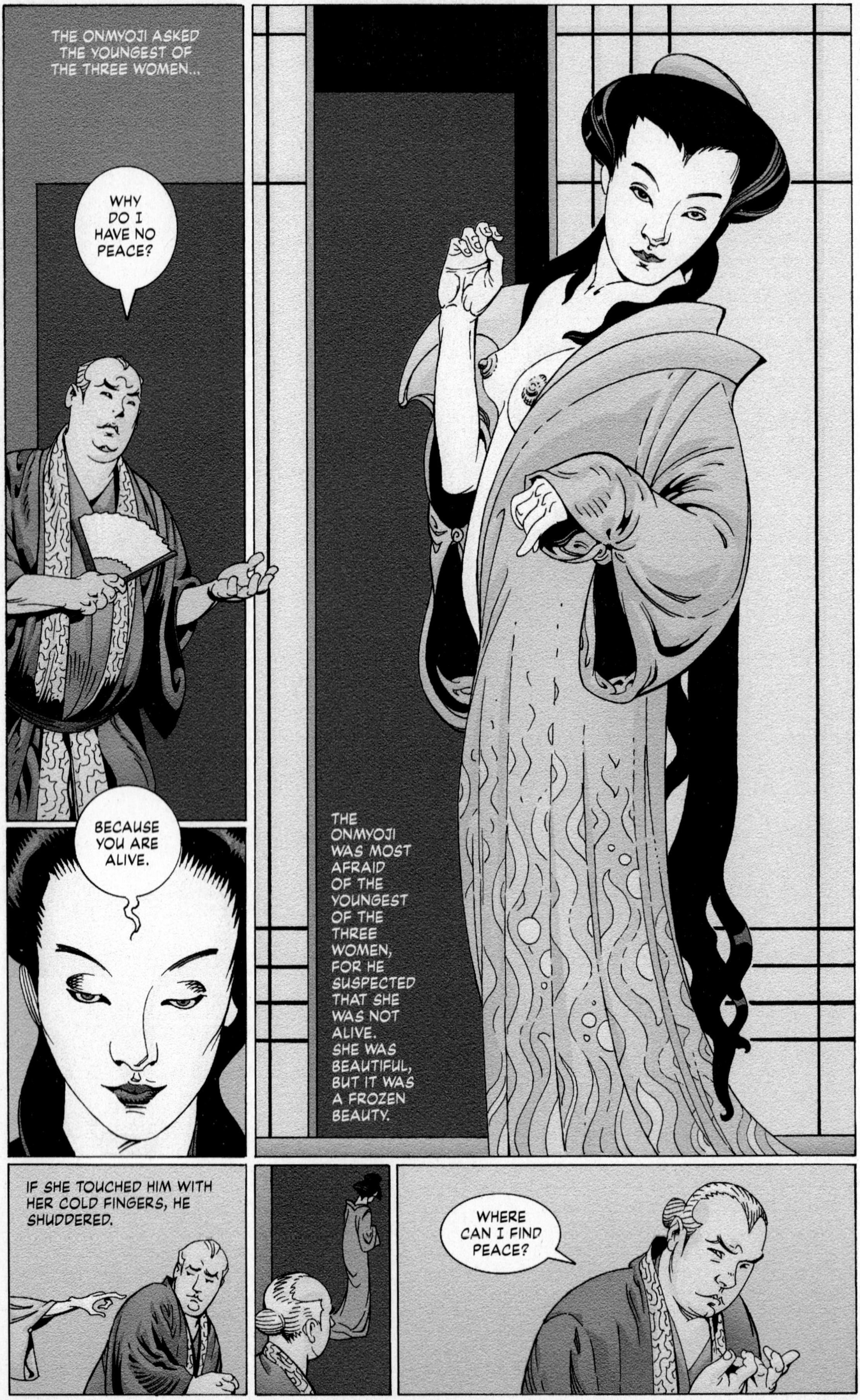
THE ONMYOJI ASKED THE YOUNGEST OF THE THREE WOMEN...
WHY DO I HAVE NO PEACE?
BECAUSE YOU ARE ALIVE.
THE ONMYOJI WAS MOST AFRAID OF THE YOUNGEST OF THE THREE WOMEN, FOR HE SUSPECTED THAT SHE WAS NOT ALIVE. SHE WAS BEAUTIFUL, BUT IT WAS A FROZEN BEAUTY.
IF SHE TOUCHED HIM WITH HER COLD FINGERS, HE SHUDDERED.
WHERE CAN I FIND PEACE?

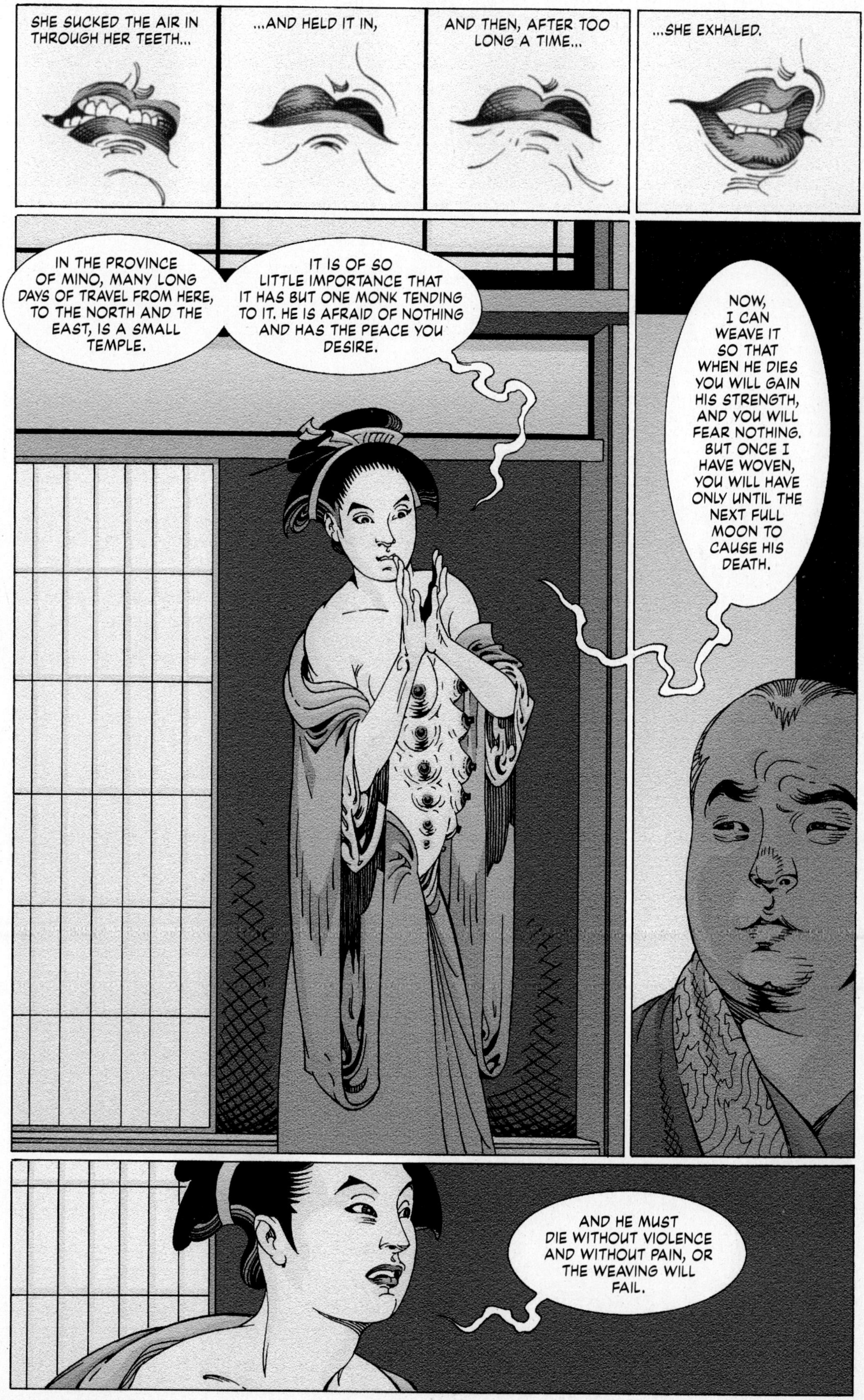
SHE SUCKED THE AIR IN THROUGH HER TEETH...
...AND HELD IT IN,
AND THEN, AFTER TOO LONG A TIME...
...SHE EXHALED.
IN THE PROVINCE OF MINO, MANY LONG DAYS OF TRAVEL FROM HERE, TO THE NORTH AND THE EAST, IS A SMALL TEMPLE.
IT IS OF SO LITTLE IMPORTANCE THAT IT HAS BUT ONE MONK TENDING TO IT. HE IS AFRAID OF NOTHING AND HAS THE PEACE YOU DESIRE.
NOW, I CAN WEAVE IT SO THAT WHEN HE DIES YOU WILL GAIN HIS STRENGTH, AND YOU WILL FEAR NOTHING. BUT ONCE I HAVE WOVEN, YOU WILL HAVE ONLY UNTIL THE NEXT FULL MOON TO CAUSE HIS DEATH.
AND HE MUST DIE WITHOUT VIOLENCE AND WITHOUT PAIN, OR THE WEAVING WILL FAIL.

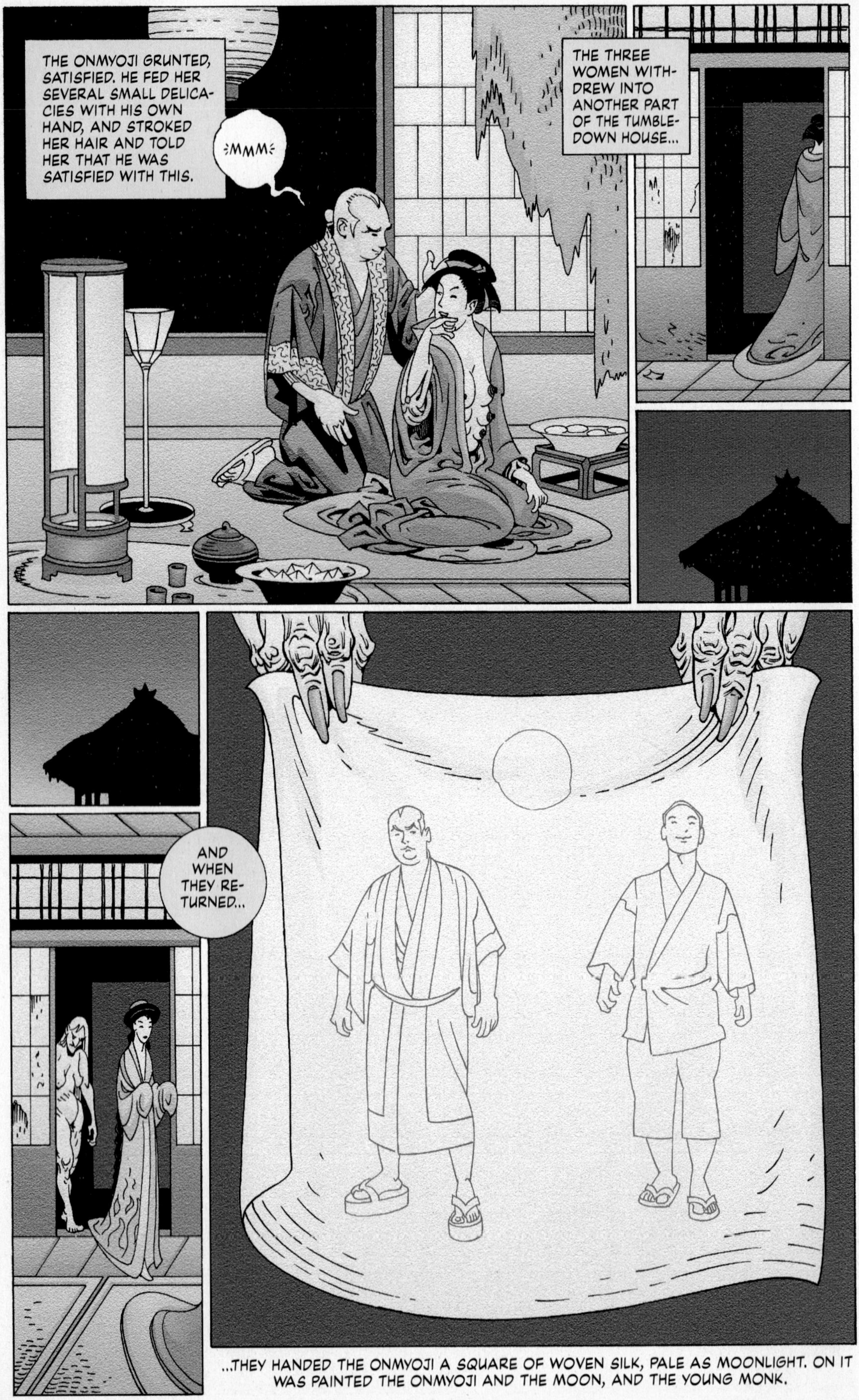
THE ONMYOJI GRUNTED, SATISFIED. HE FED HER SEVERAL SMALL DELICACIES WITH HIS OWN HAND, AND STROKED HER HAIR AND TOLD HER THAT HE WAS SATISFIED WITH THIS.
MMM
THE THREE WOMEN WITHDREW INTO ANOTHER PART OF THE TUMBLEDOWN HOUSE...
AND WHEN THEY RETURNED...
...THEY HANDED THE ONMYOJI A SQUARE OF WOVEN SILK, PALE AS MOONLIGHT. ON IT WAS PAINTED THE ONMYOJI AND THE MOON, AND THE YOUNG MONK.

THE ONMYOJI NODDED, SATISFIED. HE WOULD HAVE THANKED THEM, BUT HE KNEW THAT ONE MUST NOT THANK CREATURES OF THEIR KIND.

SO HE PLACED THEIR PAYMENT ON THE FLOOR...

...AND HURRIED HOME.

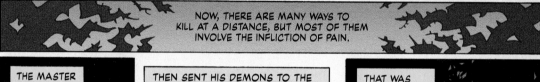

NOW, THERE ARE MANY WAYS TO KILL AT A DISTANCE, BUT MOST OF THEM INVOLVE THE INFLICTION OF PAIN.

THE MASTER OF YIN-YANG CONSULTED HIS SCROLLS.

THEN SENT HIS DEMONS TO THE MOUNTAIN WHERE THE MONK LIVED, TO OBTAIN FOR HIM THINGS THE MONK HAD TOUCHED.

THAT WAS WHERE THE FOX HAD OVER-HEARD THEM.

SO WE ARE COMMANDED AND THE MONK SHALL DIE.

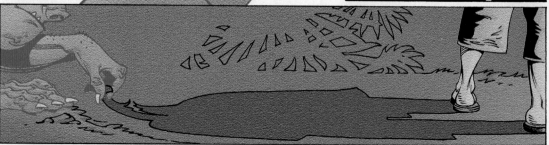

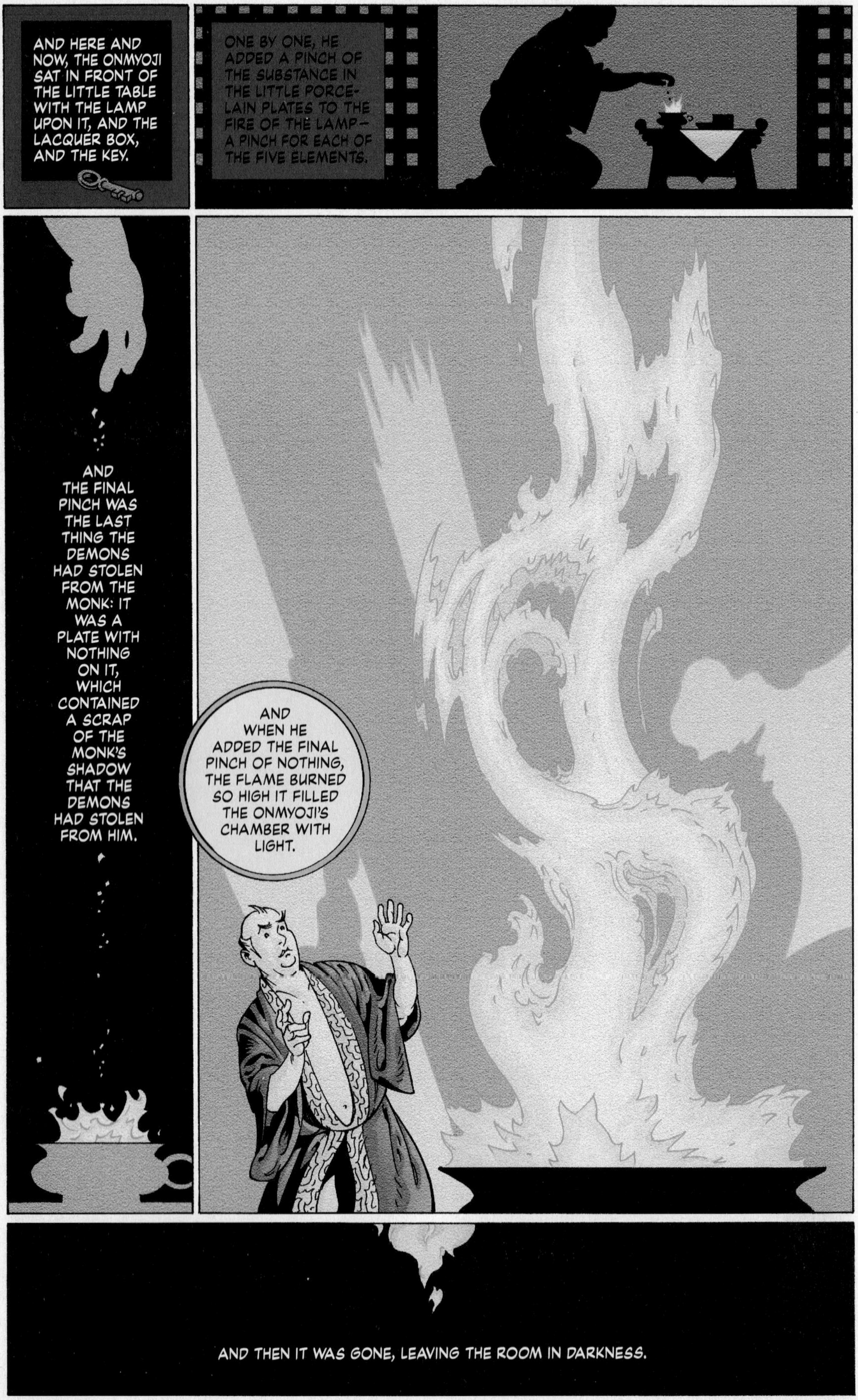
AND HERE AND NOW, THE ONMYOJI SAT IN FRONT OF THE LITTLE TABLE WITH THE LAMP UPON IT, AND THE LACQUER BOX, AND THE KEY.
ONE BY ONE, HE ADDED A PINCH OF THE SUBSTANCE IN THE LITTLE PORCELAIN PLATES TO THE FIRE OF THE LAMP— A PINCH FOR EACH OF THE FIVE ELEMENTS.
AND THE FINAL PINCH WAS THE LAST THING THE DEMONS HAD STOLEN FROM THE MONK: IT WAS A PLATE WITH NOTHING ON IT, WHICH CONTAINED A SCRAP OF THE MONK'S SHADOW THAT THE DEMONS HAD STOLEN FROM HIM.
AND WHEN HE ADDED THE FINAL PINCH OF NOTHING, THE FLAME BURNED SO HIGH IT FILLED THE ONMYOJI'S CHAMBER WITH LIGHT.
AND THEN IT WAS GONE, LEAVING THE ROOM IN DARKNESS.

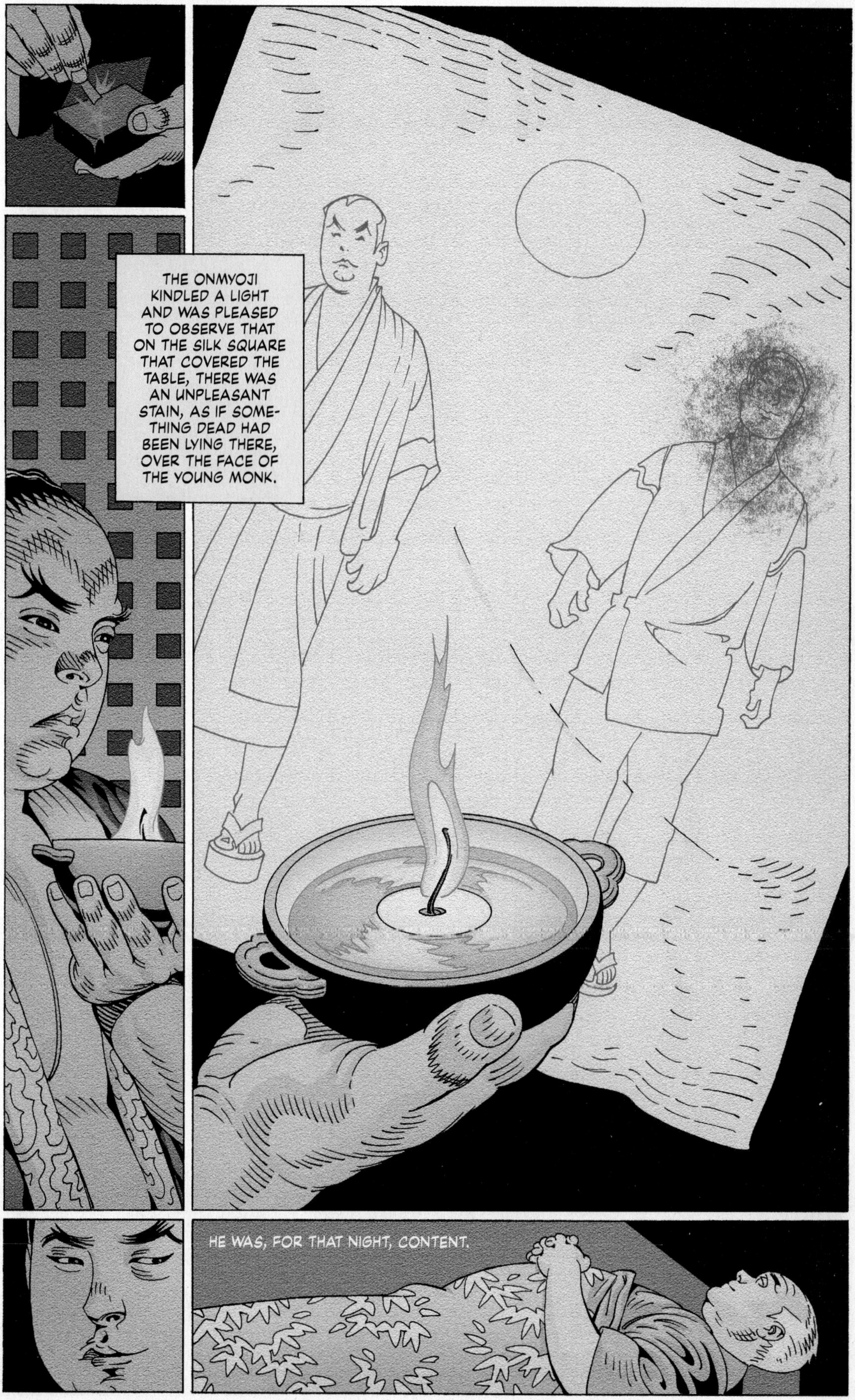
THE ONMYOJI KINDLED A LIGHT AND WAS PLEASED TO OBSERVE THAT ON THE SILK SQUARE THAT COVERED THE TABLE, THERE WAS AN UNPLEASANT STAIN, AS IF SOMETHING DEAD HAD BEEN LYING THERE, OVER THE FACE OF THE YOUNG MONK.
HE WAS, FOR THAT NIGHT, CONTENT.

IN THE MONK'S DREAM THAT NIGHT, HE WAS STANDING IN HIS FATHER'S HOUSE, BEFORE HIS FATHER HAD LOST HIS HOUSE AND ALL HE OWNED IN HIS DISGRACE, FOR HIS FATHER HAD POWERFUL ENEMIES AND HAD DIED BY HIS OWN HAND.

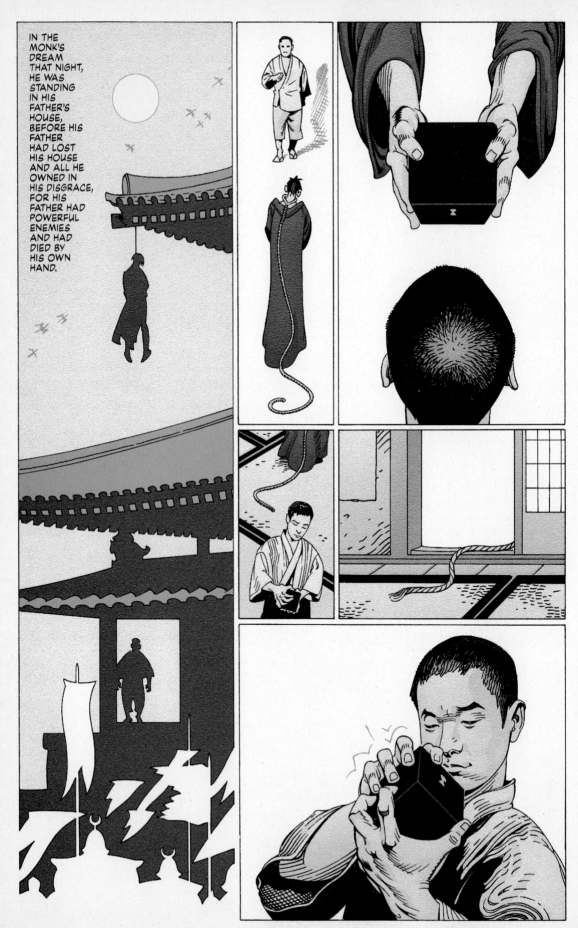

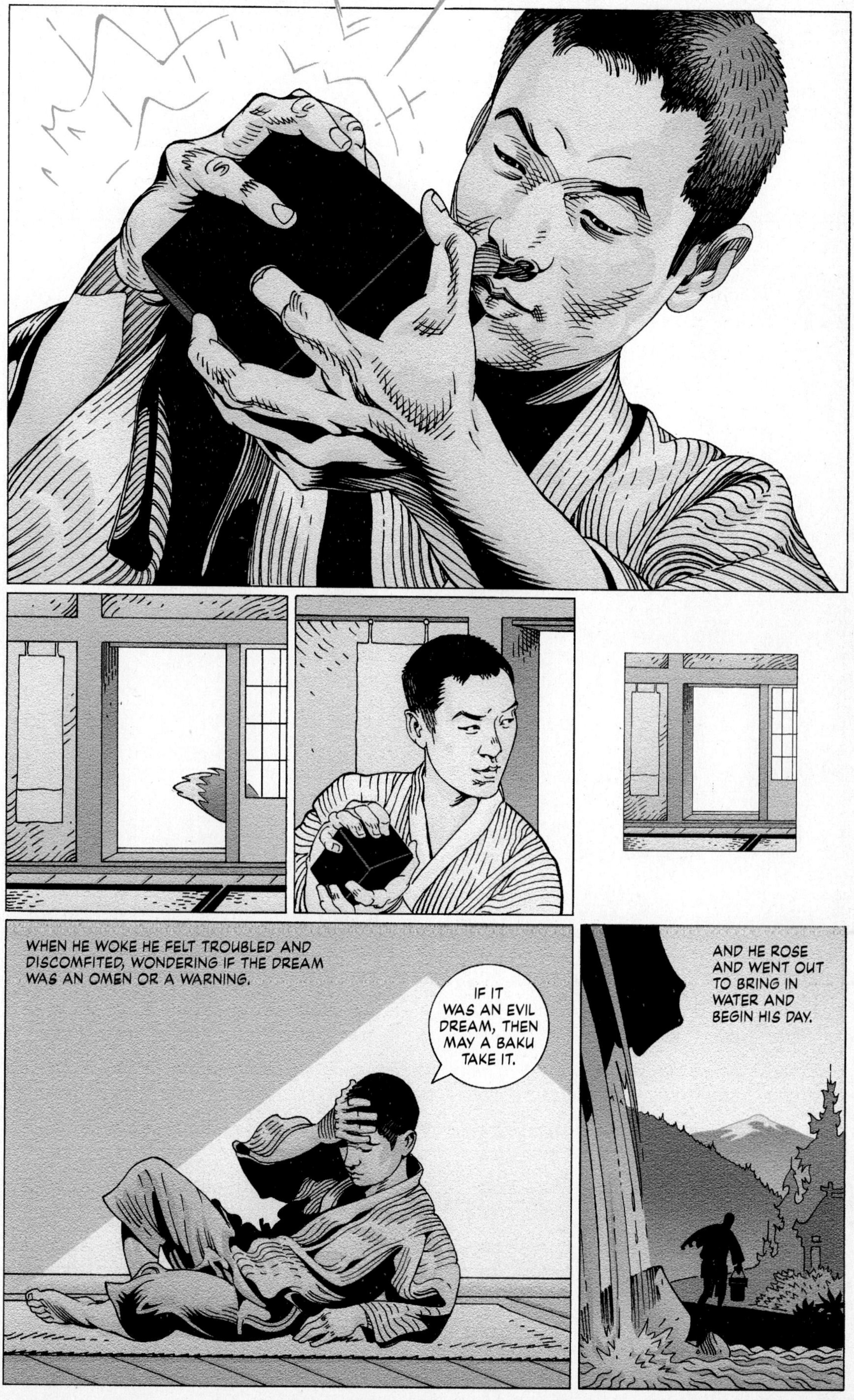
WHEN HE WOKE HE FELT TROUBLED AND DISCOMFITED, WONDERING IF THE DREAM WAS AN OMEN OR A WARNING.
IF IT WAS AN EVIL DREAM, THEN MAY A BAKU TAKE IT.
AND HE ROSE AND WENT OUT TO BRING IN WATER AND BEGIN HIS DAY.

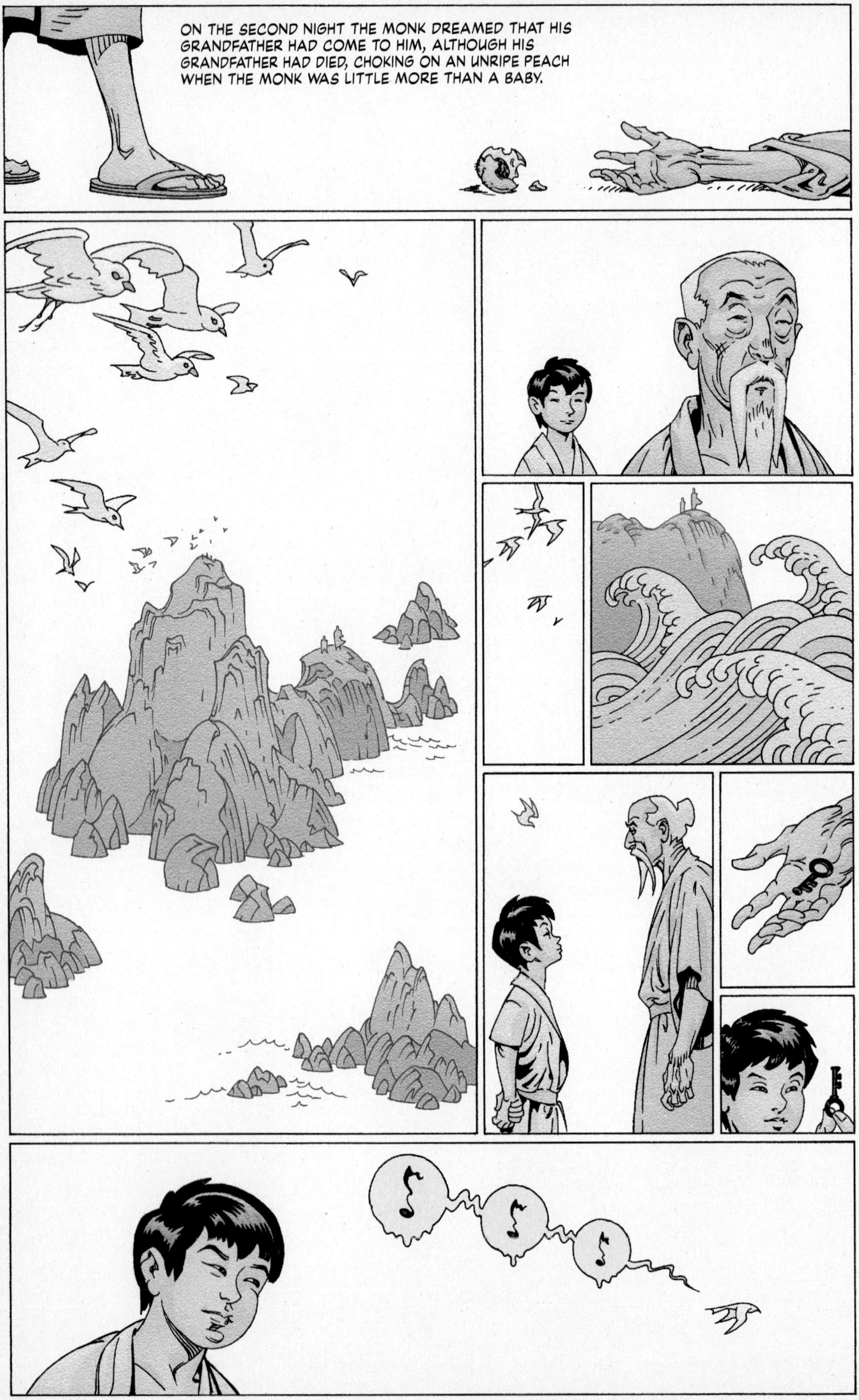
ON THE SECOND NIGHT THE MONK DREAMED THAT HIS GRANDFATHER HAD COME TO HIM, ALTHOUGH HIS GRANDFATHER HAD DIED, CHOKING ON AN UNRIPE PEACH WHEN THE MONK WAS LITTLE MORE THAN A BABY.

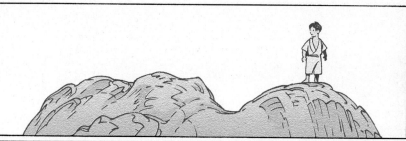

HE WOKE WITH HIS HAND CLOSED ABOUT A NONEXISTENT KEY, FEELING THAT THE EYES OF A FOX WERE UPON HIM.

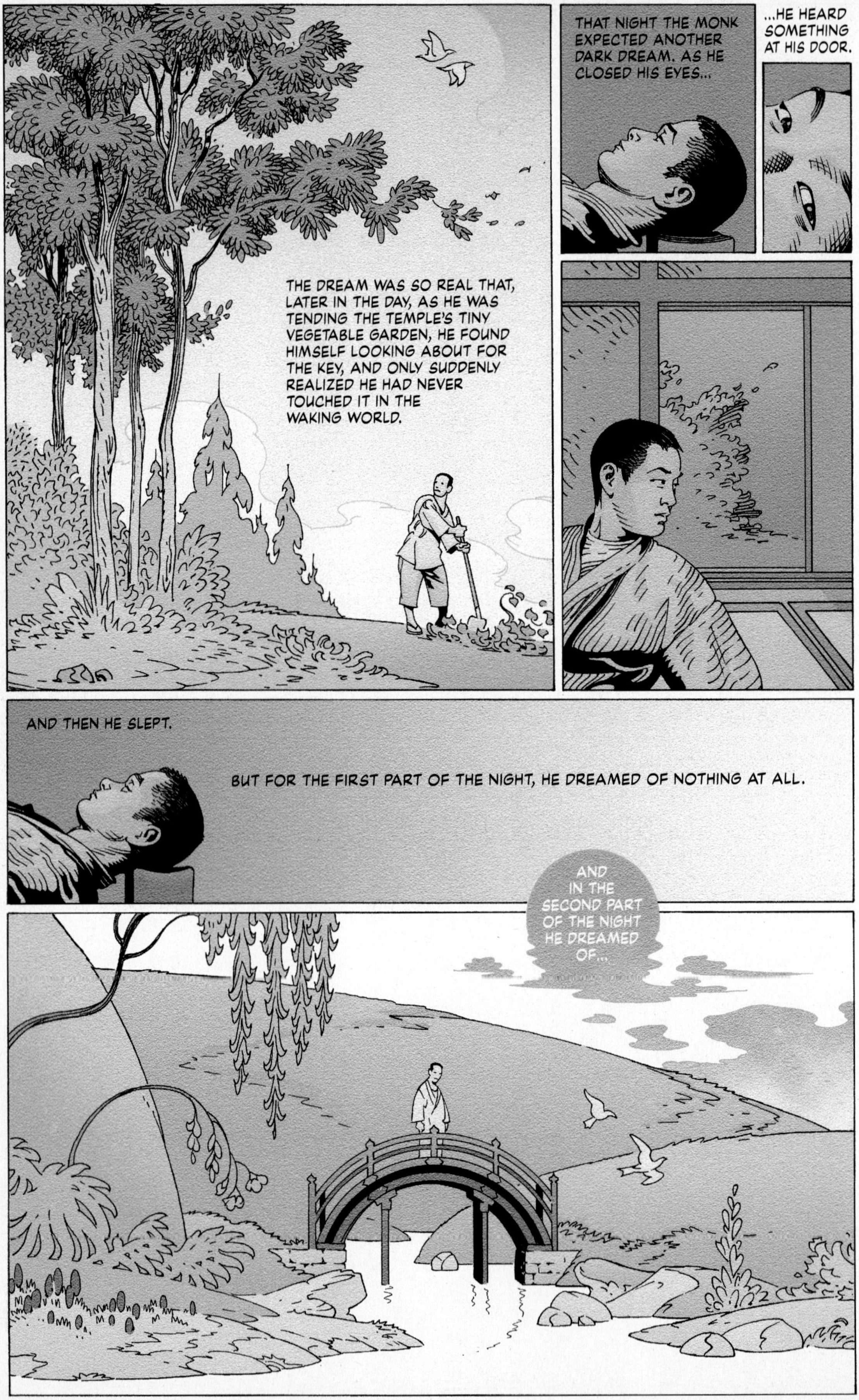
THE DREAM WAS SO REAL THAT, LATER IN THE DAY, AS HE WAS TENDING THE TEMPLE'S TINY VEGETABLE GARDEN, HE FOUND HIMSELF LOOKING ABOUT FOR THE KEY, AND ONLY SUDDENLY REALIZED HE HAD NEVER TOUCHED IT IN THE WAKING WORLD.
THAT NIGHT THE MONK EXPECTED ANOTHER DARK DREAM. AS HE CLOSED HIS EYES...
...HE HEARD SOMETHING AT HIS DOOR.
AND THEN HE SLEPT.
BUT FOR THE FIRST PART OF THE NIGHT, HE DREAMED OF NOTHING AT ALL.
AND IN THE SECOND PART OF THE NIGHT HE DREAMED OF...

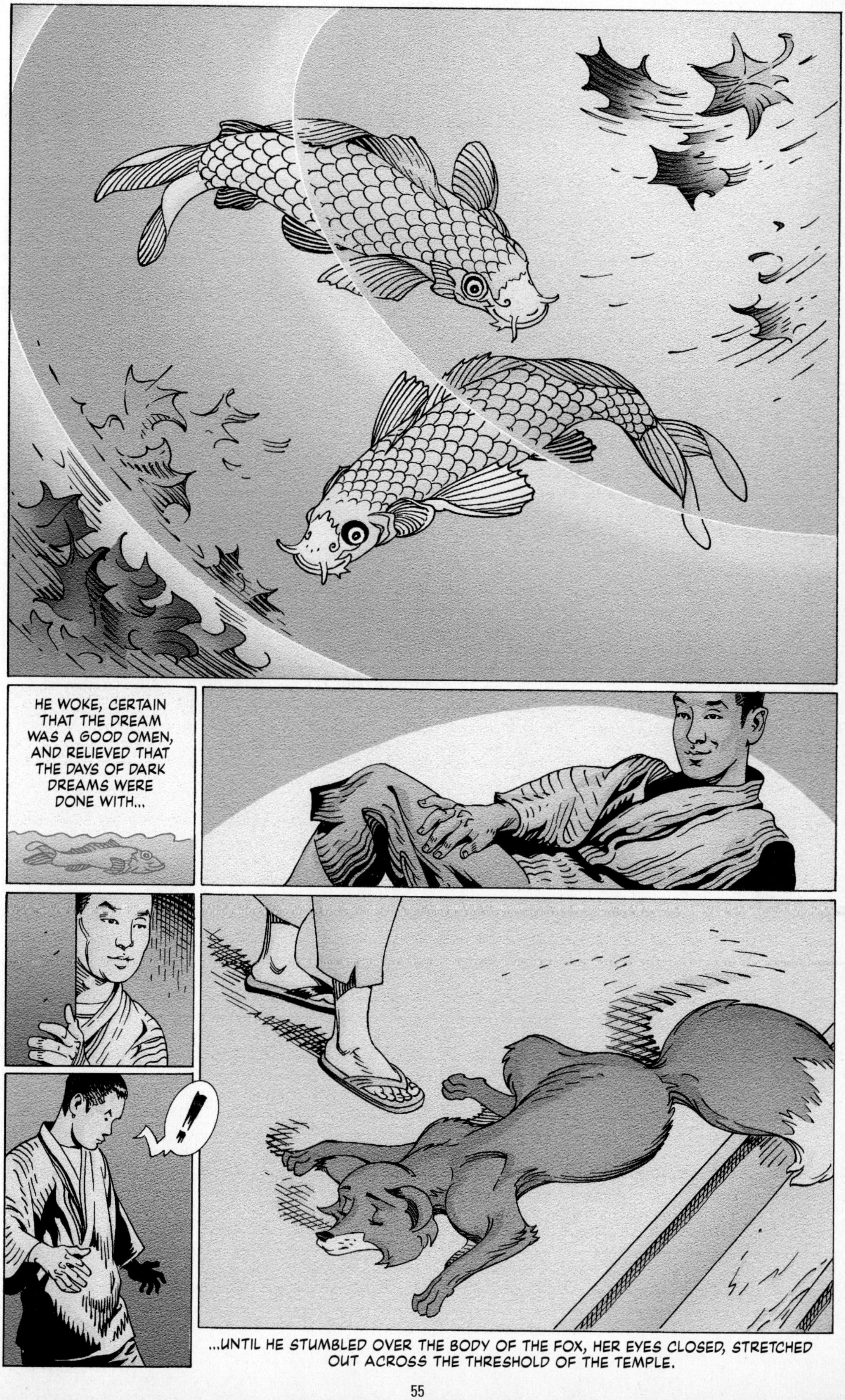
HE WOKE, CERTAIN THAT THE DREAM WAS A GOOD OMEN, AND RELIEVED THAT THE DAYS OF DARK DREAMS WERE DONE WITH...
!

...UNTIL HE STUMBLED OVER THE BODY OF THE FOX, HER EYES CLOSED, STRETCHED OUT ACROSS THE THRESHOLD OF THE TEMPLE.

4

AT FIRST, THE MONK BELIEVED THE FOX WAS DEAD. THEN HE PERCEIVED THAT SHE WAS BREATHING SO SHALLOWLY THAT ONE COULD SCARCELY TELL THAT SHE WAS BREATHING AT ALL, BUT STILL, SHE WAS ALIVE.

THE MONK TOOK THE FOX INTO THE LITTLE TEMPLE AND SET HER DOWN BESIDE THE BRAZIER TO WARM HERSELF.

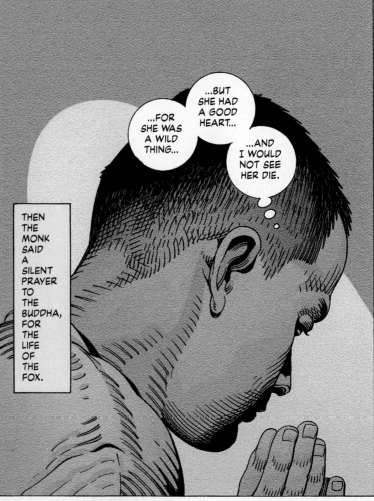

THEN THE MONK SAID A SILENT PRAYER TO THE BUDDHA, FOR THE LIFE OF THE FOX.

...FOR SHE WAS A WILD THING...

...BUT SHE HAD A GOOD HEART...

...AND I WOULD NOT SEE HER DIE.

HE STROKED HER FUR, AS SOFT AS THISTLEDOWN, AND FELT THE WEAK BEAT OF HER HEART.

WHEN I WAS A BOY...

...BEFORE MY FATHER'S DISGRACE...

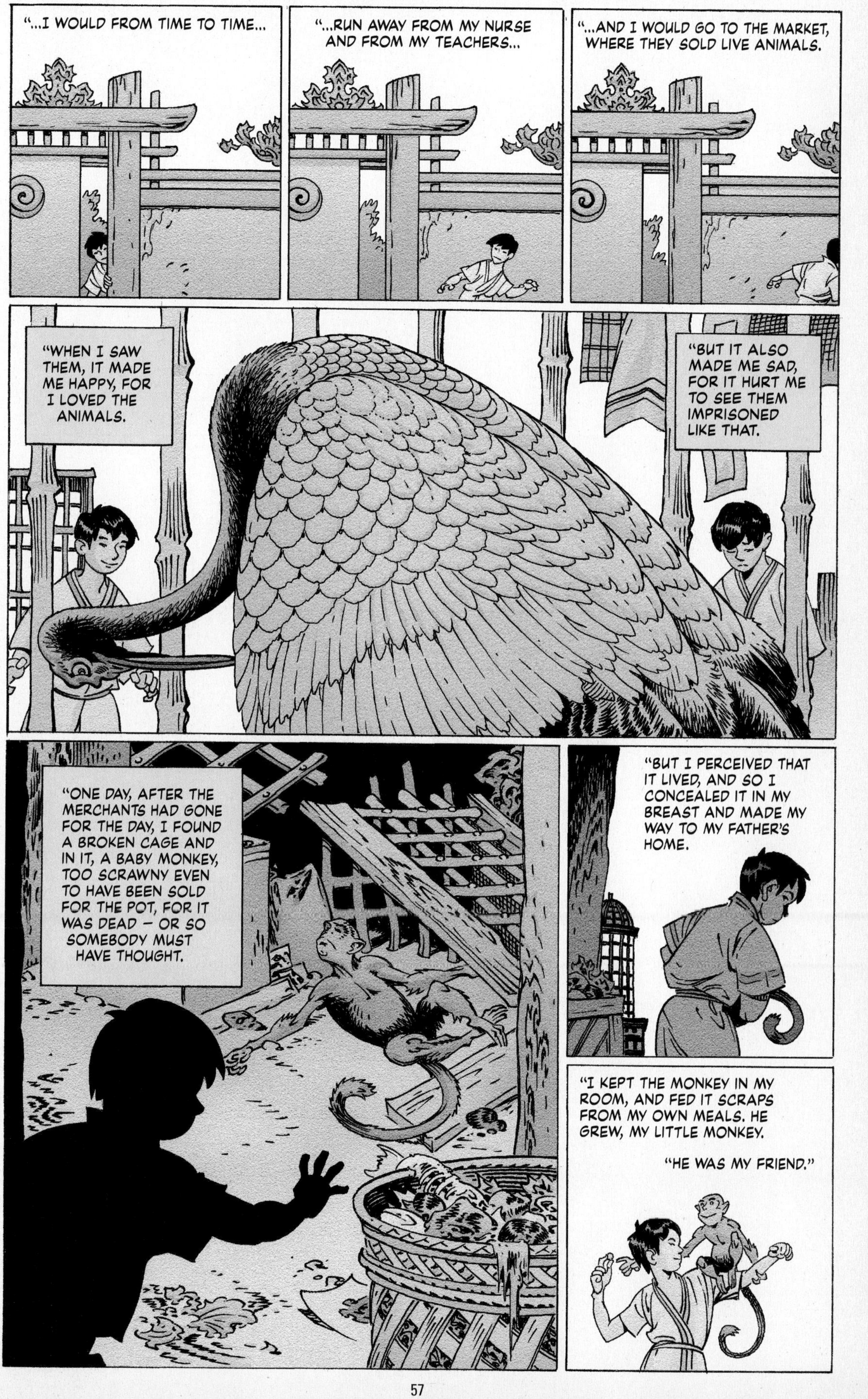
"...I WOULD FROM TIME TO TIME...
"...RUN AWAY FROM MY NURSE AND FROM MY TEACHERS...
"...AND I WOULD GO TO THE MARKET, WHERE THEY SOLD LIVE ANIMALS.
"WHEN I SAW THEM, IT MADE ME HAPPY, FOR I LOVED THE ANIMALS.
"BUT IT ALSO MADE ME SAD, FOR IT HURT ME TO SEE THEM IMPRISONED LIKE THAT.
"ONE DAY, AFTER THE MERCHANTS HAD GONE FOR THE DAY, I FOUND A BROKEN CAGE AND IN IT, A BABY MONKEY, TOO SCRAWNY EVEN TO HAVE BEEN SOLD FOR THE POT, FOR IT WAS DEAD – OR SO SOMEBODY MUST HAVE THOUGHT.
"BUT I PERCEIVED THAT IT LIVED, AND SO I CONCEALED IT IN MY BREAST AND MADE MY WAY TO MY FATHER'S HOME.
"I KEPT THE MONKEY IN MY ROOM, AND FED IT SCRAPS FROM MY OWN MEALS. HE GREW, MY LITTLE MONKEY.
"HE WAS MY FRIEND."

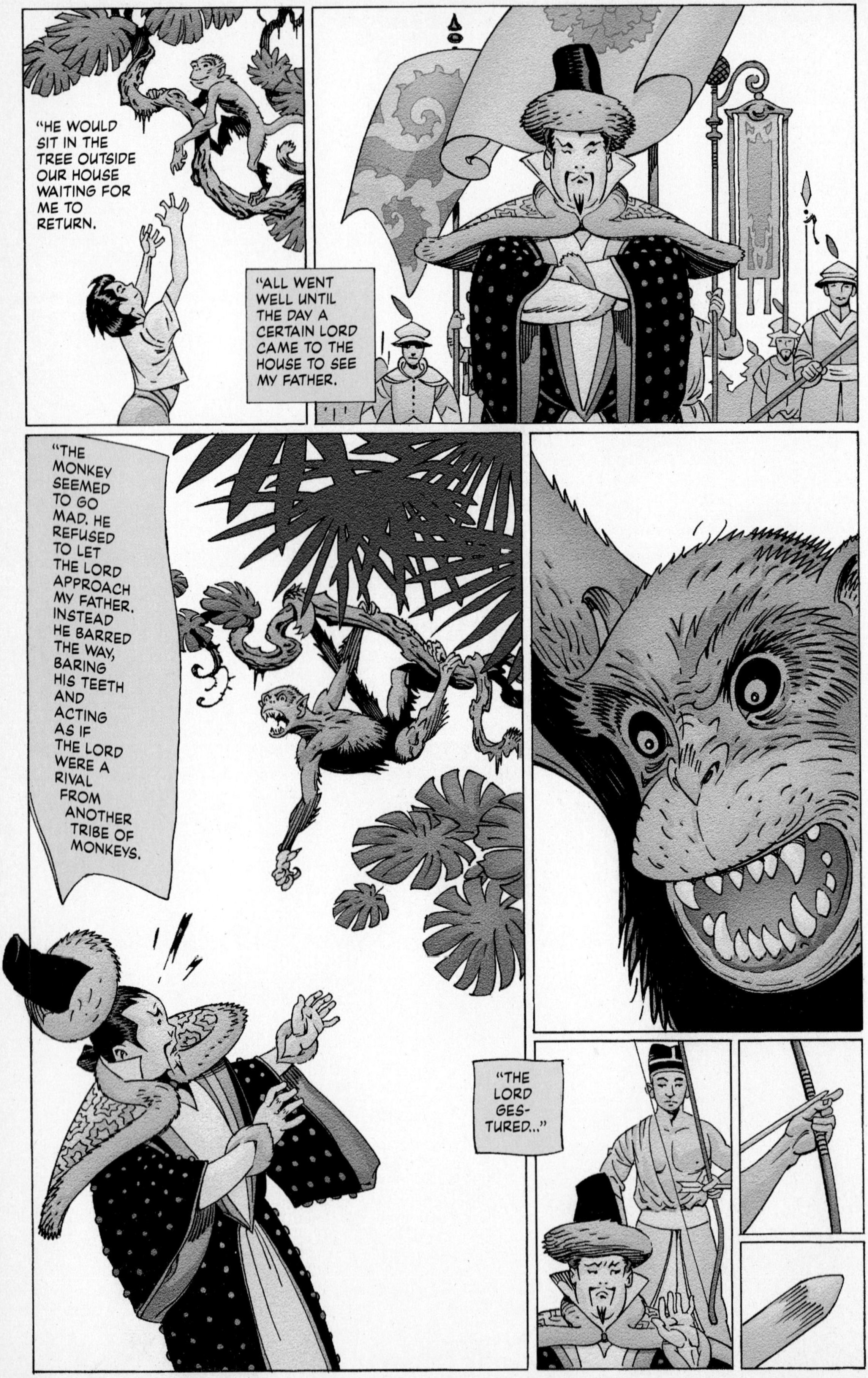
"HE WOULD SIT IN THE TREE OUTSIDE OUR HOUSE WAITING FOR ME TO RETURN.
"ALL WENT WELL UNTIL THE DAY A CERTAIN LORD CAME TO THE HOUSE TO SEE MY FATHER.
"THE MONKEY SEEMED TO GO MAD. HE REFUSED TO LET THE LORD APPROACH MY FATHER. INSTEAD HE BARRED THE WAY, BARING HIS TEETH AND ACTING AS IF THE LORD WERE A RIVAL FROM ANOTHER TRIBE OF MONKEYS.
"THE LORD GES-TURED..."

"...AND ONE OF HIS RETAINERS PUT AN ARROW THROUGH THE MONKEY'S CHEST, ALTHOUGH I BEGGED HIM NOT TO.

"I CARRIED THE MONKEY OUT OF THE HOUSE, AND HE LOOKED INTO MY EYES AS HE DIED.

"LATER, WHEN MY FATHER WAS DISGRACED, IT WAS THROUGH THE MACHINATIONS OF THAT SELFSAME LORD. AND SOMETIMES I THINK THAT THE MONKEY WAS BUT A SPIRIT SENT BY AMIDA BUDDHA TO PROTECT US, IF ONLY WE HAD LISTENED AND SEEN."

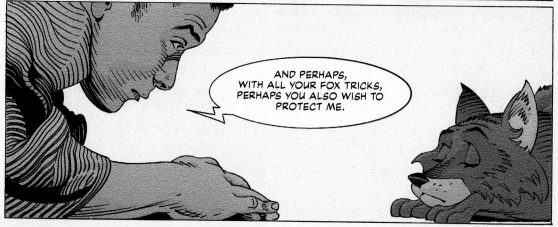

AND PERHAPS, WITH ALL YOUR FOX TRICKS, PERHAPS YOU ALSO WISH TO PROTECT ME.

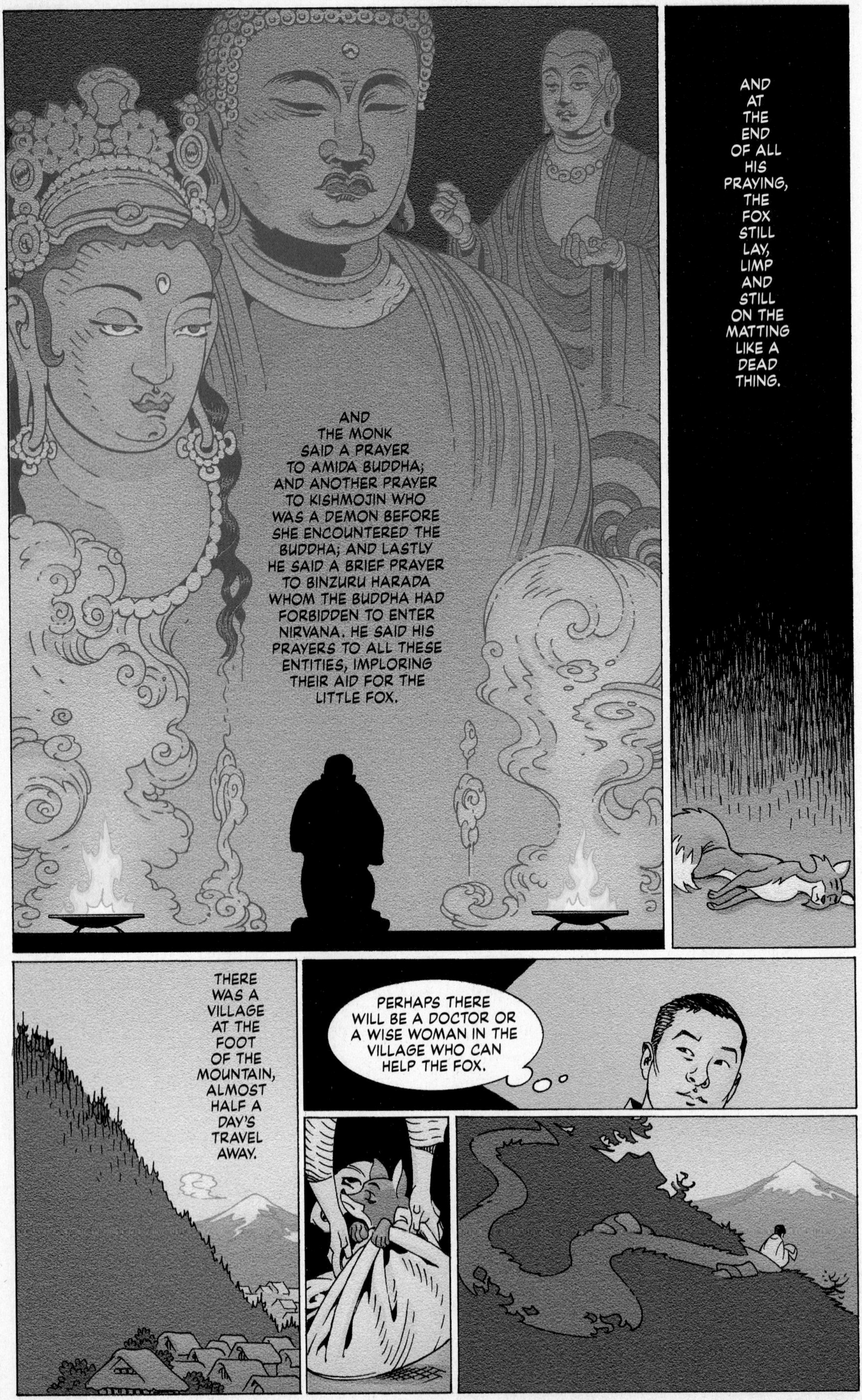
AND THE MONK SAID A PRAYER TO AMIDA BUDDHA; AND ANOTHER PRAYER TO KISHMOJIN WHO WAS A DEMON BEFORE SHE ENCOUNTERED THE BUDDHA; AND LASTLY HE SAID A BRIEF PRAYER TO BINZURU HARADA WHOM THE BUDDHA HAD FORBIDDEN TO ENTER NIRVANA. HE SAID HIS PRAYERS TO ALL THESE ENTITIES, IMPLORING THEIR AID FOR THE LITTLE FOX.
AND AT THE END OF ALL HIS PRAYING, THE FOX STILL LAY, LIMP AND STILL ON THE MATTING LIKE A DEAD THING.
THERE WAS A VILLAGE AT THE FOOT OF THE MOUNTAIN, ALMOST HALF A DAY'S TRAVEL AWAY.
PERHAPS THERE WILL BE A DOCTOR OR A WISE WOMAN IN THE VILLAGE WHO CAN HELP THE FOX.

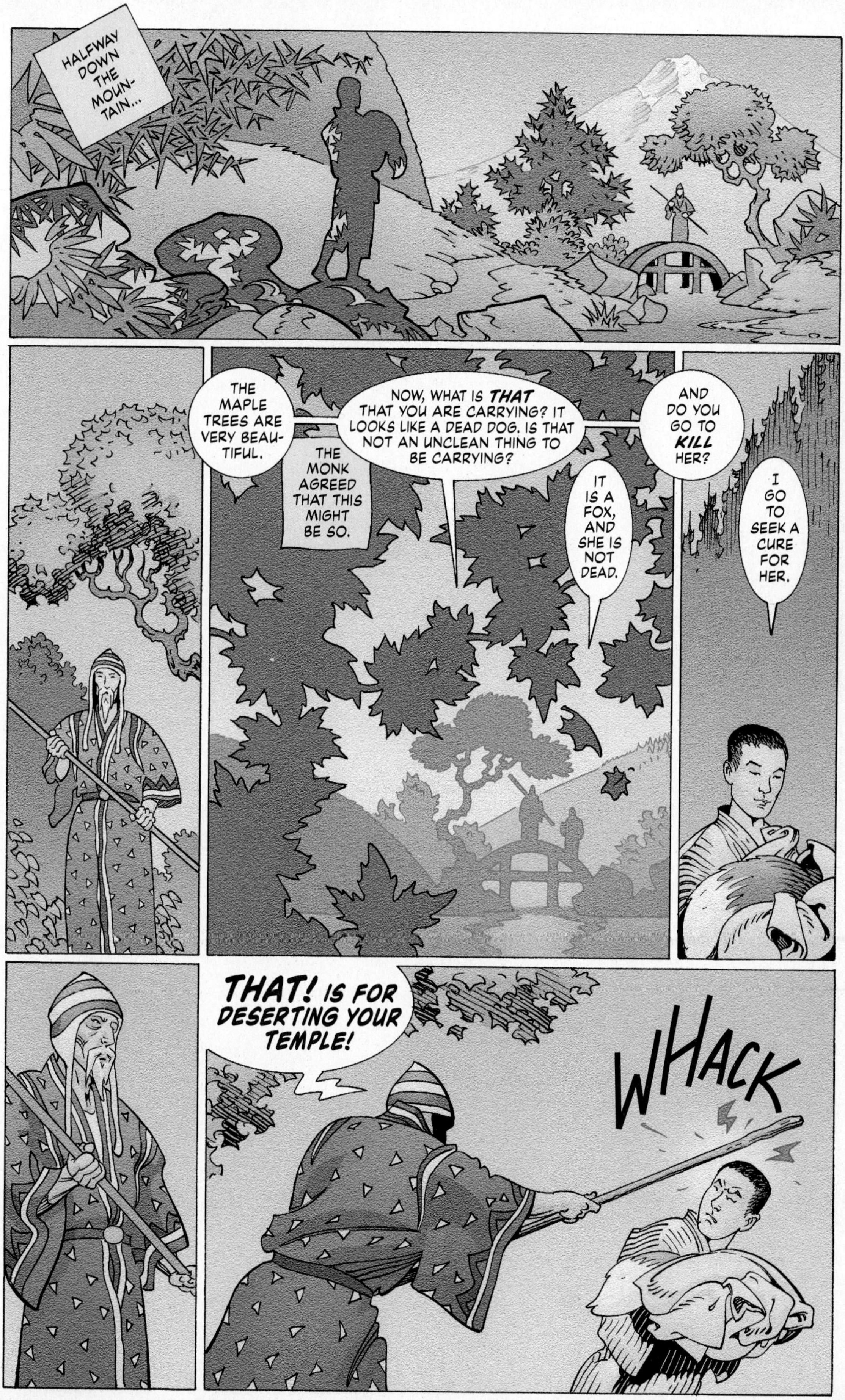
HALFWAY DOWN THE MOUN-TAIN...
THE MAPLE TREES ARE VERY BEAU-TIFUL.
THE MONK AGREED THAT THIS MIGHT BE SO.
NOW, WHAT IS THAT THAT YOU ARE CARRYING? IT LOOKS LIKE A DEAD DOG. IS THAT NOT AN UNCLEAN THING TO BE CARRYING?
IT IS A FOX, AND SHE IS NOT DEAD.
AND DO YOU GO TO KILL HER?
I GO TO SEEK A CURE FOR HER.
THAT! IS FOR DESERTING YOUR TEMPLE!
WHACK

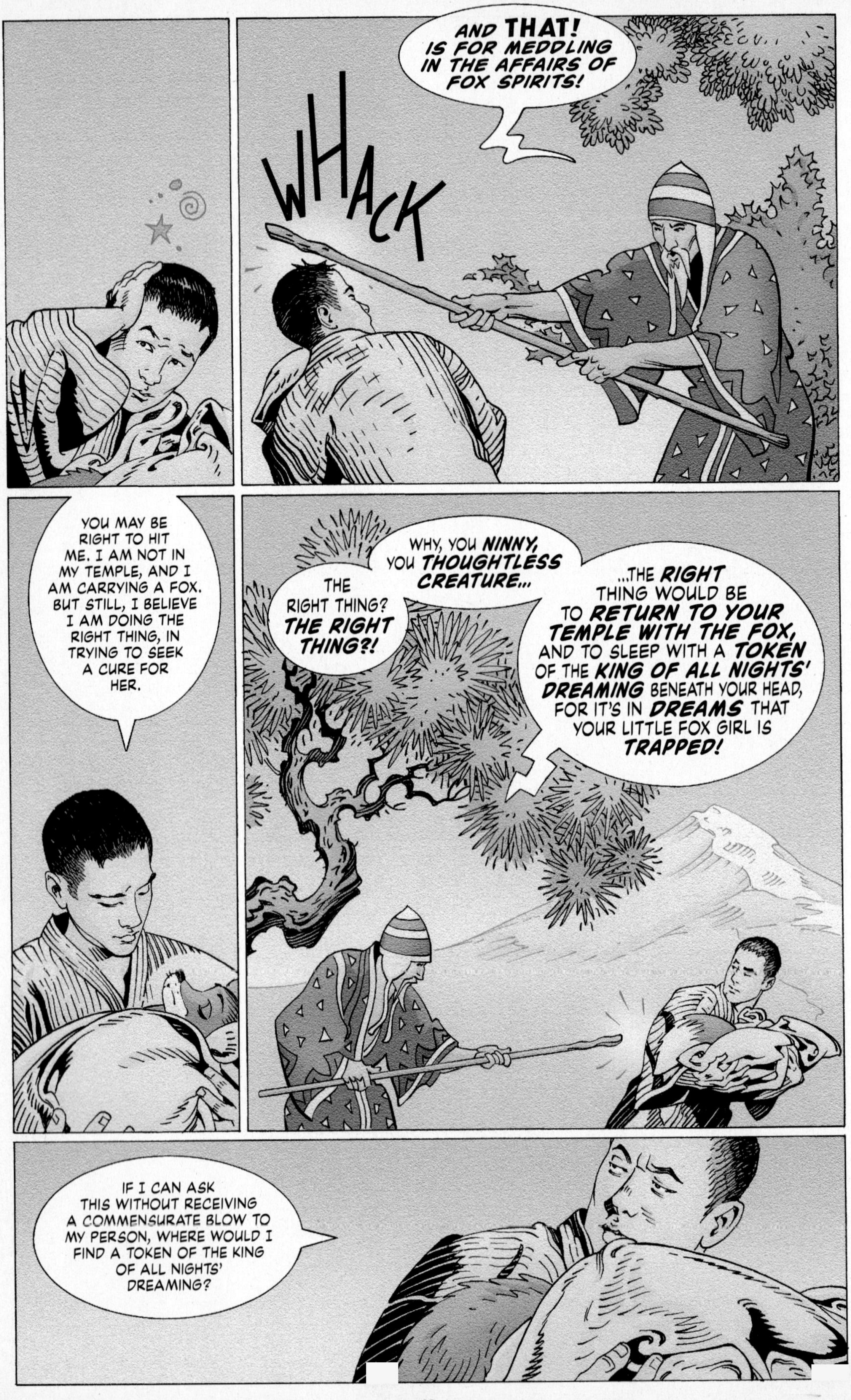
AND THAT! IS FOR MEDDLING IN THE AFFAIRS OF FOX SPIRITS!
WHACK
YOU MAY BE RIGHT TO HIT ME. I AM NOT IN MY TEMPLE, AND I AM CARRYING A FOX. BUT STILL, I BELIEVE I AM DOING THE RIGHT THING, IN TRYING TO SEEK A CURE FOR HER.
THE RIGHT THING? THE RIGHT THING?!
WHY, YOU NINNY, YOU THOUGHTLESS CREATURE...
...THE RIGHT THING WOULD BE TO RETURN TO YOUR TEMPLE WITH THE FOX, AND TO SLEEP WITH A TOKEN OF THE KING OF ALL NIGHTS' DREAMING BENEATH YOUR HEAD, FOR IT'S IN DREAMS THAT YOUR LITTLE FOX GIRL IS TRAPPED!
IF I CAN ASK THIS WITHOUT RECEIVING A COMMENSURATE BLOW TO MY PERSON, WHERE WOULD I FIND A TOKEN OF THE KING OF ALL NIGHTS' DREAMING?

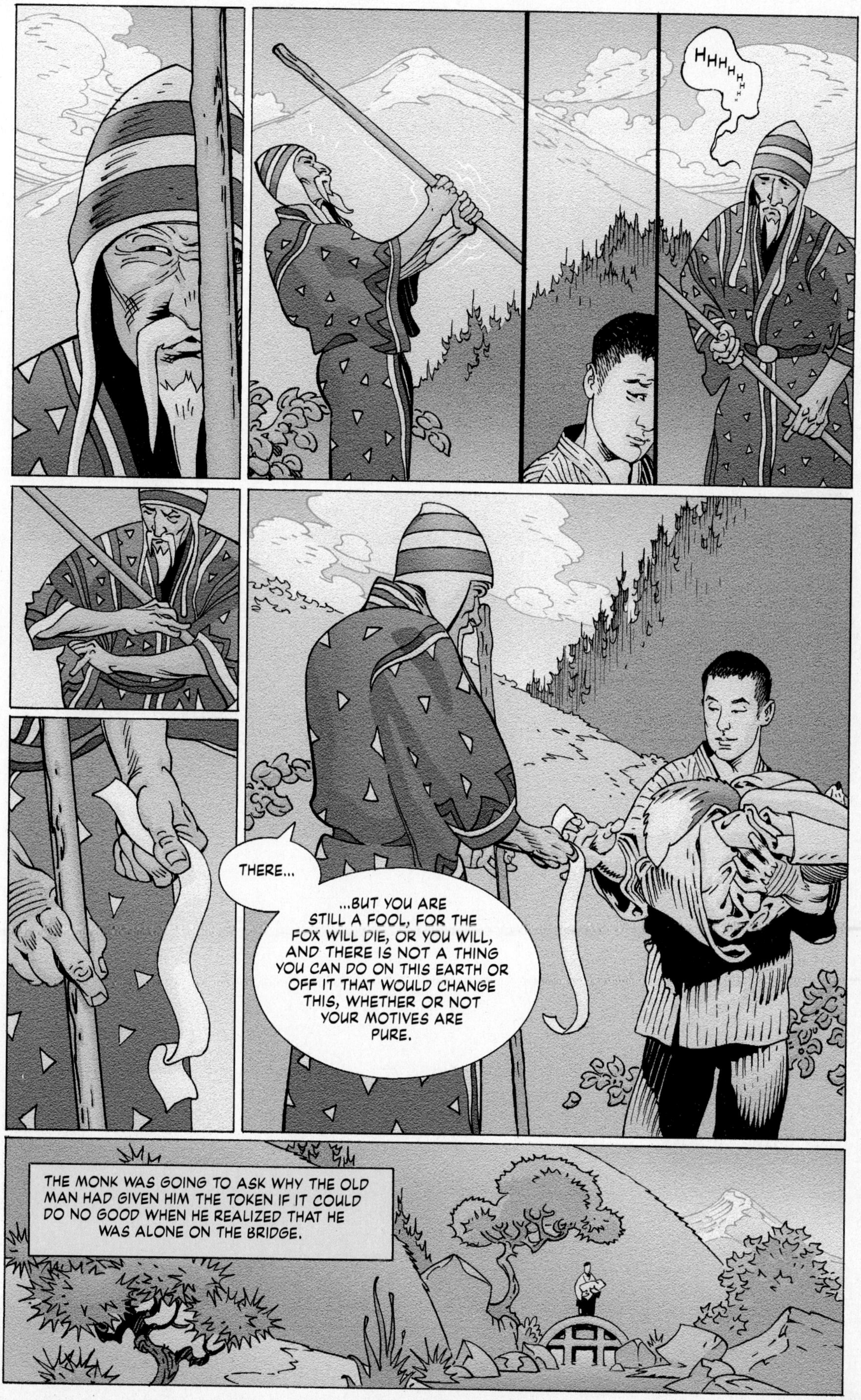
HHHHHHHH
THERE...
...BUT YOU ARE STILL A FOOL, FOR THE FOX WILL DIE, OR YOU WILL, AND THERE IS NOT A THING YOU CAN DO ON THIS EARTH OR OFF IT THAT WOULD CHANGE THIS, WHETHER OR NOT YOUR MOTIVES ARE PURE.
THE MONK WAS GOING TO ASK WHY THE OLD MAN HAD GIVEN HIM THE TOKEN IF IT COULD DO NO GOOD WHEN HE REALIZED THAT HE WAS ALONE ON THE BRIDGE.

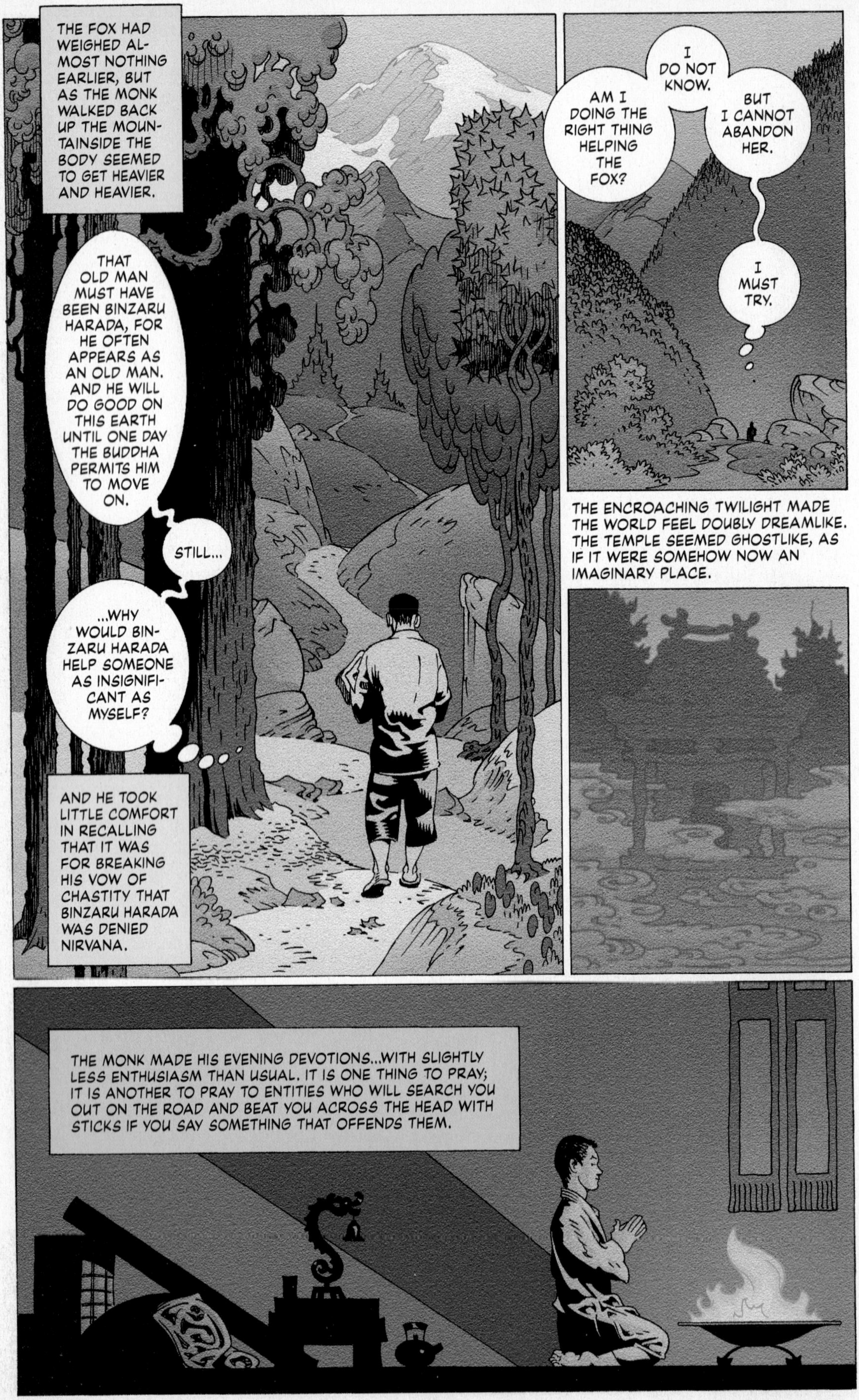
THE FOX HAD WEIGHED AL-MOST NOTHING EARLIER, BUT AS THE MONK WALKED BACK UP THE MOUN-TAINSIDE THE BODY SEEMED TO GET HEAVIER AND HEAVIER.
THAT OLD MAN MUST HAVE BEEN BINZARU HARADA, FOR HE OFTEN APPEARS AS AN OLD MAN. AND HE WILL DO GOOD ON THIS EARTH UNTIL ONE DAY THE BUDDHA PERMITS HIM TO MOVE ON.
STILL...
...WHY WOULD BIN-ZARU HARADA HELP SOMEONE AS INSIGNIFI-CANT AS MYSELF?
AND HE TOOK LITTLE COMFORT IN RECALLING THAT IT WAS FOR BREAKING HIS VOW OF CHASTITY THAT BINZARU HARADA WAS DENIED NIRVANA.
AM I DOING THE RIGHT THING HELPING THE FOX?
I DO NOT KNOW.
BUT I CANNOT ABANDON HER.
I MUST TRY.
THE ENCROACHING TWILIGHT MADE THE WORLD FEEL DOUBLY DREAMLIKE. THE TEMPLE SEEMED GHOSTLIKE, AS IF IT WERE SOMEHOW NOW AN IMAGINARY PLACE.
THE MONK MADE HIS EVENING DEVOTIONS...WITH SLIGHTLY LESS ENTHUSIASM THAN USUAL. IT IS ONE THING TO PRAY; IT IS ANOTHER TO PRAY TO ENTITIES WHO WILL SEARCH YOU OUT ON THE ROAD AND BEAT YOU ACROSS THE HEAD WITH STICKS IF YOU SAY SOMETHING THAT OFFENDS THEM.

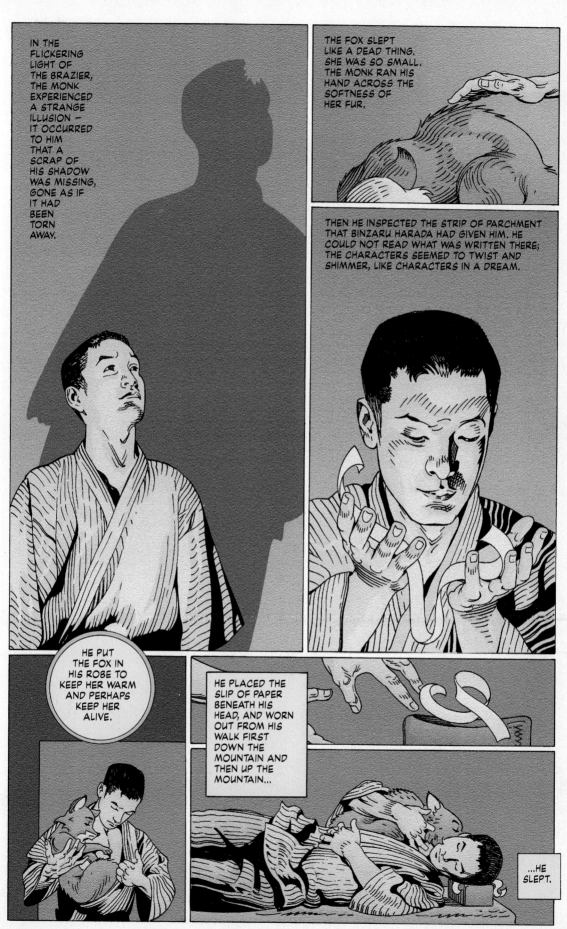

IN THE FLICKERING LIGHT OF THE BRAZIER, THE MONK EXPERIENCED A STRANGE ILLUSION — IT OCCURRED TO HIM THAT A SCRAP OF HIS SHADOW WAS MISSING, GONE AS IF IT HAD BEEN TORN AWAY.

THE FOX SLEPT LIKE A DEAD THING, SHE WAS SO SMALL. THE MONK RAN HIS HAND ACROSS THE SOFTNESS OF HER FUR.

THEN HE INSPECTED THE STRIP OF PARCHMENT THAT BINZARU HARADA HAD GIVEN HIM. HE COULD NOT READ WHAT WAS WRITTEN THERE; THE CHARACTERS SEEMED TO TWIST AND SHIMMER, LIKE CHARACTERS IN A DREAM.

HE PUT THE FOX IN HIS ROBE TO KEEP HER WARM AND PERHAPS KEEP HER ALIVE.

HE PLACED THE SLIP OF PAPER BENEATH HIS HEAD, AND WORN OUT FROM HIS WALK FIRST DOWN THE MOUNTAIN AND THEN UP THE MOUNTAIN...

...HE SLEPT.

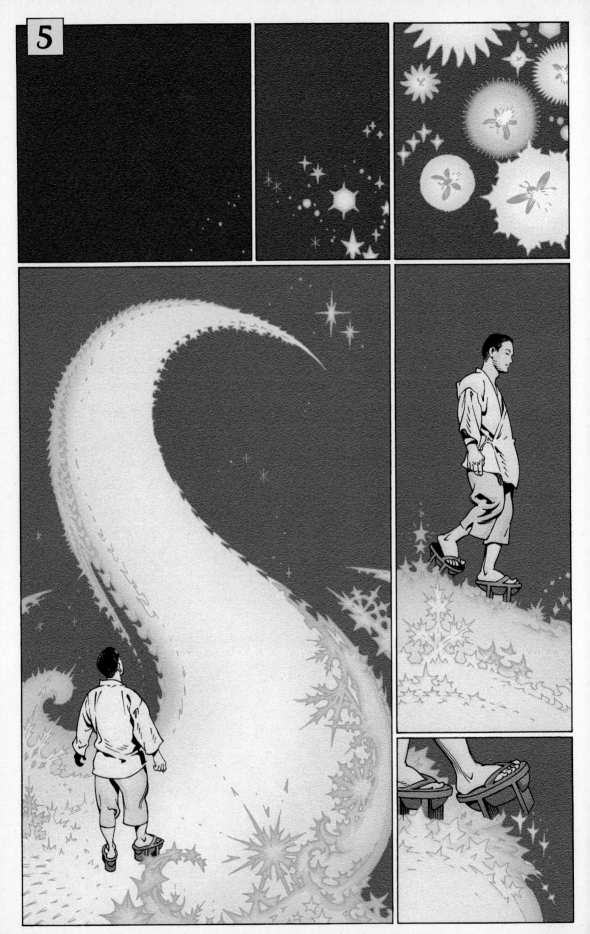

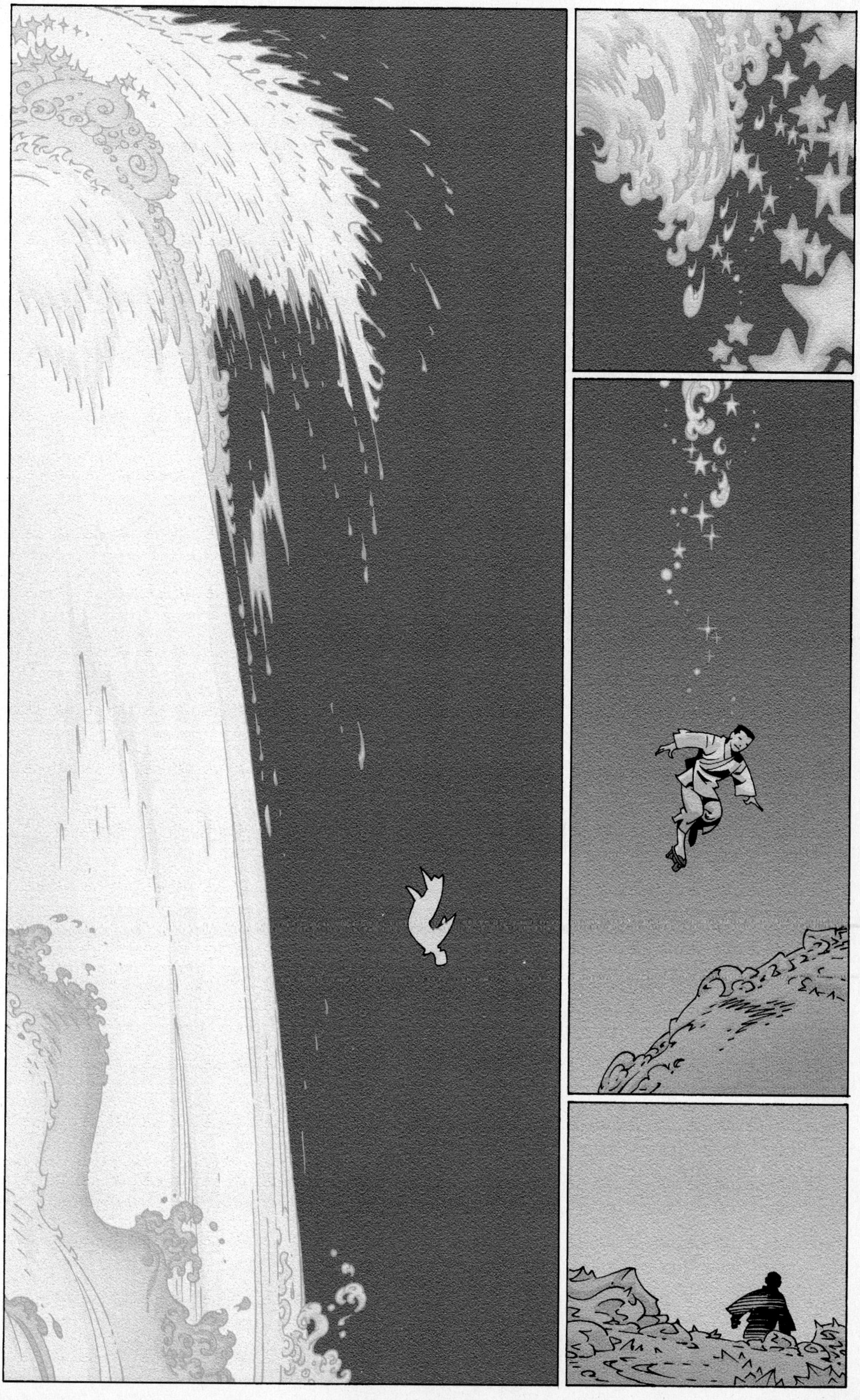

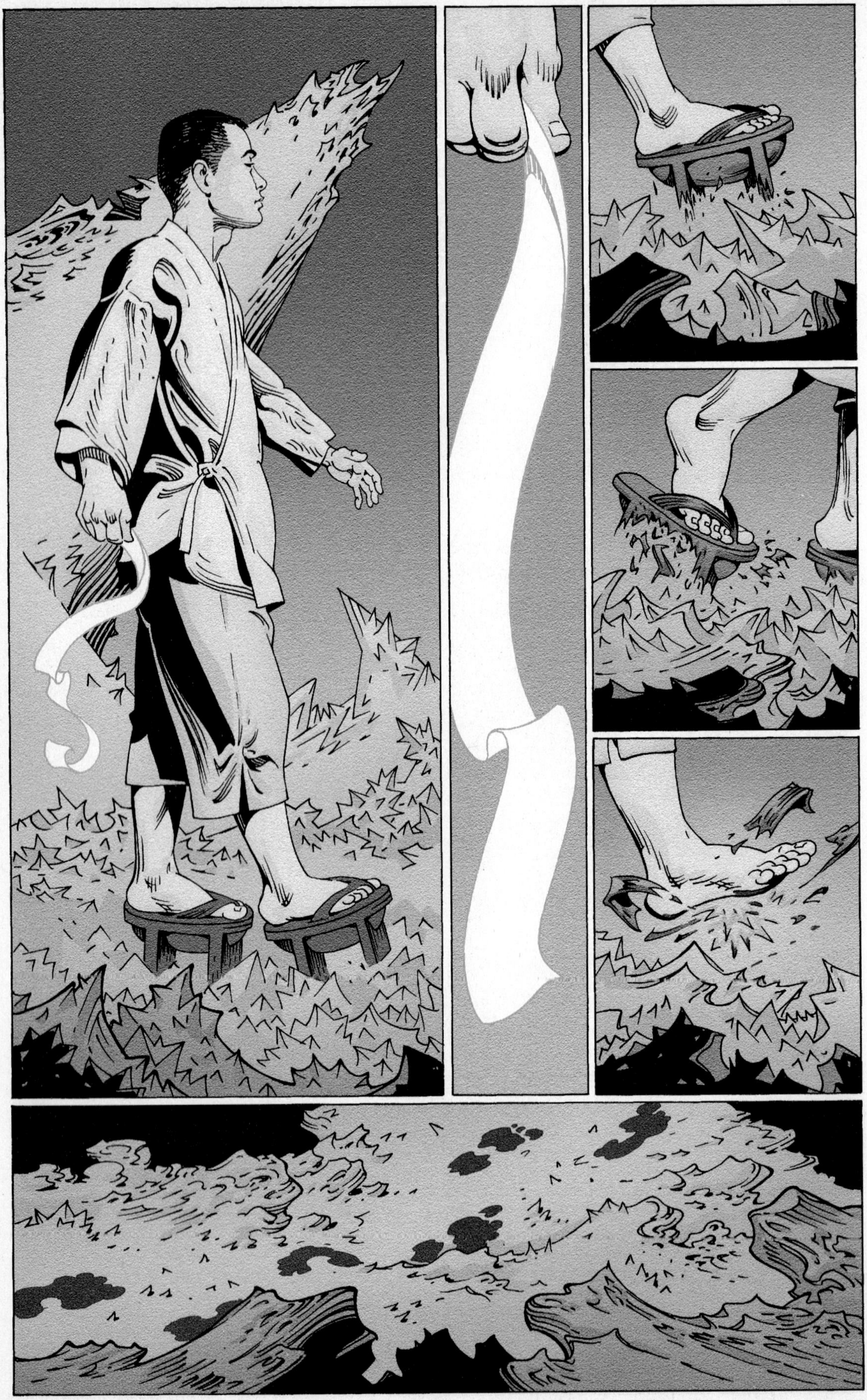

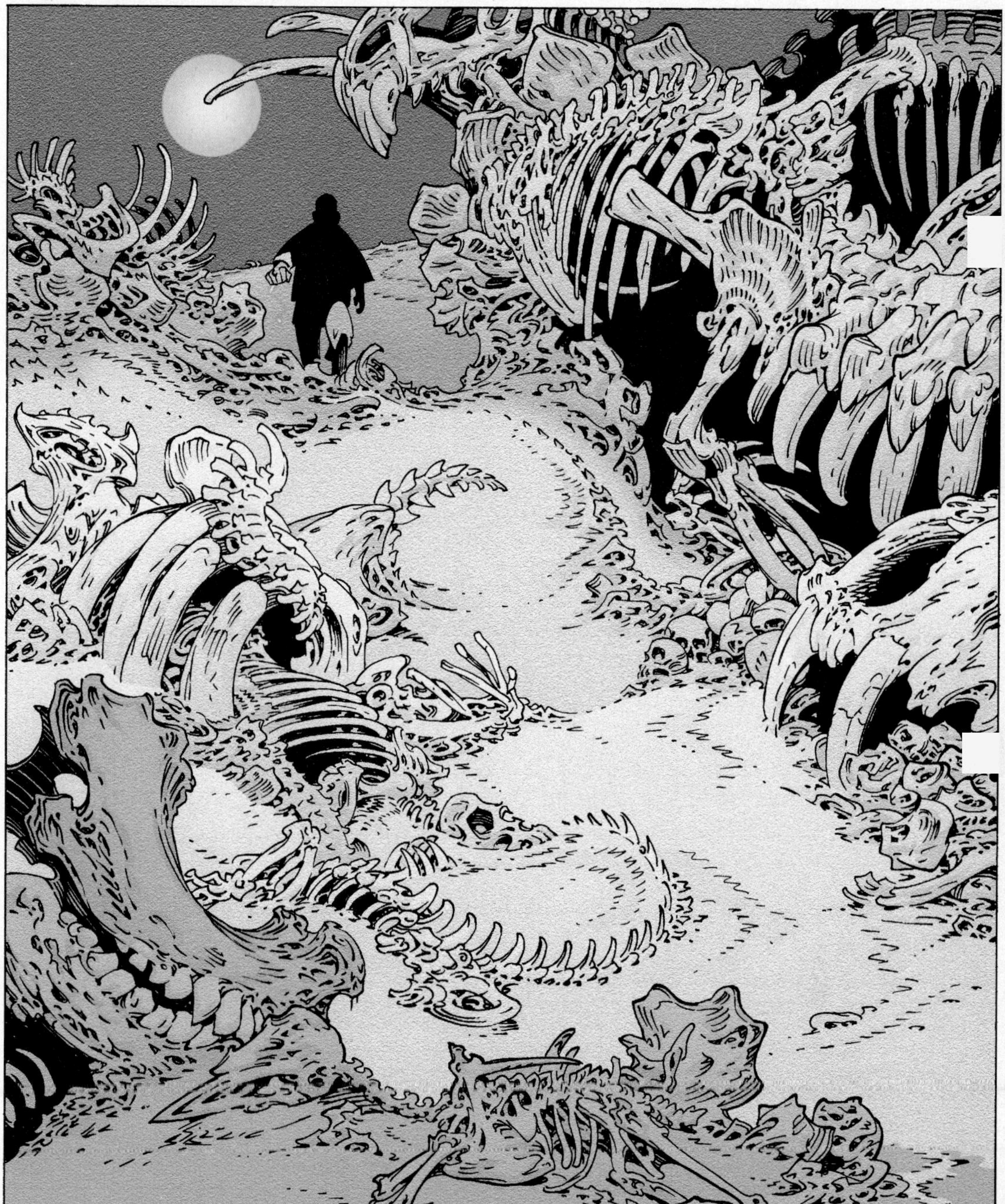

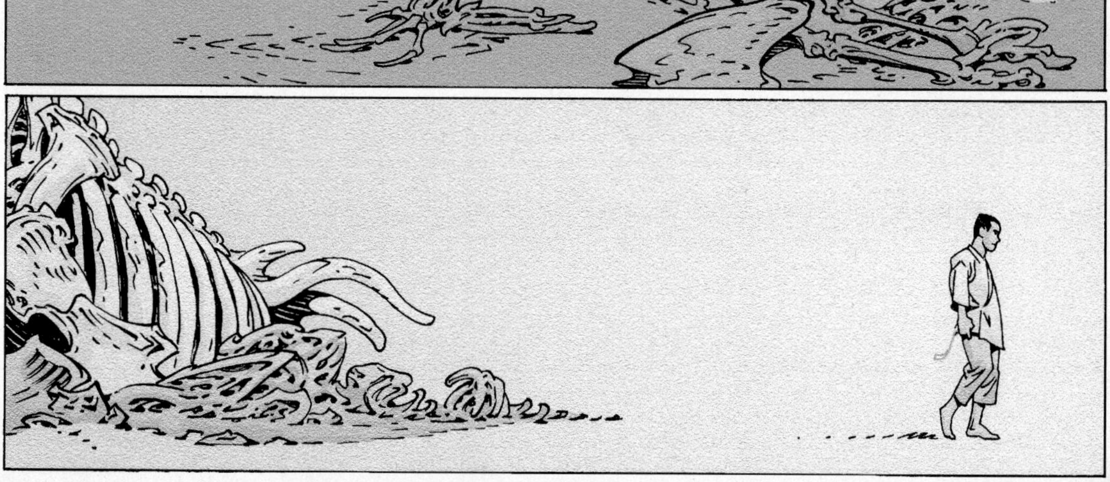

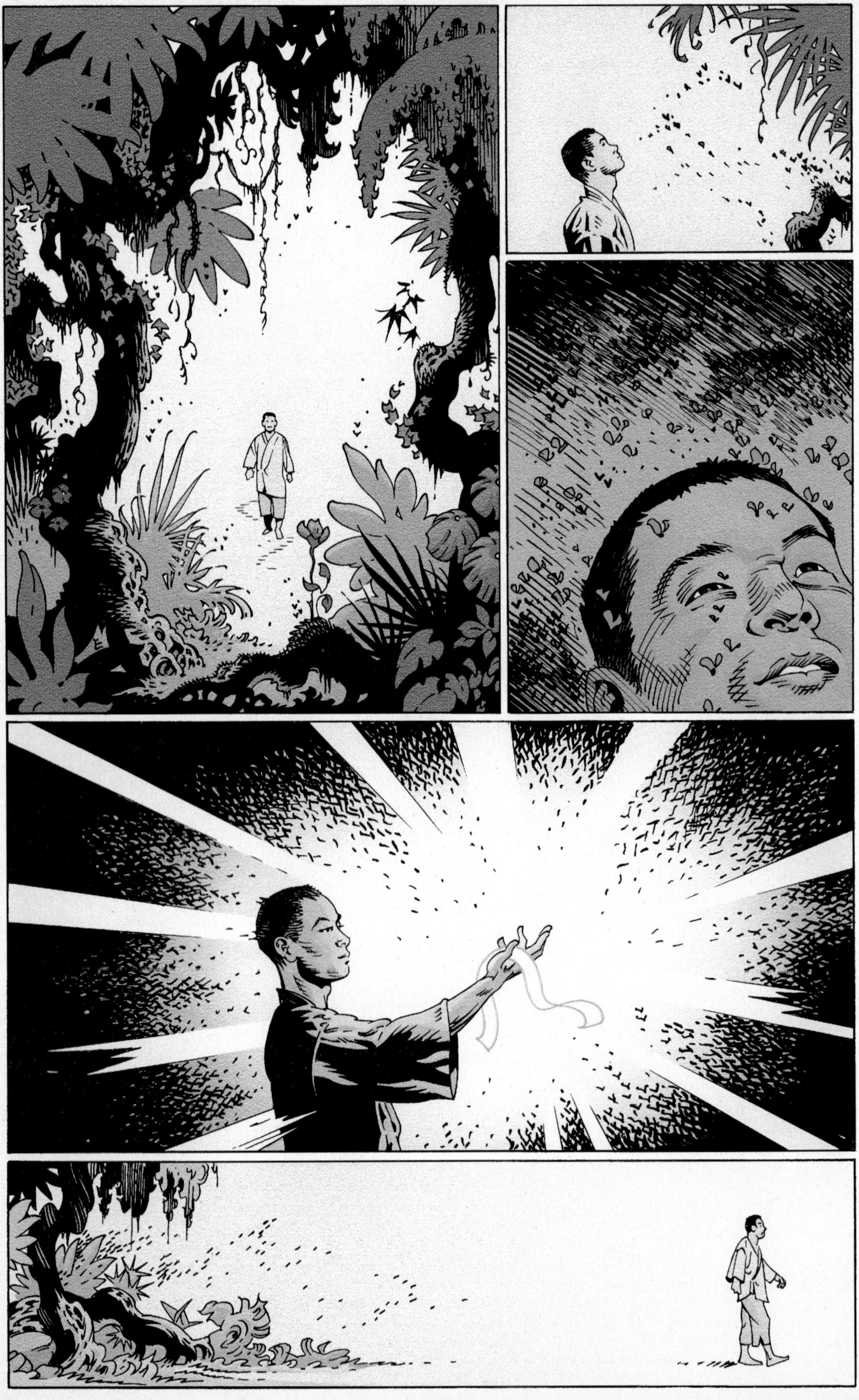

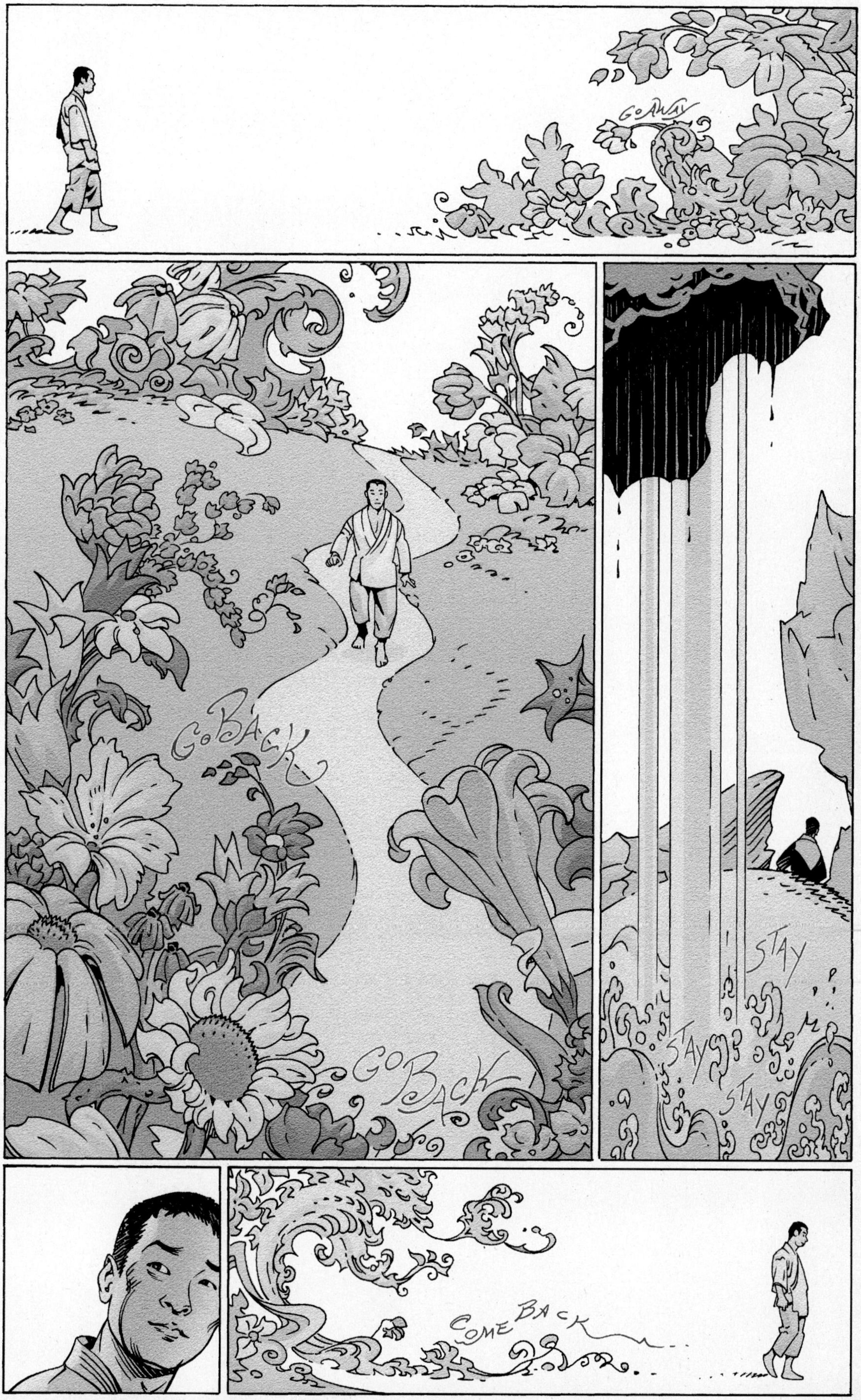
GO AWAY
GO BACK
GO BACK
STAY
STAY
STAY
COME BACK

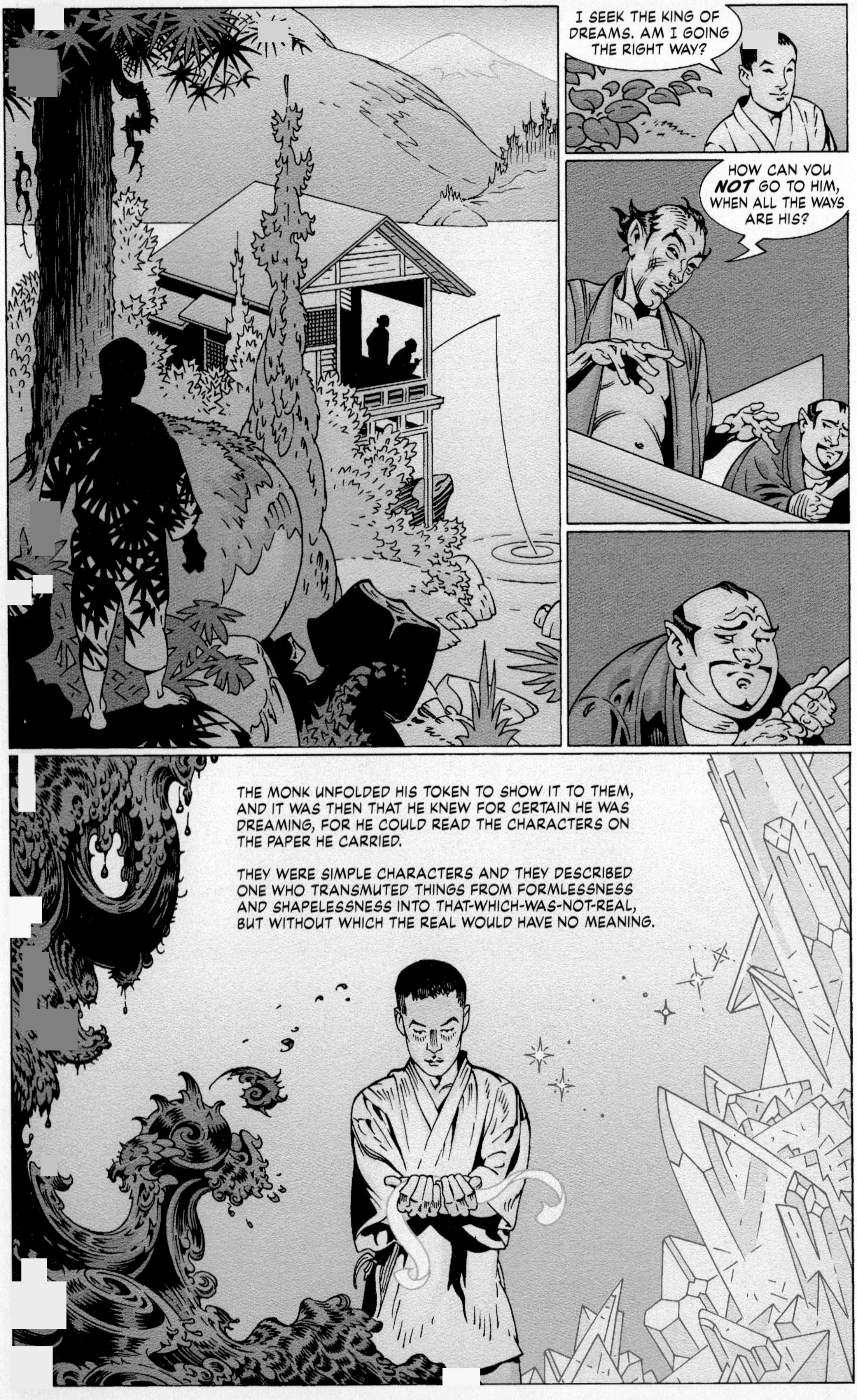
I SEEK THE KING OF DREAMS. AM I GOING THE RIGHT WAY?
HOW CAN YOU **NOT** GO TO HIM, WHEN ALL THE WAYS ARE HIS?
THE MONK UNFOLDED HIS TOKEN TO SHOW IT TO THEM, AND IT WAS THEN THAT HE KNEW FOR CERTAIN HE WAS DREAMING, FOR HE COULD READ THE CHARACTERS ON THE PAPER HE CARRIED.
THEY WERE SIMPLE CHARACTERS AND THEY DESCRIBED ONE WHO TRANSMUTED THINGS FROM FORMLESSNESS AND SHAPELESSNESS INTO THAT-WHICH-WAS-NOT-REAL, BUT WITHOUT WHICH THE REAL WOULD HAVE NO MEANING.

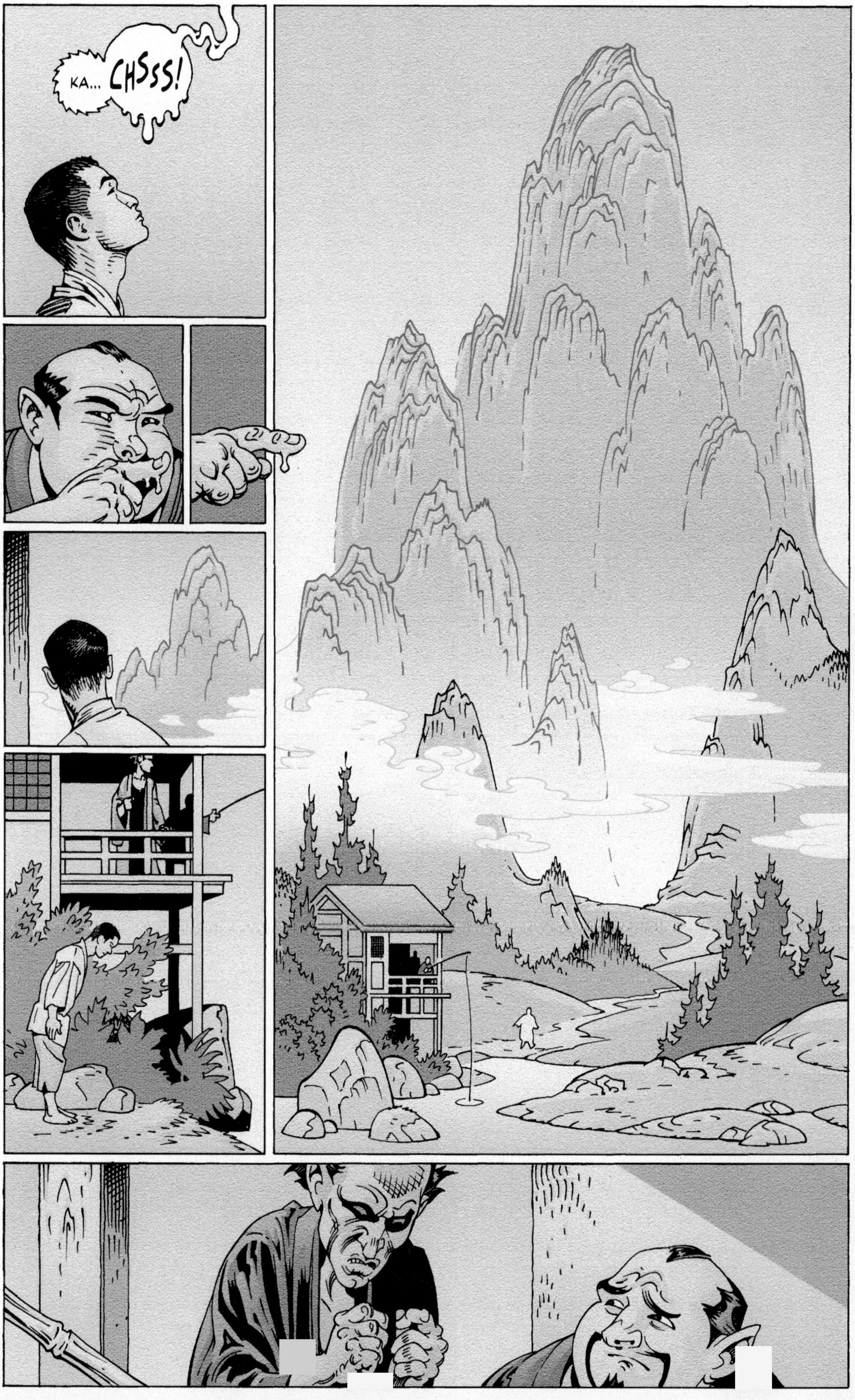
KA... CHSSS!

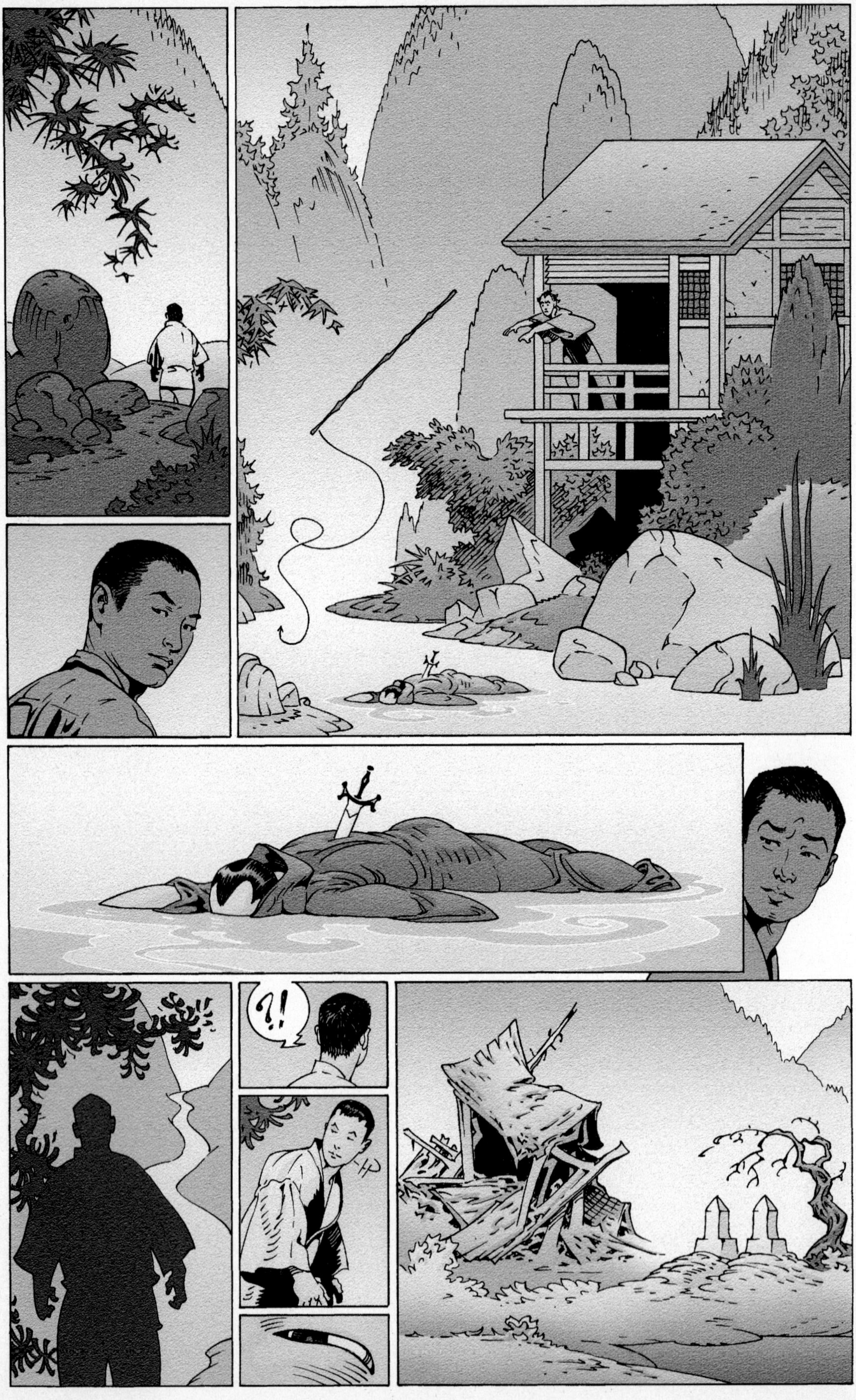
?!

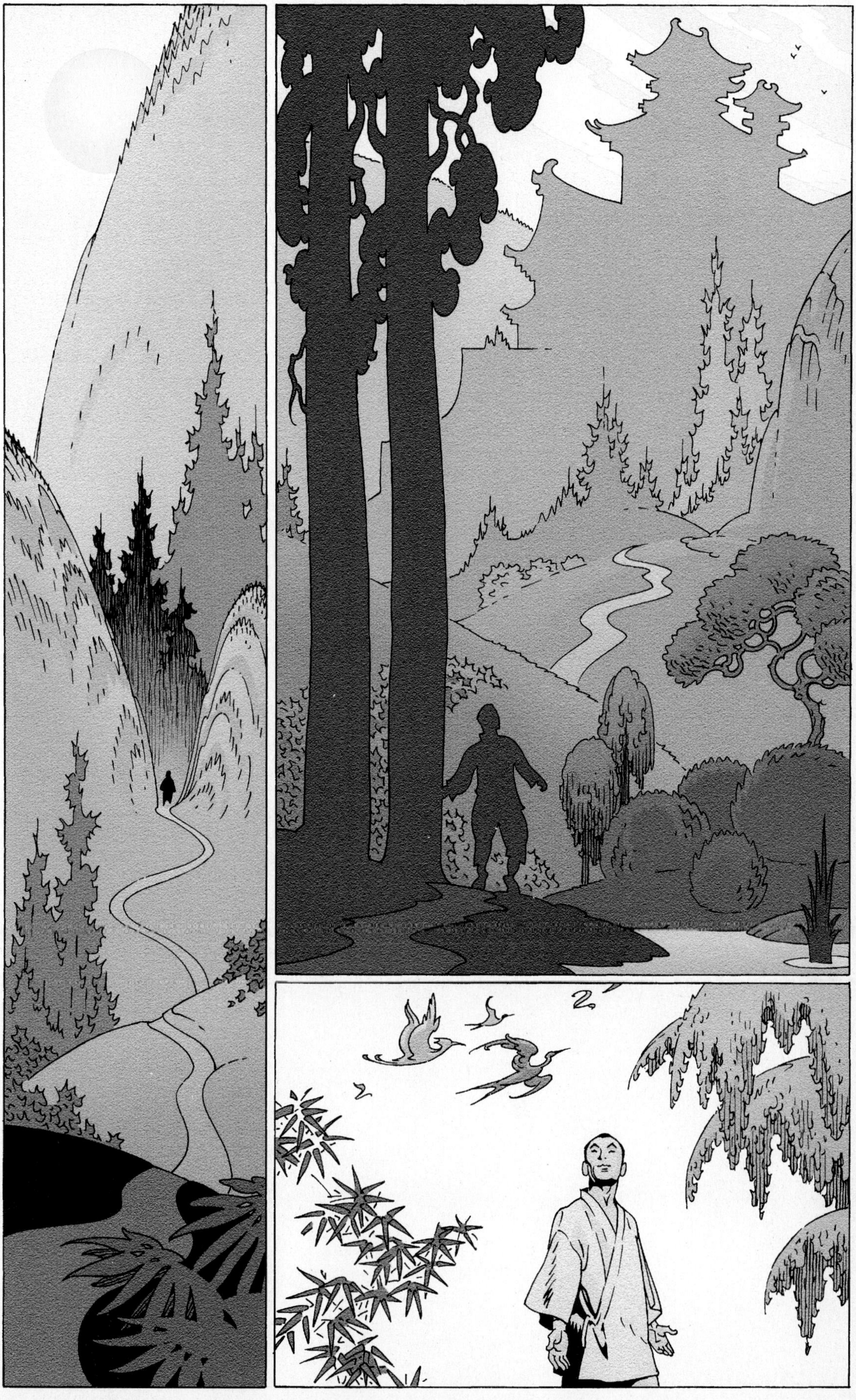

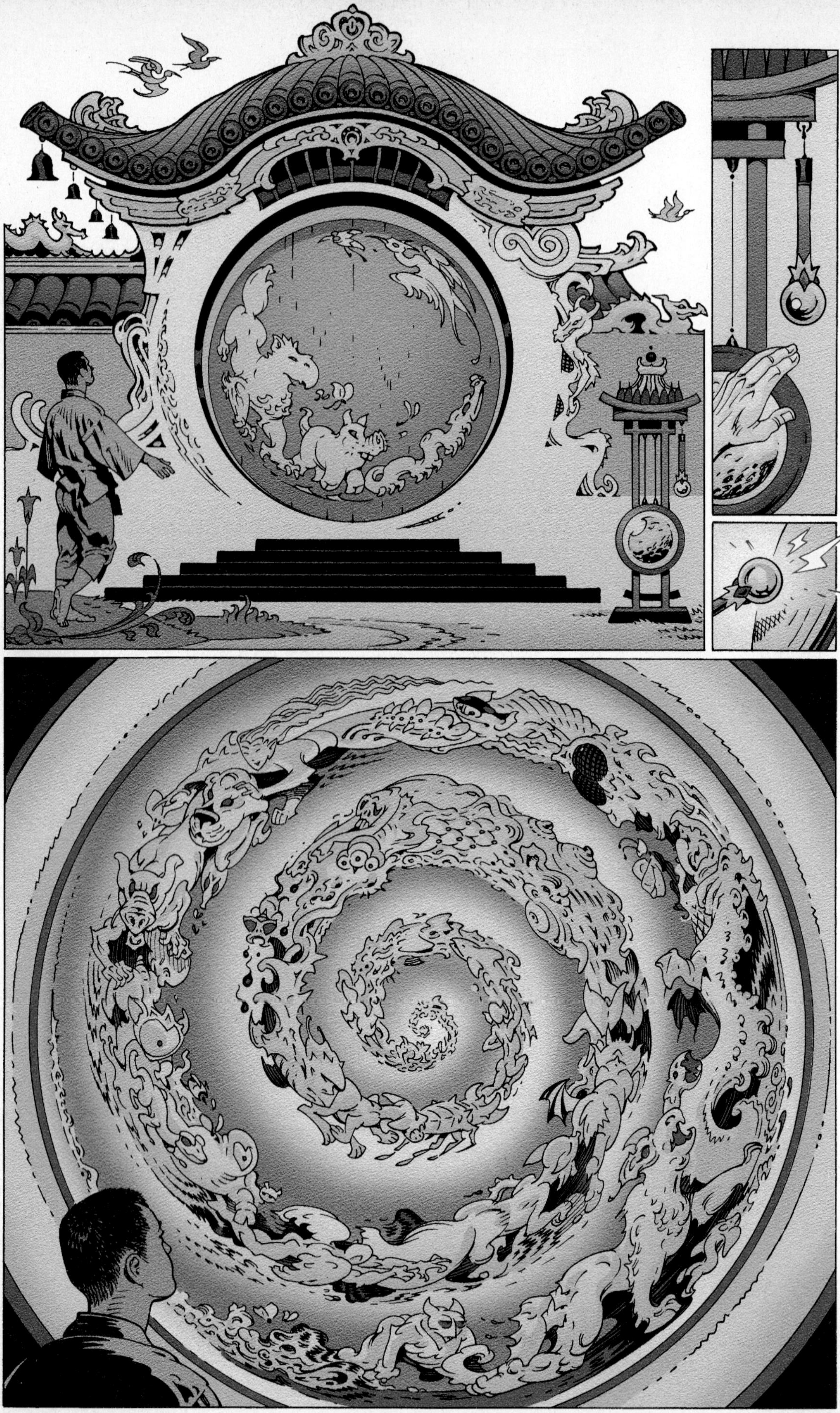

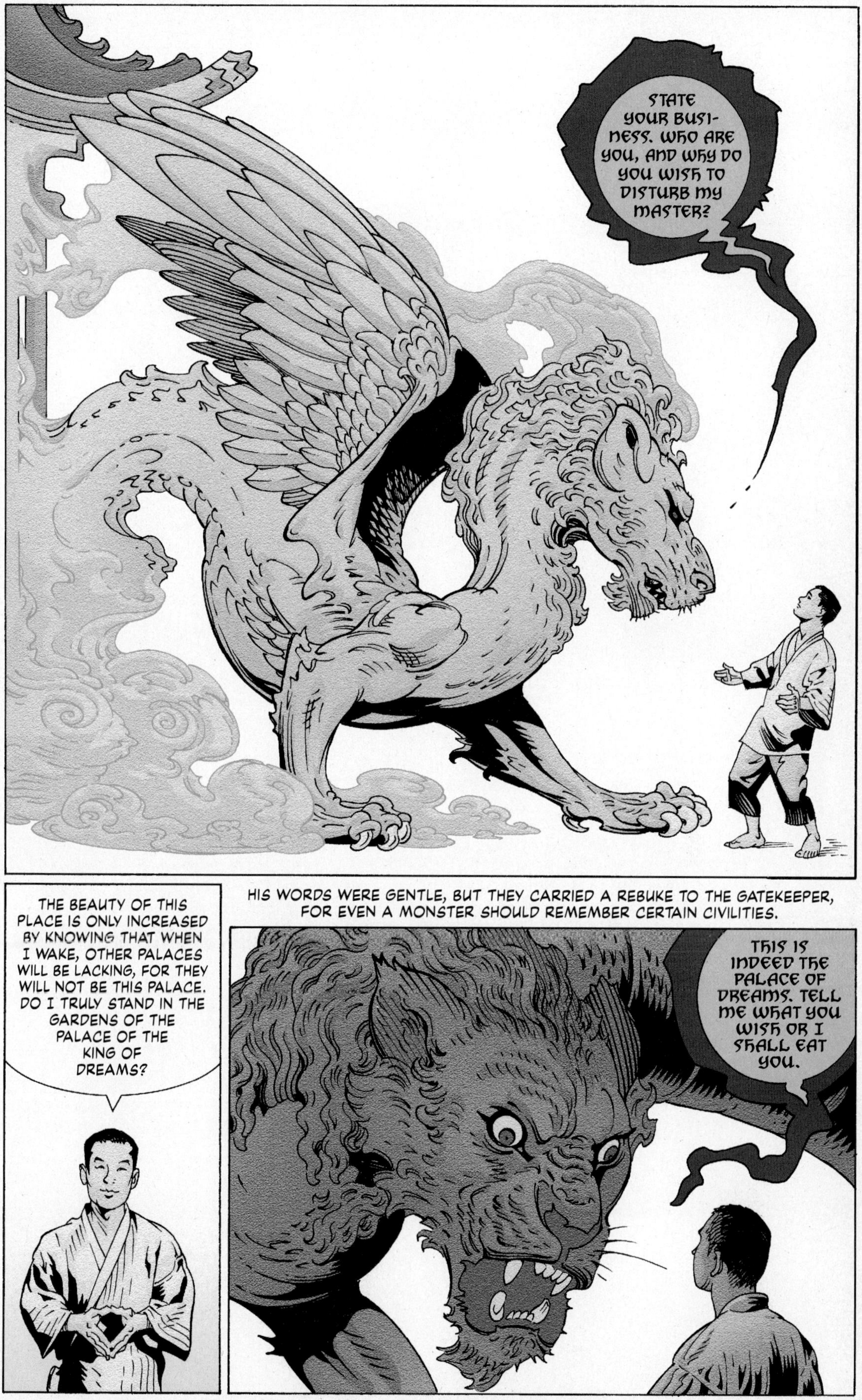
STATE YOUR BUSI-NESS. WHO ARE YOU, AND WHY DO YOU WISH TO DISTURB MY MASTER?
THE BEAUTY OF THIS PLACE IS ONLY INCREASED BY KNOWING THAT WHEN I WAKE, OTHER PALACES WILL BE LACKING, FOR THEY WILL NOT BE THIS PALACE. DO I TRULY STAND IN THE GARDENS OF THE PALACE OF THE KING OF DREAMS?
HIS WORDS WERE GENTLE, BUT THEY CARRIED A REBUKE TO THE GATEKEEPER, FOR EVEN A MONSTER SHOULD REMEMBER CERTAIN CIVILITIES.
THIS IS INDEED THE PALACE OF DREAMS. TELL ME WHAT YOU WISH OR I SHALL EAT YOU.

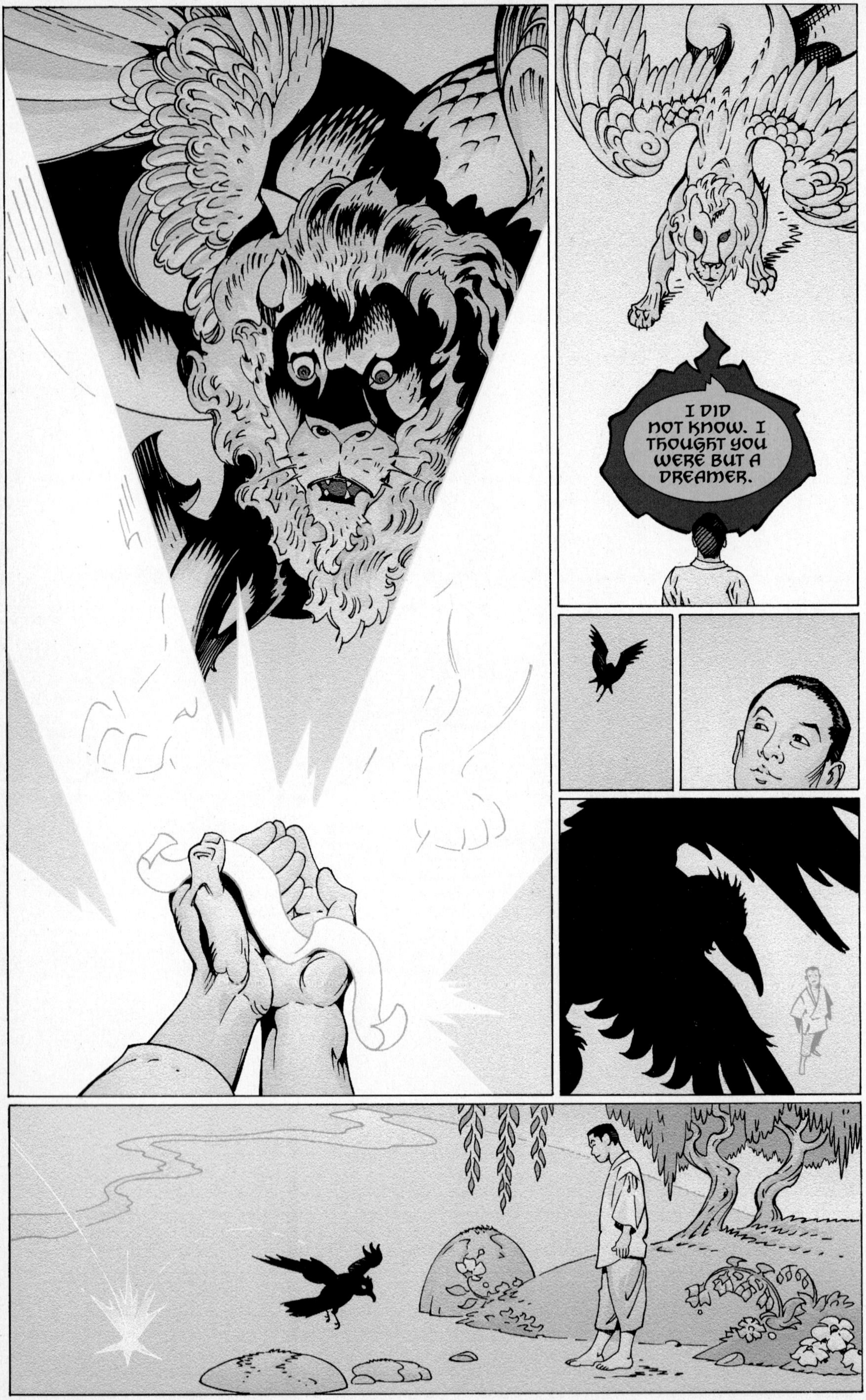
I DID NOT KNOW. I THOUGHT YOU WERE BUT A DREAMER.

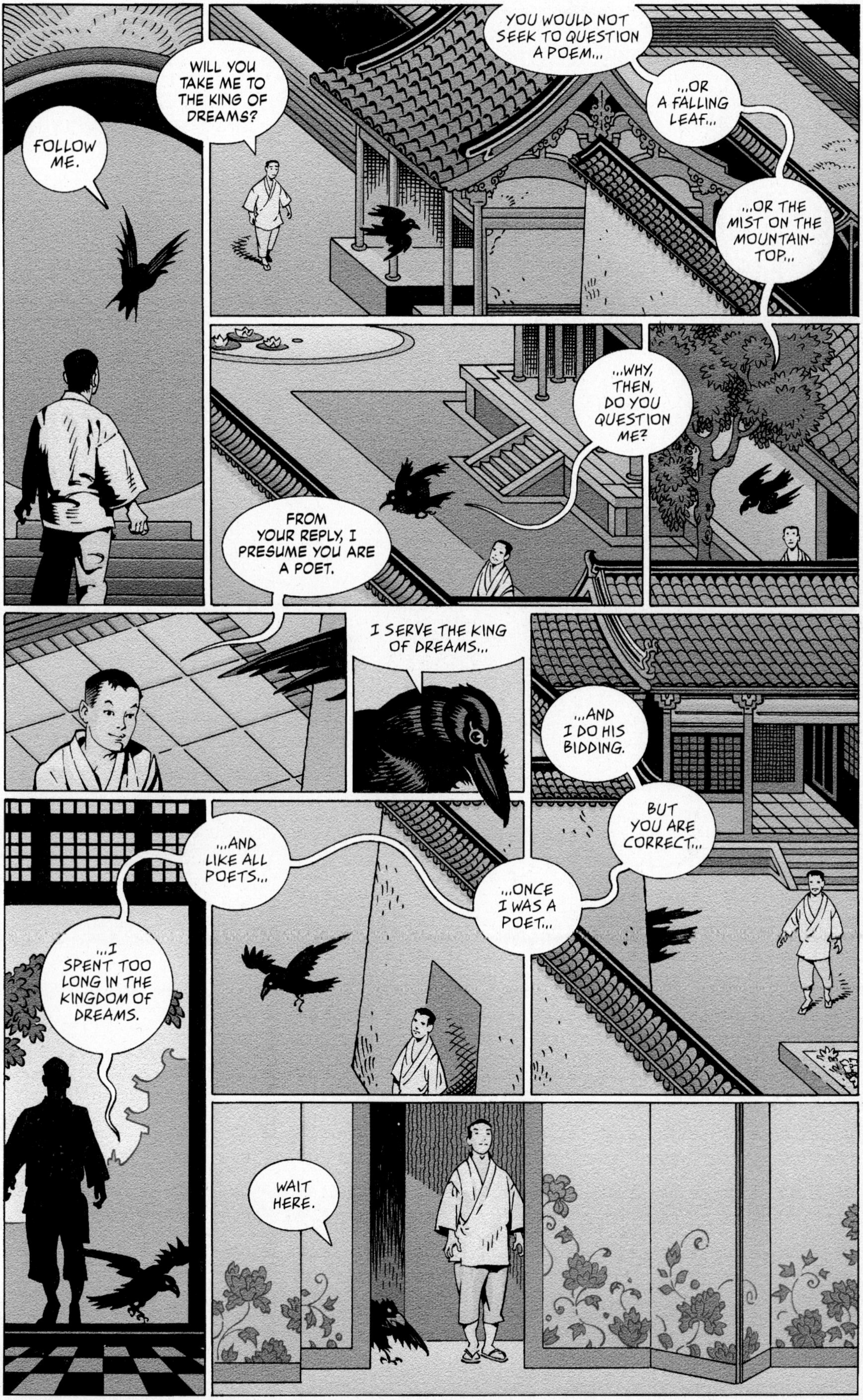
FOLLOW ME.
WILL YOU TAKE ME TO THE KING OF DREAMS?
YOU WOULD NOT SEEK TO QUESTION A POEM...
...OR A FALLING LEAF...
...OR THE MIST ON THE MOUNTAIN-TOP...
...WHY, THEN, DO YOU QUESTION ME?
FROM YOUR REPLY, I PRESUME YOU ARE A POET.
I SERVE THE KING OF DREAMS...
...AND I DO HIS BIDDING.
BUT YOU ARE CORRECT...
...ONCE I WAS A POET...
...AND LIKE ALL POETS...
...I SPENT TOO LONG IN THE KINGDOM OF DREAMS.
WAIT HERE.

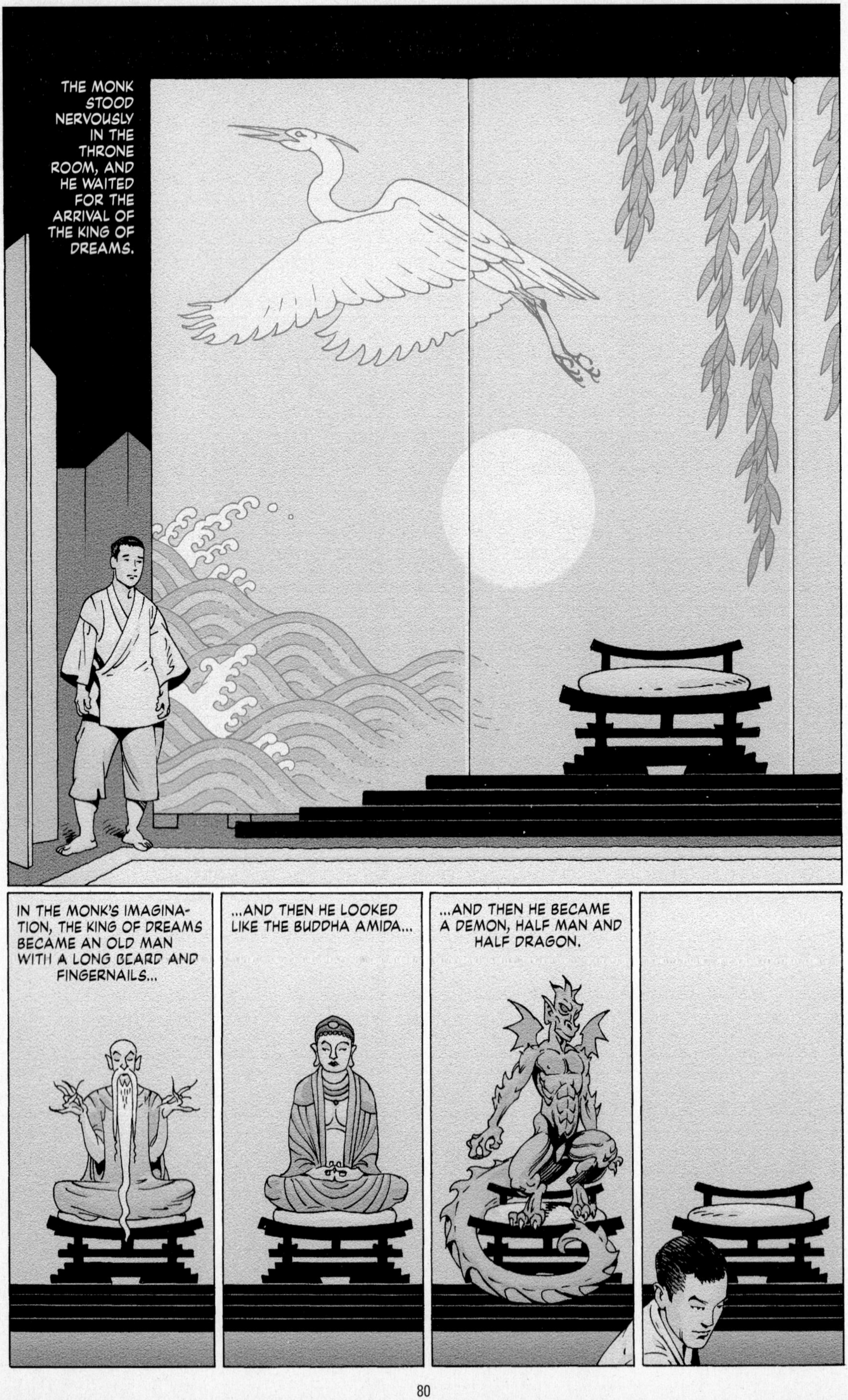
THE MONK STOOD NERVOUSLY IN THE THRONE ROOM, AND HE WAITED FOR THE ARRIVAL OF THE KING OF DREAMS.
IN THE MONK'S IMAGINATION, THE KING OF DREAMS BECAME AN OLD MAN WITH A LONG BEARD AND FINGERNAILS...
...AND THEN HE LOOKED LIKE THE BUDDHA AMIDA...
...AND THEN HE BECAME A DEMON, HALF MAN AND HALF DRAGON.

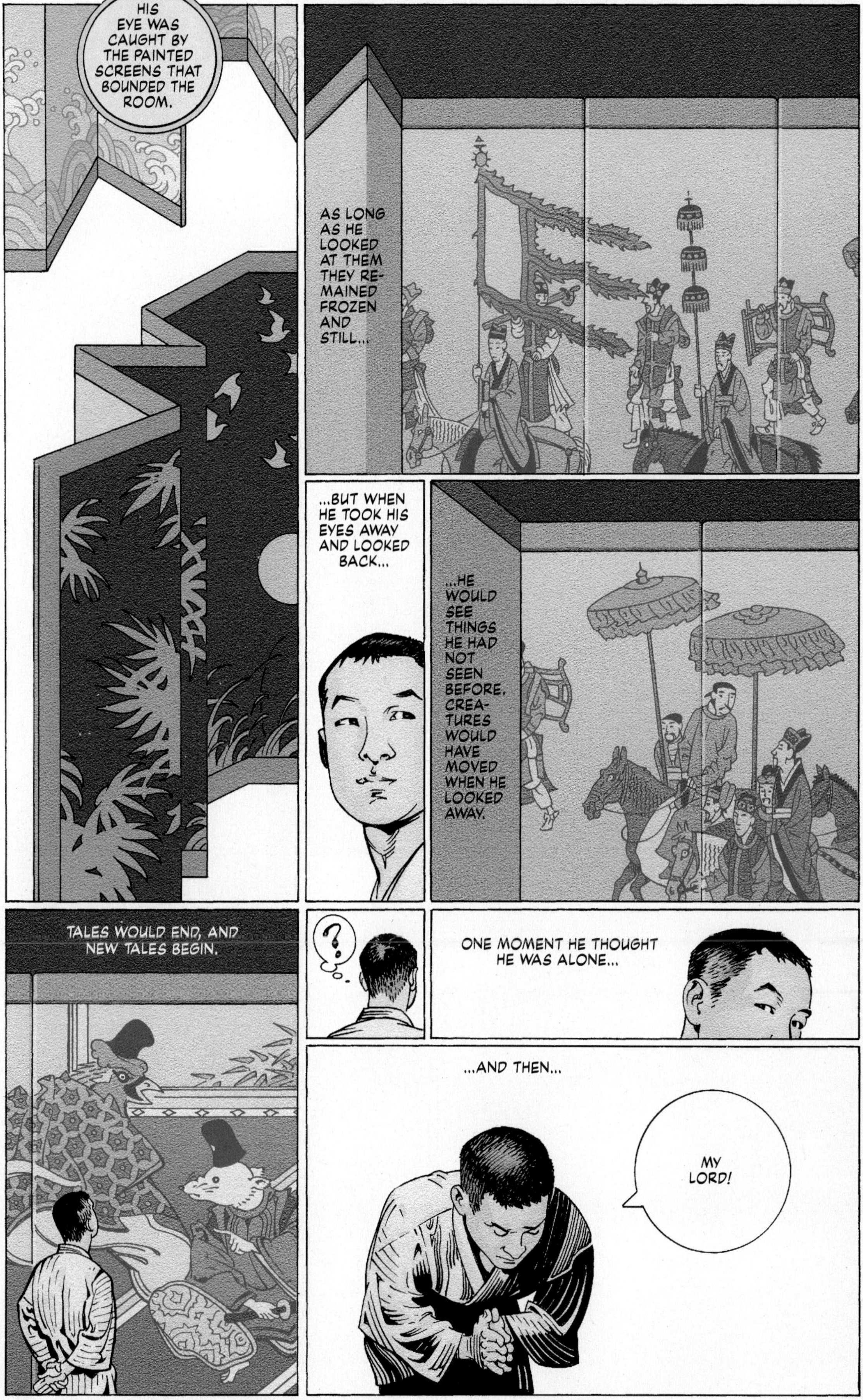
HIS EYE WAS CAUGHT BY THE PAINTED SCREENS THAT BOUNDED THE ROOM.
AS LONG AS HE LOOKED AT THEM THEY RE-MAINED FROZEN AND STILL...
...BUT WHEN HE TOOK HIS EYES AWAY AND LOOKED BACK...
...HE WOULD SEE THINGS HE HAD NOT SEEN BEFORE. CREA-TURES WOULD HAVE MOVED WHEN HE LOOKED AWAY.
TALES WOULD END, AND NEW TALES BEGIN.
?
ONE MOMENT HE THOUGHT HE WAS ALONE...
...AND THEN...
MY LORD!

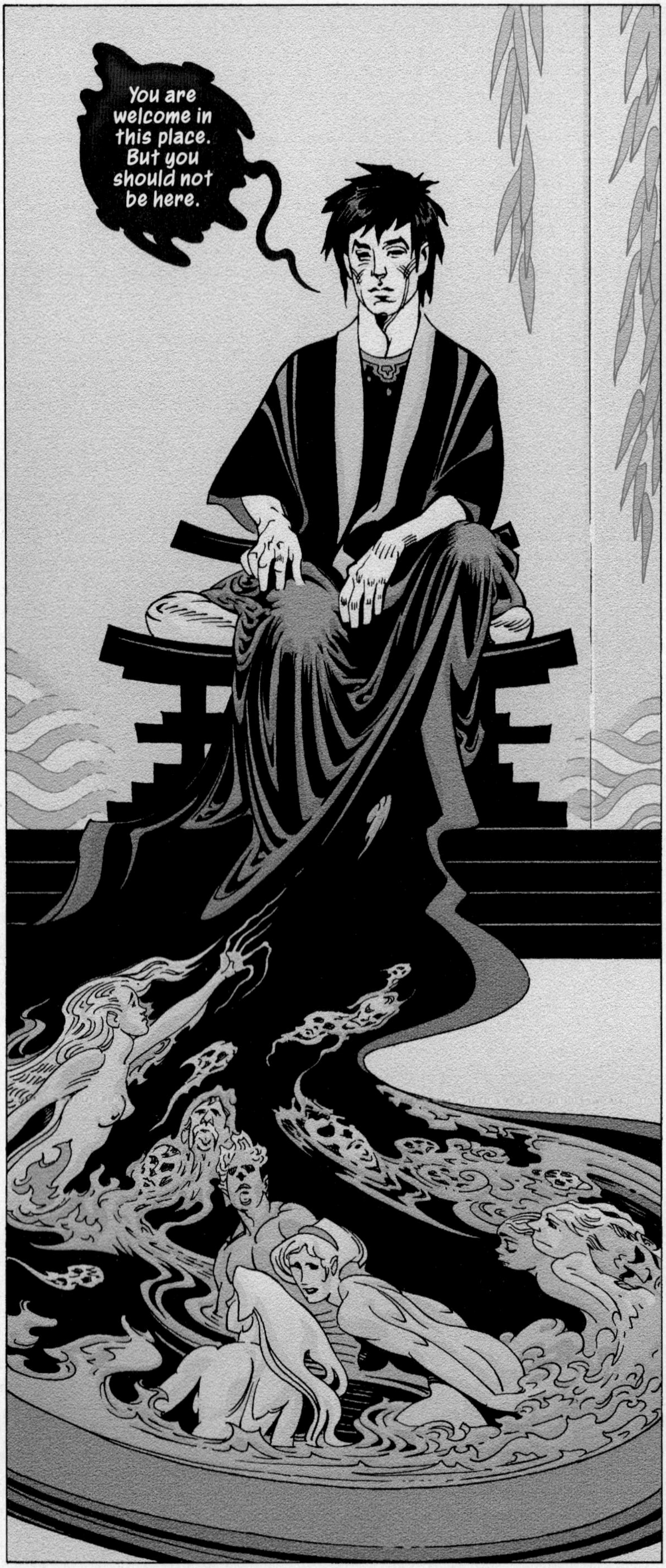
You are welcome in this place. But you should not be here.
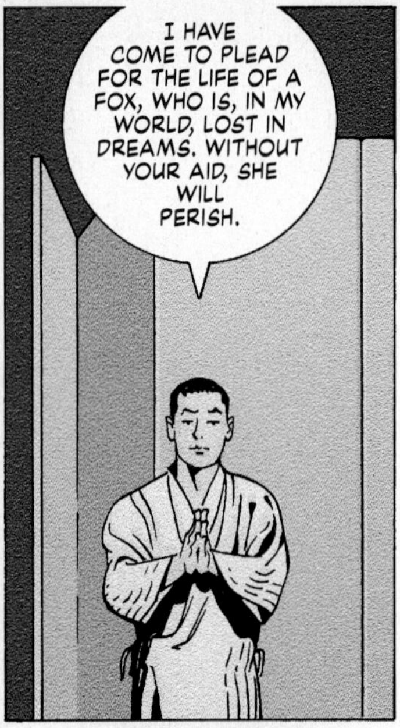
I HAVE COME TO PLEAD FOR THE LIFE OF A FOX, WHO IS, IN MY WORLD, LOST IN DREAMS. WITHOUT YOUR AID, SHE WILL PERISH.
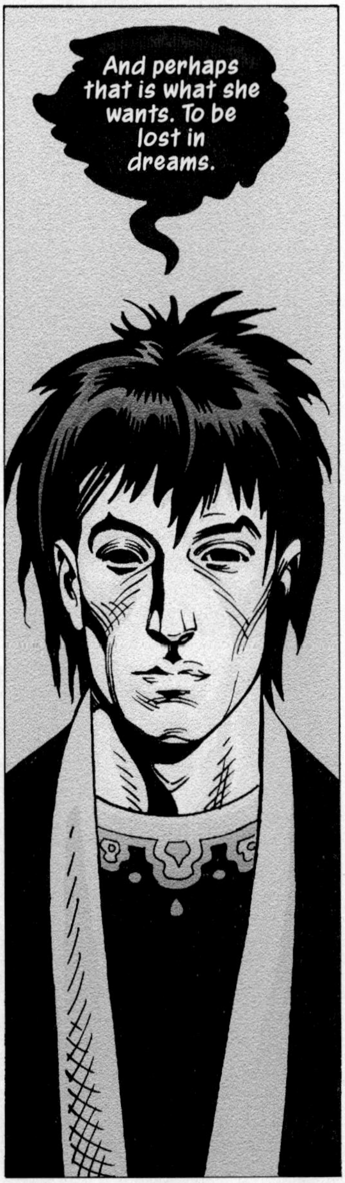
And perhaps that is what she wants. To be lost in dreams.

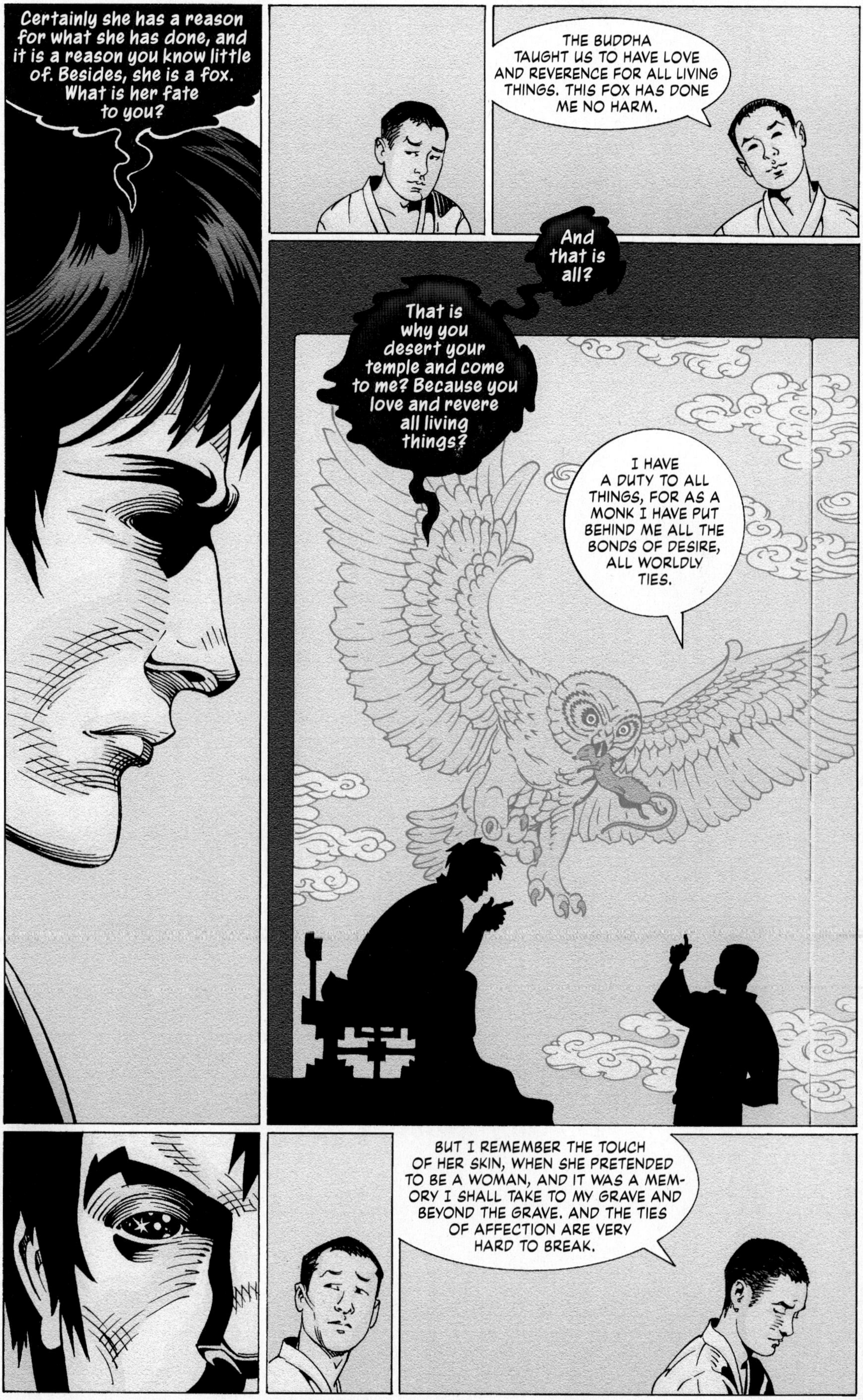
Certainly she has a reason for what she has done, and it is a reason you know little of. Besides, she is a fox. What is her fate to you?
THE BUDDHA TAUGHT US TO HAVE LOVE AND REVERENCE FOR ALL LIVING THINGS. THIS FOX HAS DONE ME NO HARM.
And that is all?
That is why you desert your temple and come to me? Because you love and revere all living things?
I HAVE A DUTY TO ALL THINGS, FOR AS A MONK I HAVE PUT BEHIND ME ALL THE BONDS OF DESIRE, ALL WORLDLY TIES.
BUT I REMEMBER THE TOUCH OF HER SKIN, WHEN SHE PRETENDED TO BE A WOMAN, AND IT WAS A MEMORY I SHALL TAKE TO MY GRAVE AND BEYOND THE GRAVE. AND THE TIES OF AFFECTION ARE VERY HARD TO BREAK.

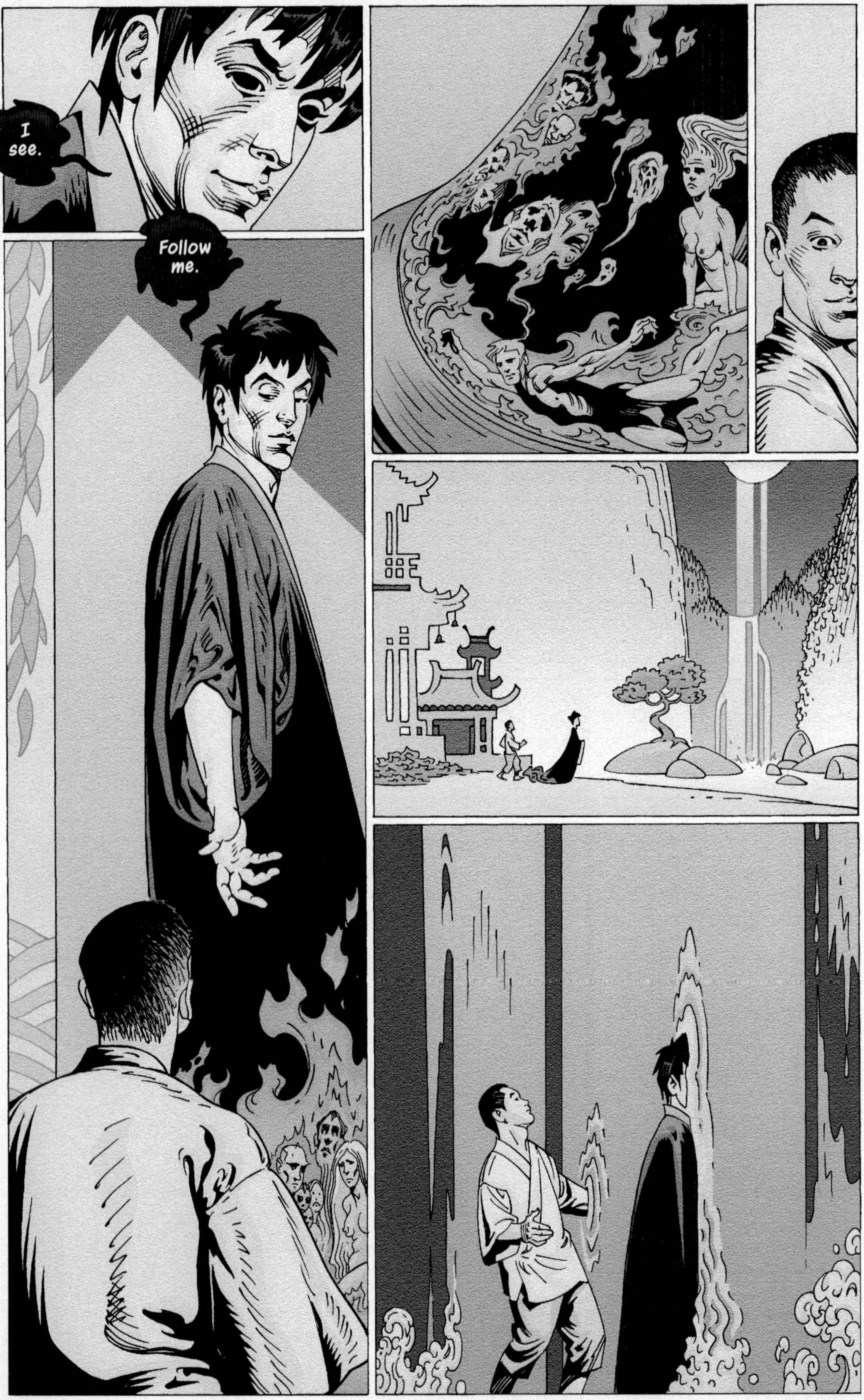
I see.
Follow me.

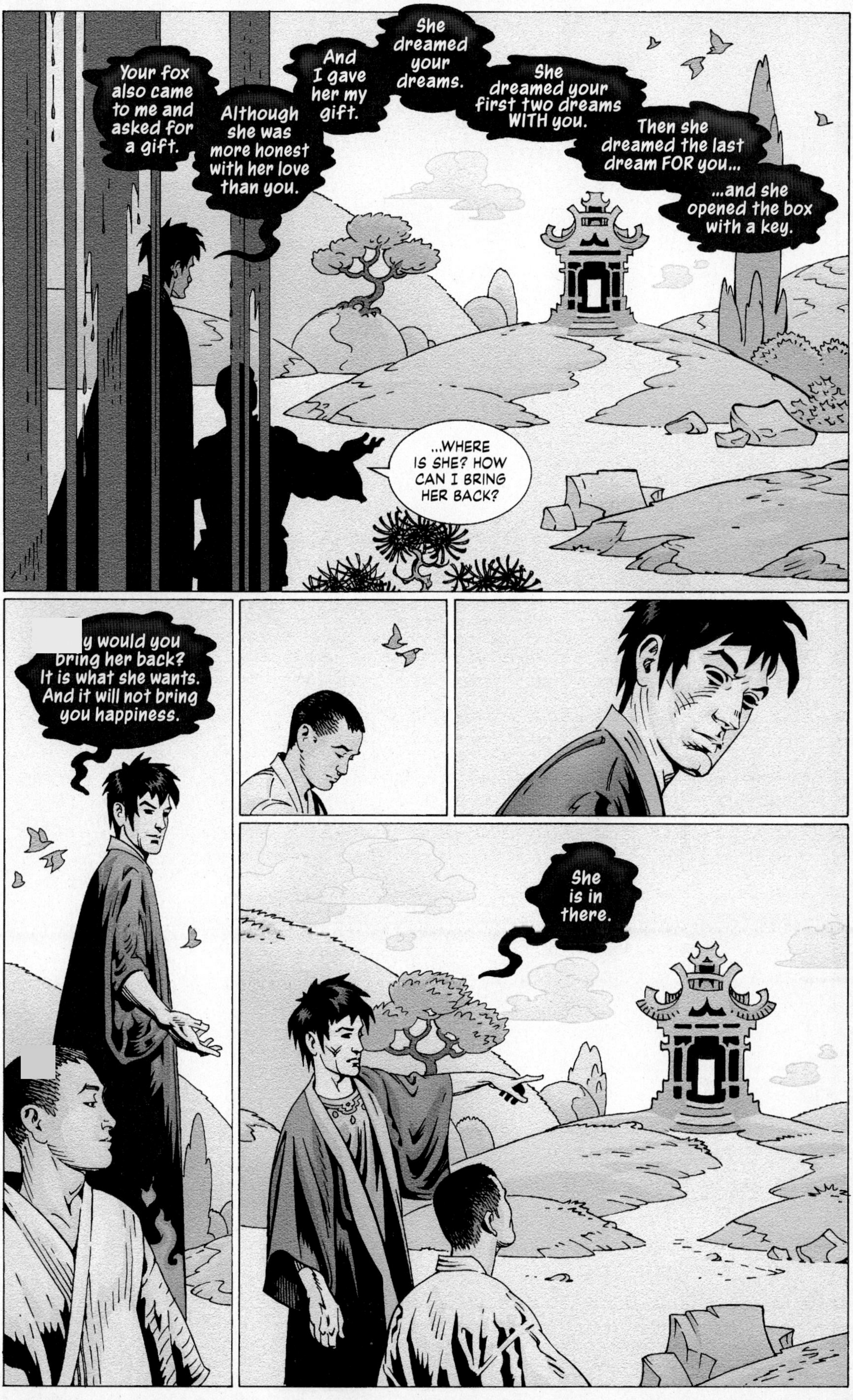
Your fox also came to me and asked for a gift.
Although she was more honest with her love than you.
And I gave her my gift.
She dreamed your dreams.
She dreamed your first two dreams WITH you.
Then she dreamed the last dream FOR you...
...and she opened the box with a key.
...WHERE IS SHE? HOW CAN I BRING HER BACK?
y would you bring her back? It is what she wants. And it will not bring you happiness.
She is in there.

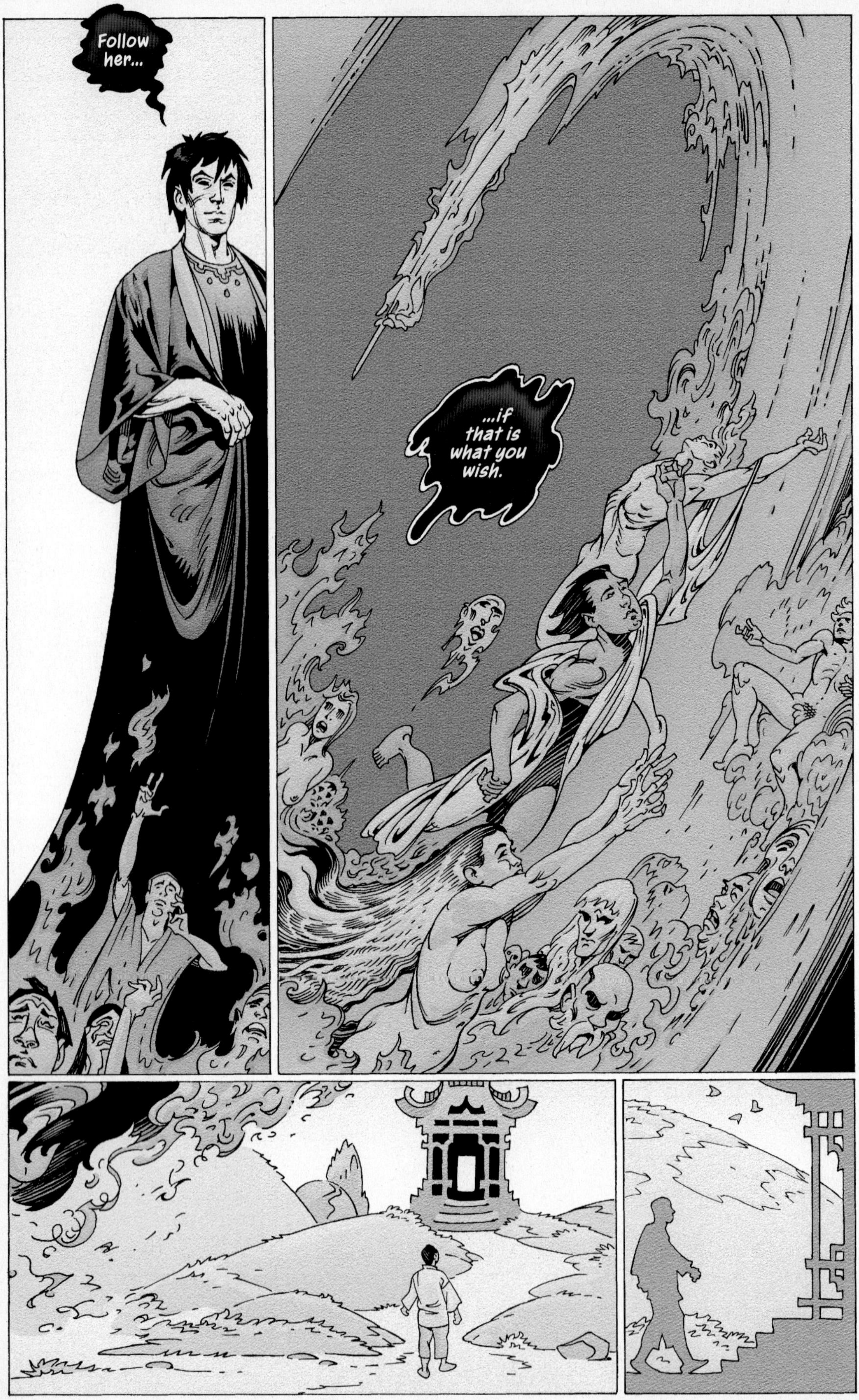
Follow her...
...if that is what you wish.

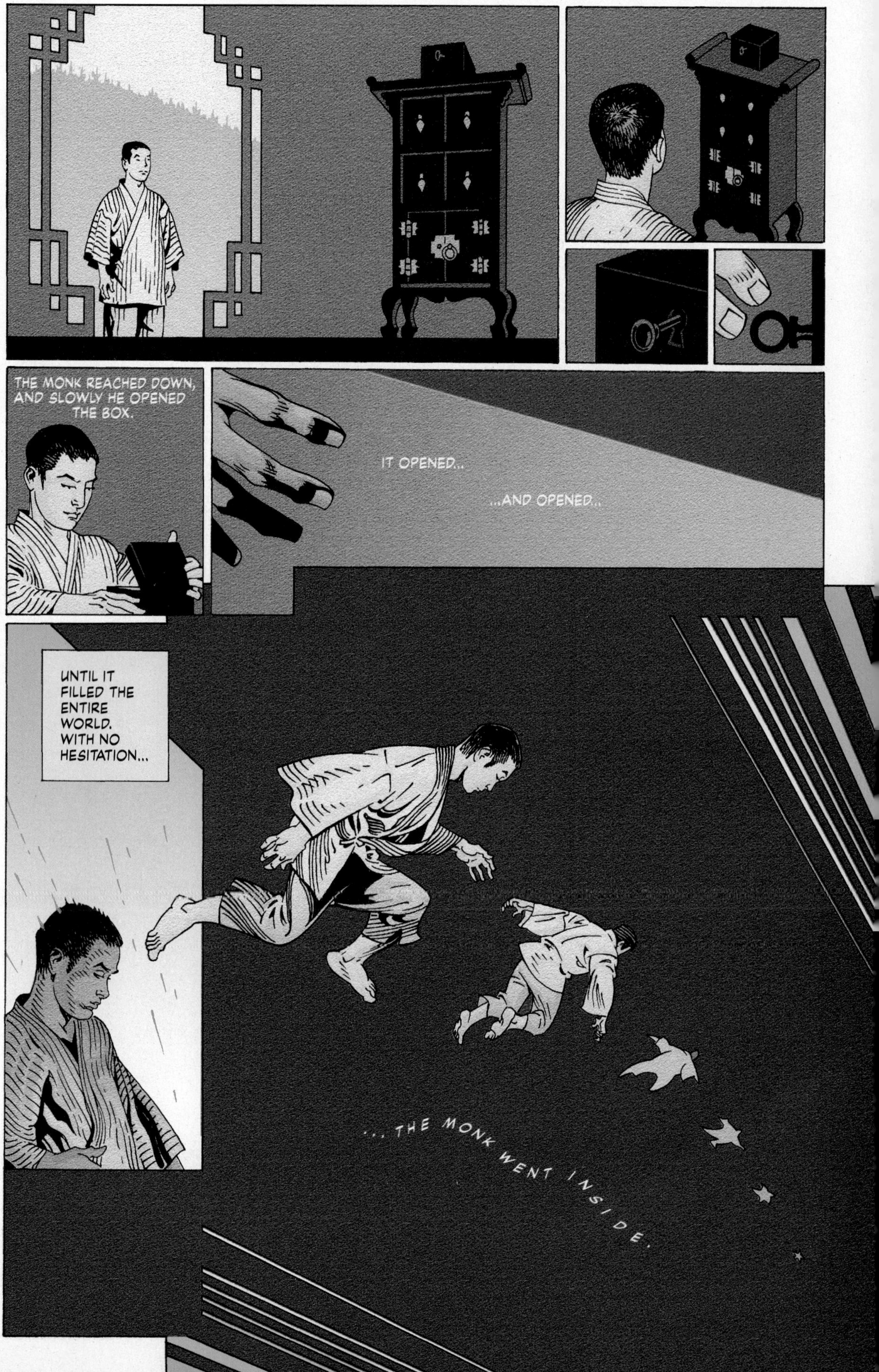
THE MONK REACHED DOWN, AND SLOWLY HE OPENED THE BOX.
IT OPENED...
...AND OPENED...
UNTIL IT FILLED THE ENTIRE WORLD. WITH NO HESITATION...
...THE MONK WENT INSIDE.

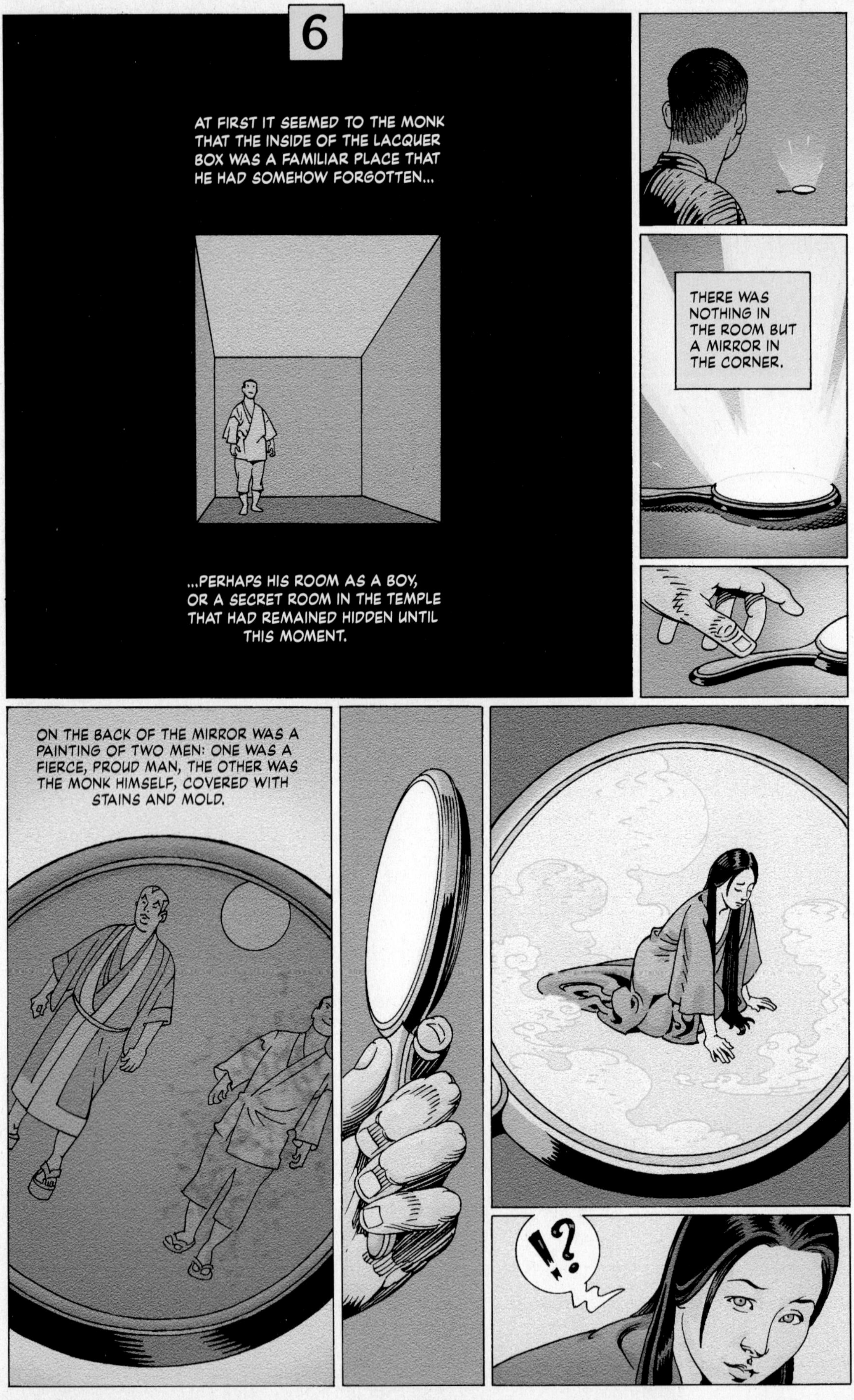
6
AT FIRST IT SEEMED TO THE MONK THAT THE INSIDE OF THE LACQUER BOX WAS A FAMILIAR PLACE THAT HE HAD SOMEHOW FORGOTTEN...
...PERHAPS HIS ROOM AS A BOY, OR A SECRET ROOM IN THE TEMPLE THAT HAD REMAINED HIDDEN UNTIL THIS MOMENT.
THERE WAS NOTHING IN THE ROOM BUT A MIRROR IN THE CORNER.
ON THE BACK OF THE MIRROR WAS A PAINTING OF TWO MEN: ONE WAS A FIERCE, PROUD MAN, THE OTHER WAS THE MONK HIMSELF, COVERED WITH STAINS AND MOLD.
!?

WHY DID YOU COME HERE? I GAVE MY LIFE FOR YOU.

YOU WERE ASLEEP AT THE DOOR OF THE THRESHOLD. I COULD NOT WAKE YOU.

I HUNTED THE BAKU. I WENT TO THE PLACE WHERE THE BAKU GO, AND WENT WITH THEM AS THEY ATE DREAMS, AND I ENTERED YOUR DREAMS, AS YOU DREAMED THEM.

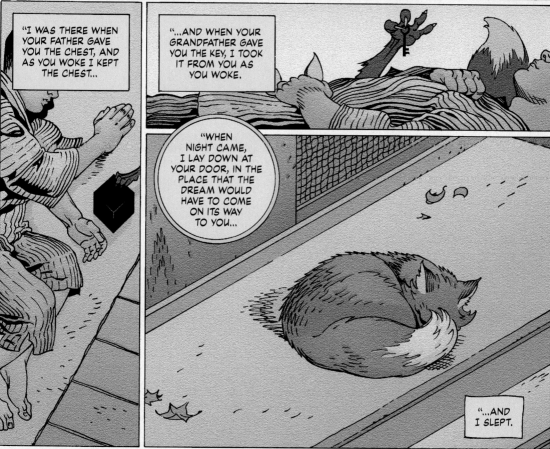

"I WAS THERE WHEN YOUR FATHER GAVE YOU THE CHEST, AND AS YOU WOKE I KEPT THE CHEST...

"...AND WHEN YOUR GRANDFATHER GAVE YOU THE KEY, I TOOK IT FROM YOU AS YOU WOKE.

"WHEN NIGHT CAME, I LAY DOWN AT YOUR DOOR, IN THE PLACE THAT THE DREAM WOULD HAVE TO COME ON ITS WAY TO YOU...

"...AND I SLEPT.

89

"I SAW THE DREAM SLIPPING THROUGH THE DARKNESS...

"...AND I SPRANG UPON IT AND MADE IT MY OWN.

"AND IN MY DREAM I OPENED THE CHEST WITH A KEY, AND IT OPENED, HUGE AS THE SKY...

"...AND I HAD NO CHOICE BUT TO ENTER.

"AND THEN I WAS VERY AFRAID, FOR I WAS LOST IN THIS BOX AND I COULD NOT FIND MY WAY OUT AGAIN. I HAD LOST THE PATH THAT WOULD TAKE ME BACK TO MY BODY. I WAS SAD AND SCARED, BUT I WAS ALSO PROUD, FOR I KNEW THAT I HAD SAVED YOUR LIFE."

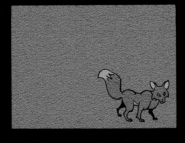

WHY WOULD YOU DO THIS FOR ME?

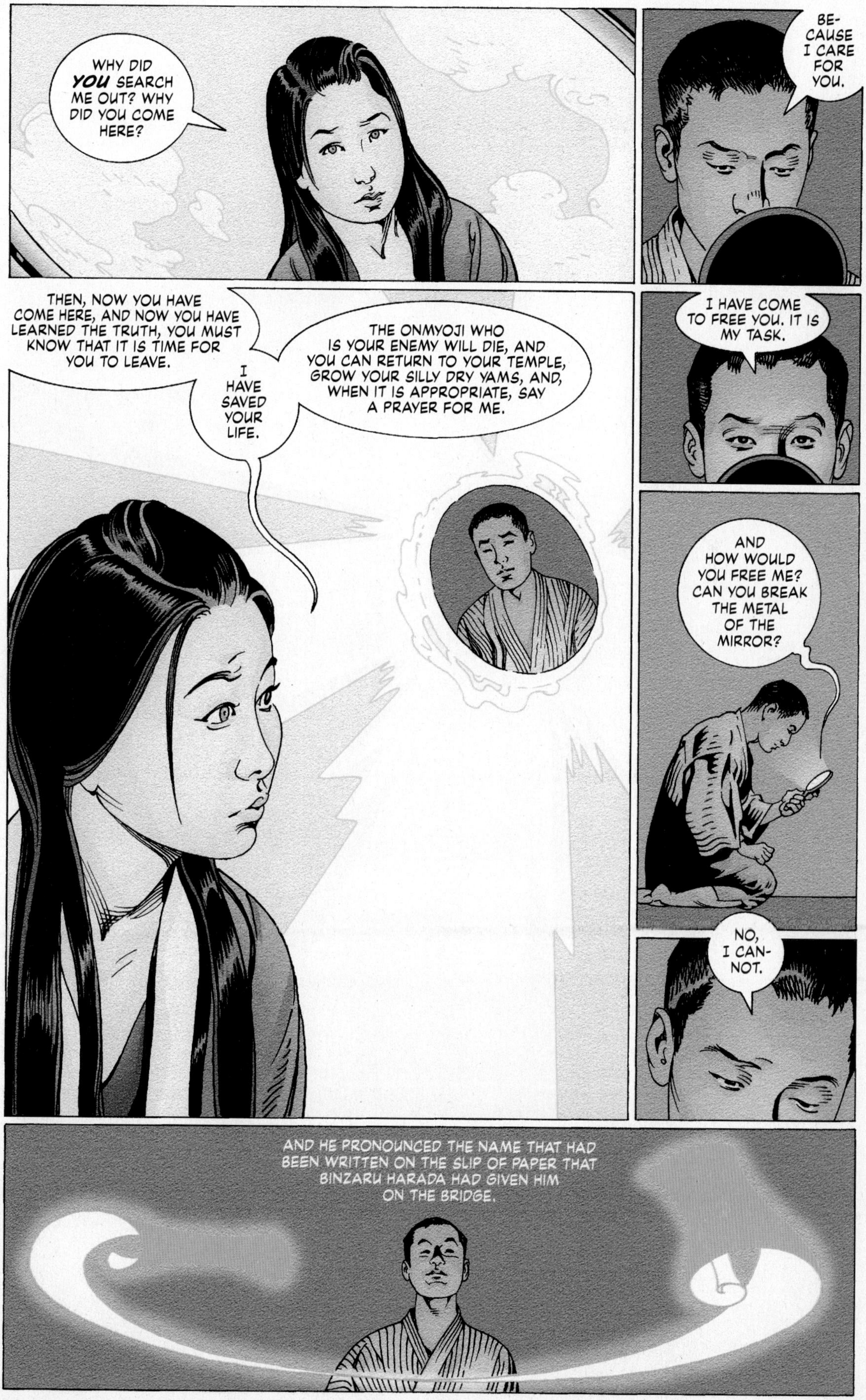
WHY DID YOU SEARCH ME OUT? WHY DID YOU COME HERE?
BE-CAUSE I CARE FOR YOU.
THEN, NOW YOU HAVE COME HERE, AND NOW YOU HAVE LEARNED THE TRUTH, YOU MUST KNOW THAT IT IS TIME FOR YOU TO LEAVE.
I HAVE SAVED YOUR LIFE.
THE ONMYOJI WHO IS YOUR ENEMY WILL DIE, AND YOU CAN RETURN TO YOUR TEMPLE, GROW YOUR SILLY DRY YAMS, AND, WHEN IT IS APPROPRIATE, SAY A PRAYER FOR ME.
I HAVE COME TO FREE YOU. IT IS MY TASK.
AND HOW WOULD YOU FREE ME? CAN YOU BREAK THE METAL OF THE MIRROR?
NO, I CAN-NOT.
AND HE PRONOUNCED THE NAME THAT HAD BEEN WRITTEN ON THE SLIP OF PAPER THAT BINZARU HARADA HAD GIVEN HIM ON THE BRIDGE.

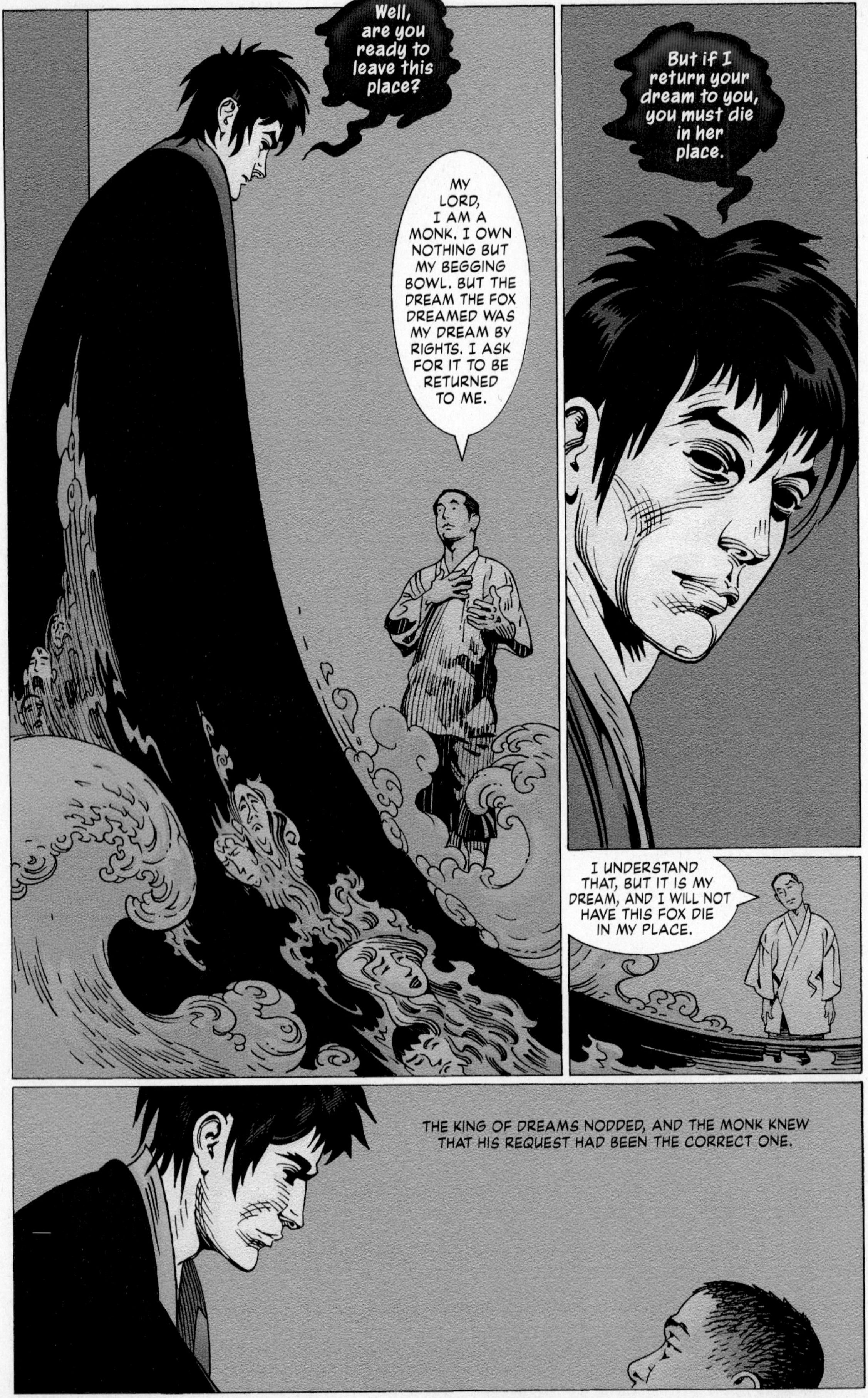
Well, are you ready to leave this place?
MY LORD, I AM A MONK. I OWN NOTHING BUT MY BEGGING BOWL. BUT THE DREAM THE FOX DREAMED WAS MY DREAM BY RIGHTS. I ASK FOR IT TO BE RETURNED TO ME.
But if I return your dream to you, you must die in her place.
I UNDERSTAND THAT, BUT IT IS MY DREAM, AND I WILL NOT HAVE THIS FOX DIE IN MY PLACE.
THE KING OF DREAMS NODDED, AND THE MONK KNEW THAT HIS REQUEST HAD BEEN THE CORRECT ONE.

THE KING GESTURED, AND THE MIRROR LAY EMPTY ON THE FLOOR, WHILE THE FOX SPIRIT STOOD BESIDE THE MONK IN THE DARK,

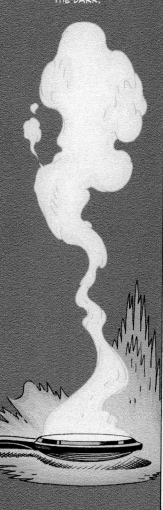

You have done the right thing, at some cost to yourself.

I shall, in my turn, do something for you.

You may have a little time to say farewell to the fox.

BUT...

...BUT YOU SWORE TO HELP ME.

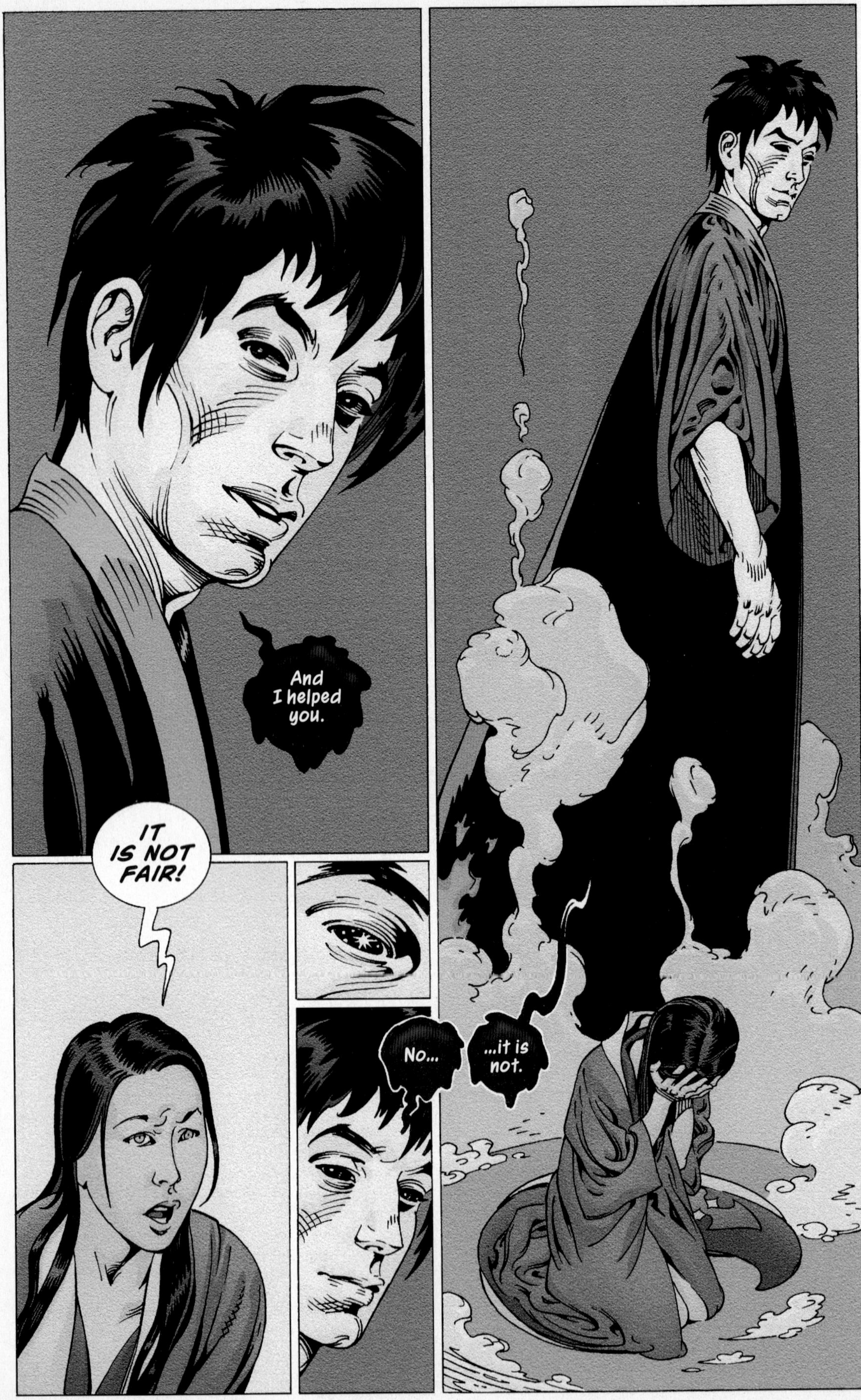
And I helped you.
IT IS NOT FAIR!
No...
...it is not.

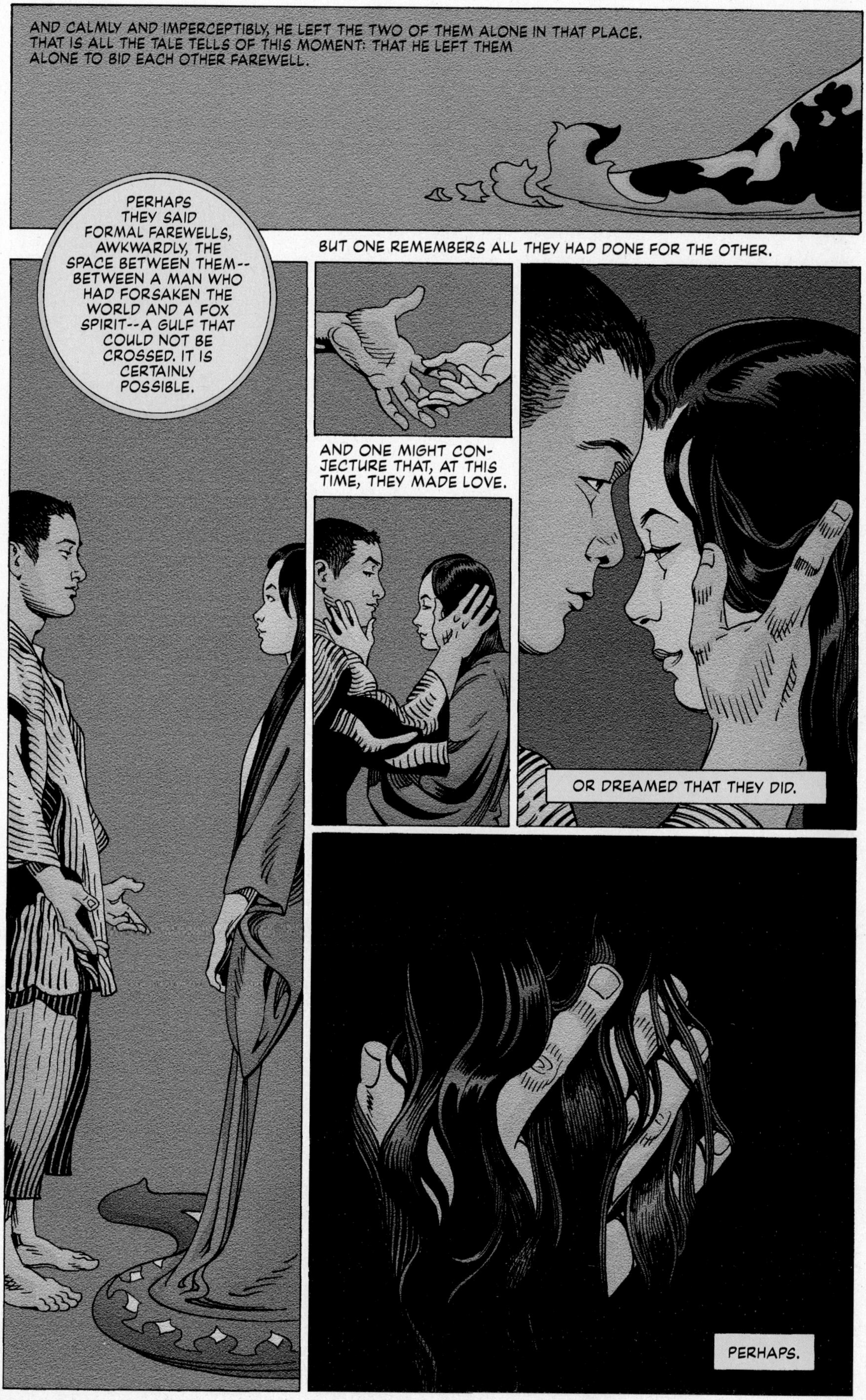
AND CALMLY AND IMPERCEPTIBLY, HE LEFT THE TWO OF THEM ALONE IN THAT PLACE. THAT IS ALL THE TALE TELLS OF THIS MOMENT: THAT HE LEFT THEM ALONE TO BID EACH OTHER FAREWELL.
PERHAPS THEY SAID FORMAL FAREWELLS, AWKWARDLY, THE SPACE BETWEEN THEM--BETWEEN A MAN WHO HAD FORSAKEN THE WORLD AND A FOX SPIRIT--A GULF THAT COULD NOT BE CROSSED. IT IS CERTAINLY POSSIBLE.
BUT ONE REMEMBERS ALL THEY HAD DONE FOR THE OTHER.
AND ONE MIGHT CONJECTURE THAT, AT THIS TIME, THEY MADE LOVE.
OR DREAMED THAT THEY DID.
PERHAPS.

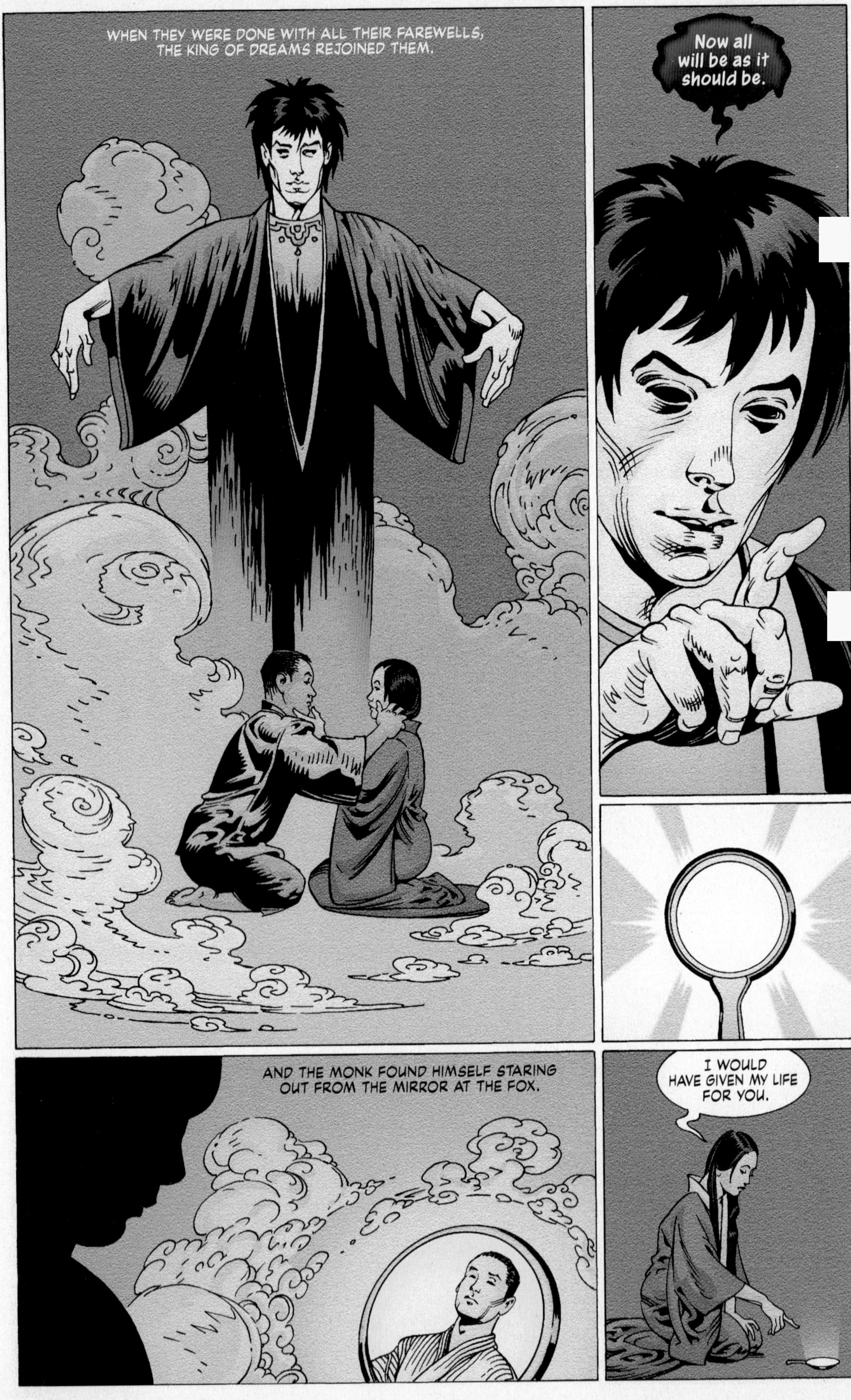
WHEN THEY WERE DONE WITH ALL THEIR FAREWELLS, THE KING OF DREAMS REJOINED THEM.
Now all will be as it should be.
AND THE MONK FOUND HIMSELF STARING OUT FROM THE MIRROR AT THE FOX.
I WOULD HAVE GIVEN MY LIFE FOR YOU.

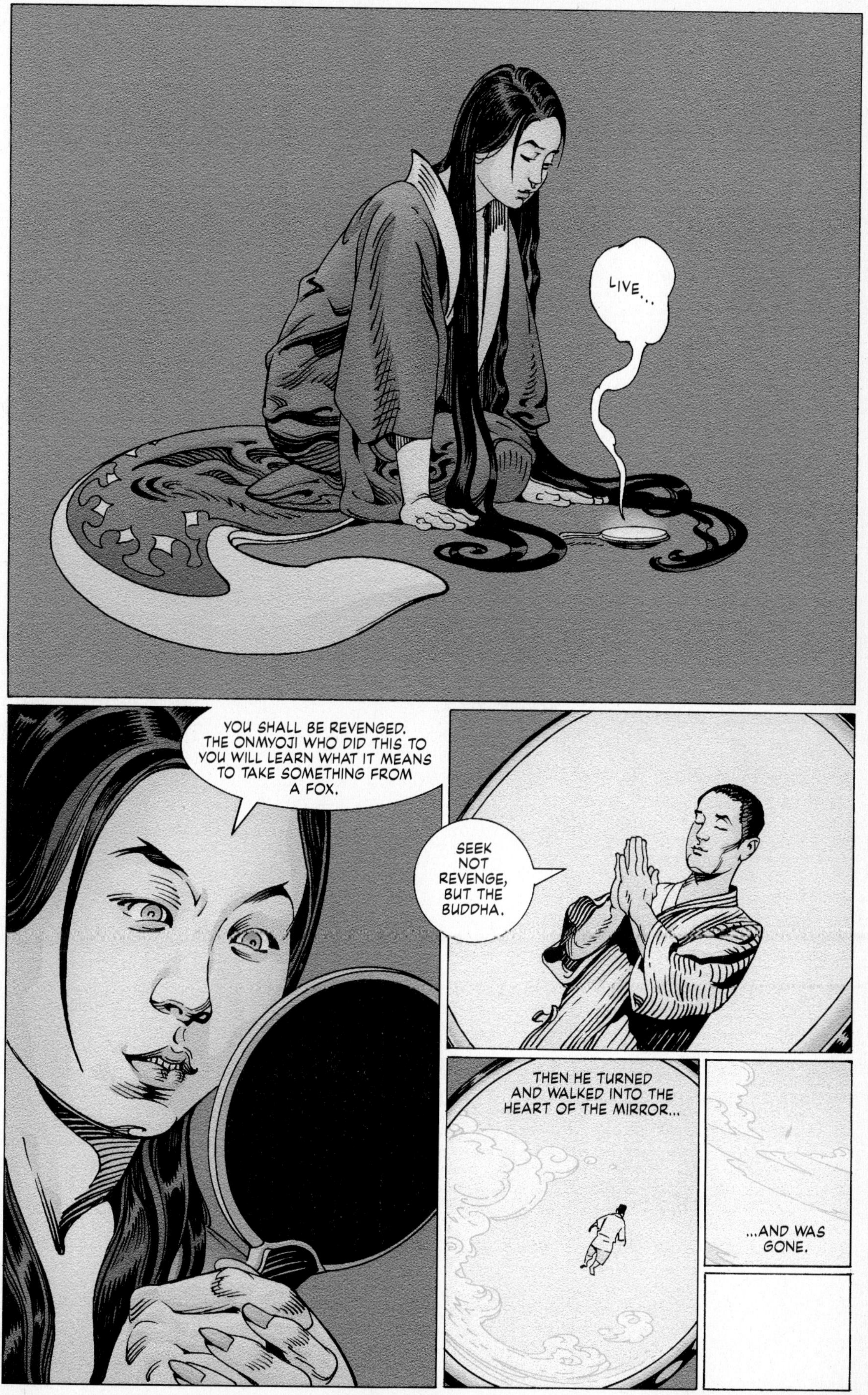
LIVE...
YOU SHALL BE REVENGED. THE ONMYOJI WHO DID THIS TO YOU WILL LEARN WHAT IT MEANS TO TAKE SOMETHING FROM A FOX.
SEEK NOT REVENGE, BUT THE BUDDHA.
THEN HE TURNED AND WALKED INTO THE HEART OF THE MIRROR...
...AND WAS GONE.

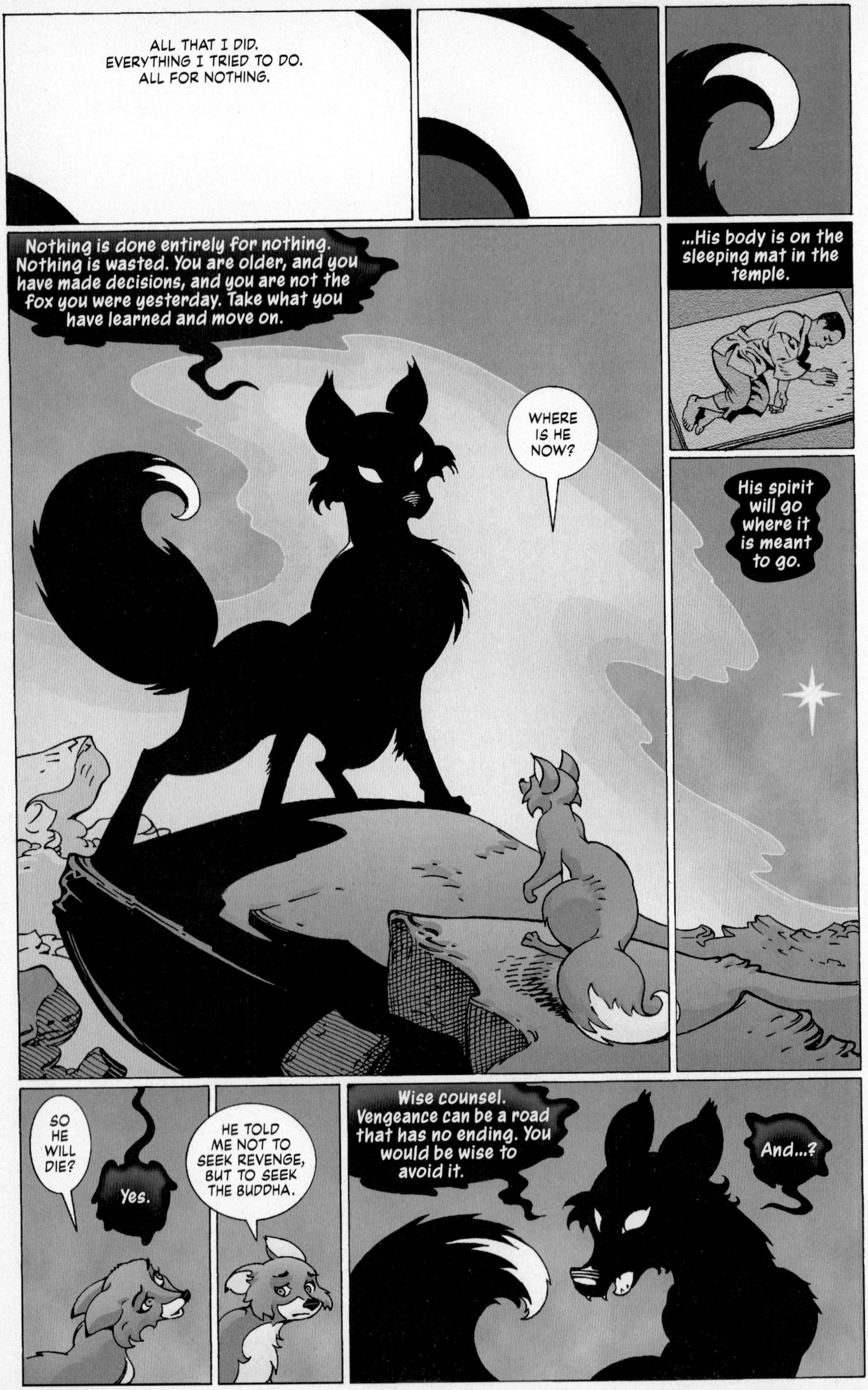
ALL THAT I DID.
EVERYTHING I TRIED TO DO.
ALL FOR NOTHING.
Nothing is done entirely for nothing. Nothing is wasted. You are older, and you have made decisions, and you are not the fox you were yesterday. Take what you have learned and move on.
WHERE IS HE NOW?
...His body is on the sleeping mat in the temple.
His spirit will go where it is meant to go.
SO HE WILL DIE?
Yes.
HE TOLD ME NOT TO SEEK REVENGE, BUT TO SEEK THE BUDDHA.
Wise counsel. Vengeance can be a road that has no ending. You would be wise to avoid it.
And...?

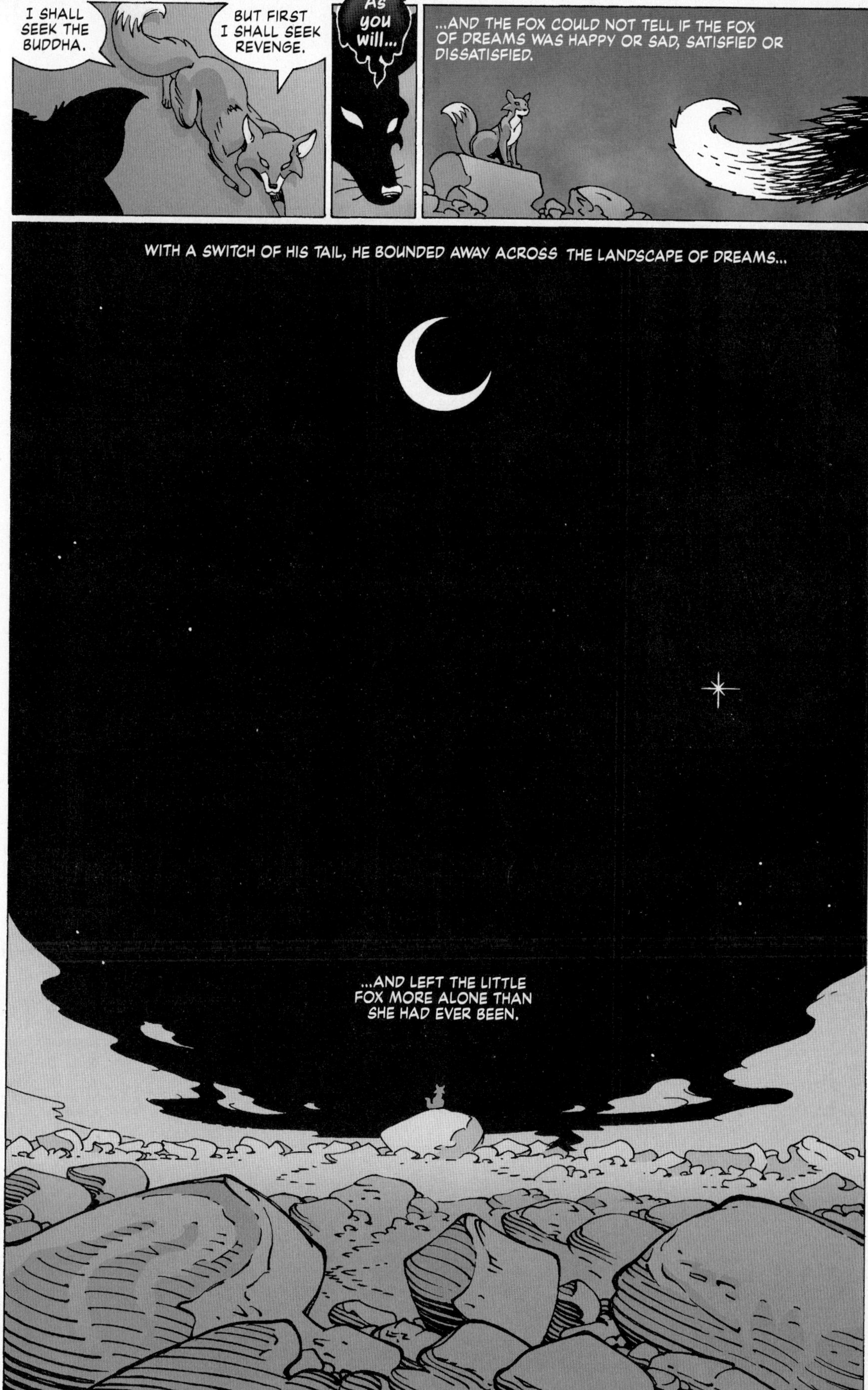
I SHALL SEEK THE BUDDHA.
BUT FIRST I SHALL SEEK REVENGE.
As you will...
...AND THE FOX COULD NOT TELL IF THE FOX OF DREAMS WAS HAPPY OR SAD, SATISFIED OR DISSATISFIED.
WITH A SWITCH OF HIS TAIL, HE BOUNDED AWAY ACROSS THE LANDSCAPE OF DREAMS...
...AND LEFT THE LITTLE FOX MORE ALONE THAN SHE HAD EVER BEEN.

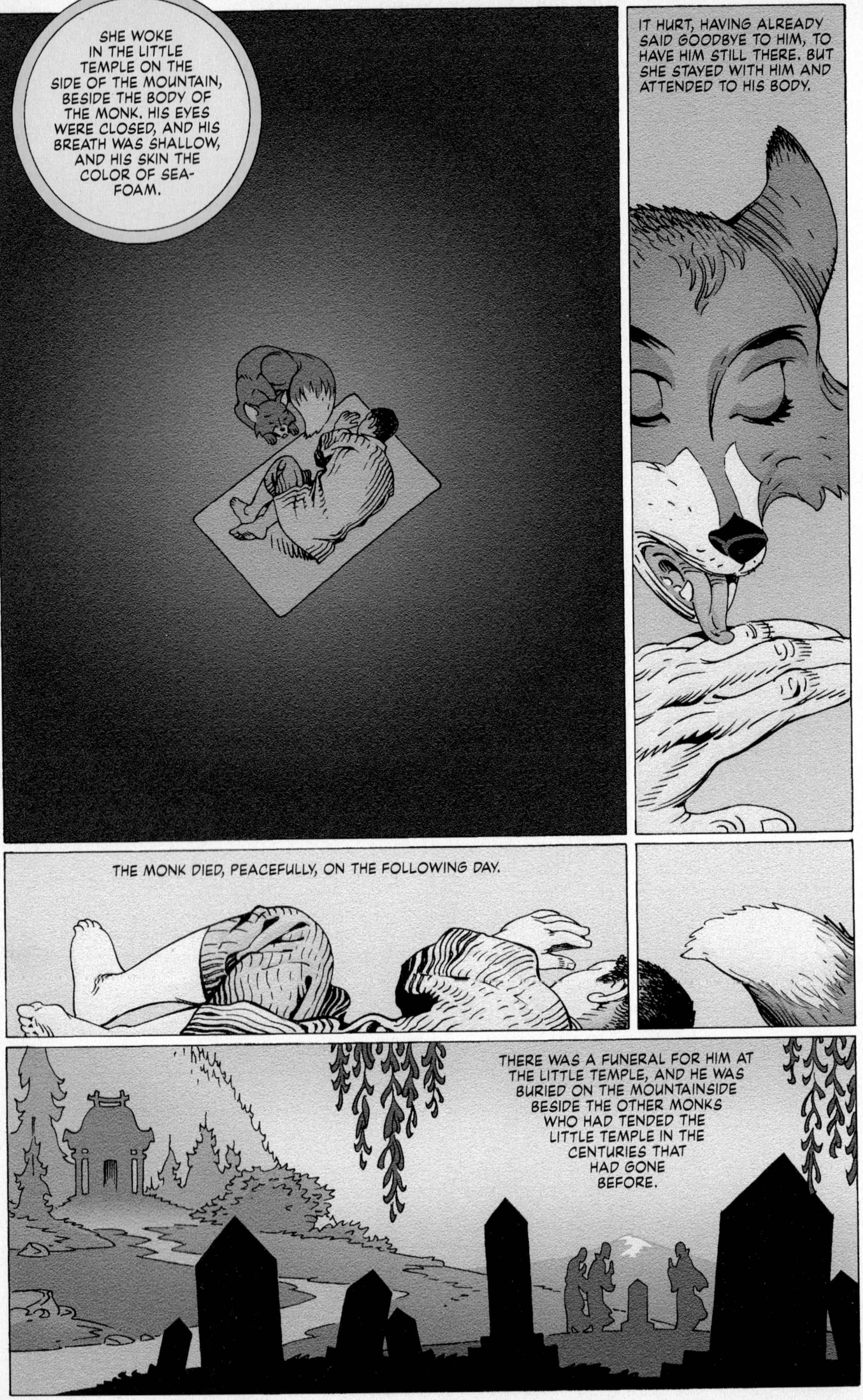
SHE WOKE IN THE LITTLE TEMPLE ON THE SIDE OF THE MOUNTAIN, BESIDE THE BODY OF THE MONK. HIS EYES WERE CLOSED, AND HIS BREATH WAS SHALLOW, AND HIS SKIN THE COLOR OF SEA-FOAM.
IT HURT, HAVING ALREADY SAID GOODBYE TO HIM, TO HAVE HIM STILL THERE. BUT SHE STAYED WITH HIM AND ATTENDED TO HIS BODY.
THE MONK DIED, PEACEFULLY, ON THE FOLLOWING DAY.
THERE WAS A FUNERAL FOR HIM AT THE LITTLE TEMPLE, AND HE WAS BURIED ON THE MOUNTAINSIDE BESIDE THE OTHER MONKS WHO HAD TENDED THE LITTLE TEMPLE IN THE CENTURIES THAT HAD GONE BEFORE.

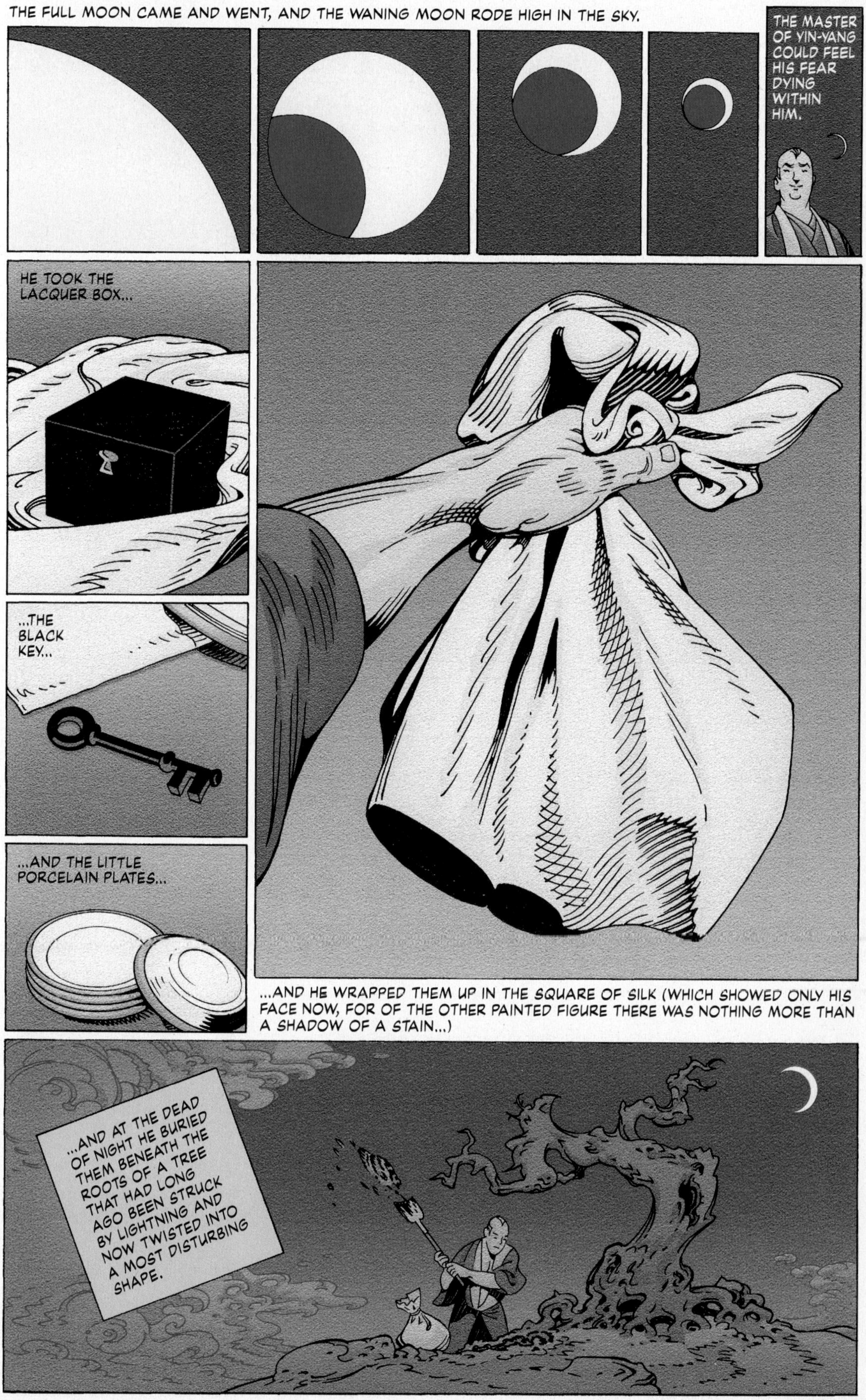
THE FULL MOON CAME AND WENT, AND THE WANING MOON RODE HIGH IN THE SKY.
THE MASTER OF YIN-YANG COULD FEEL HIS FEAR DYING WITHIN HIM.
HE TOOK THE LACQUER BOX...
...THE BLACK KEY...
...AND THE LITTLE PORCELAIN PLATES...
...AND HE WRAPPED THEM UP IN THE SQUARE OF SILK (WHICH SHOWED ONLY HIS FACE NOW, FOR OF THE OTHER PAINTED FIGURE THERE WAS NOTHING MORE THAN A SHADOW OF A STAIN...)
...AND AT THE DEAD OF NIGHT HE BURIED THEM BENEATH THE ROOTS OF A TREE THAT HAD LONG AGO BEEN STRUCK BY LIGHTNING AND NOW TWISTED INTO A MOST DISTURBING SHAPE.

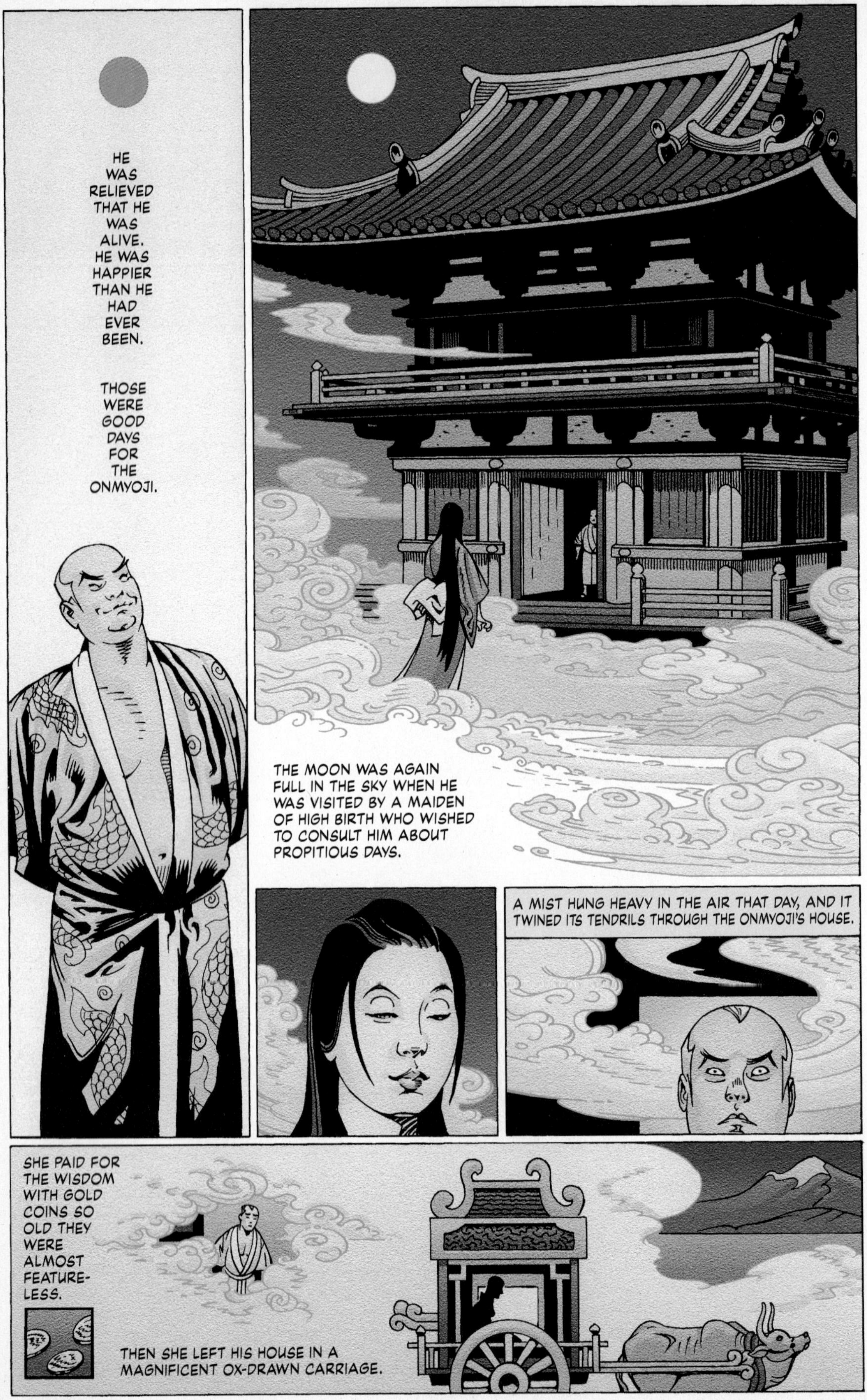

HE WAS RELIEVED THAT HE WAS ALIVE. HE WAS HAPPIER THAN HE HAD EVER BEEN.
THOSE WERE GOOD DAYS FOR THE ONMYOJI.
THE MOON WAS AGAIN FULL IN THE SKY WHEN HE WAS VISITED BY A MAIDEN OF HIGH BIRTH WHO WISHED TO CONSULT HIM ABOUT PROPITIOUS DAYS.
A MIST HUNG HEAVY IN THE AIR THAT DAY, AND IT TWINED ITS TENDRILS THROUGH THE ONMYOJI'S HOUSE.
SHE PAID FOR THE WISDOM WITH GOLD COINS SO OLD THEY WERE ALMOST FEATURE-LESS.
THEN SHE LEFT HIS HOUSE IN A MAGNIFICENT OX-DRAWN CARRIAGE.

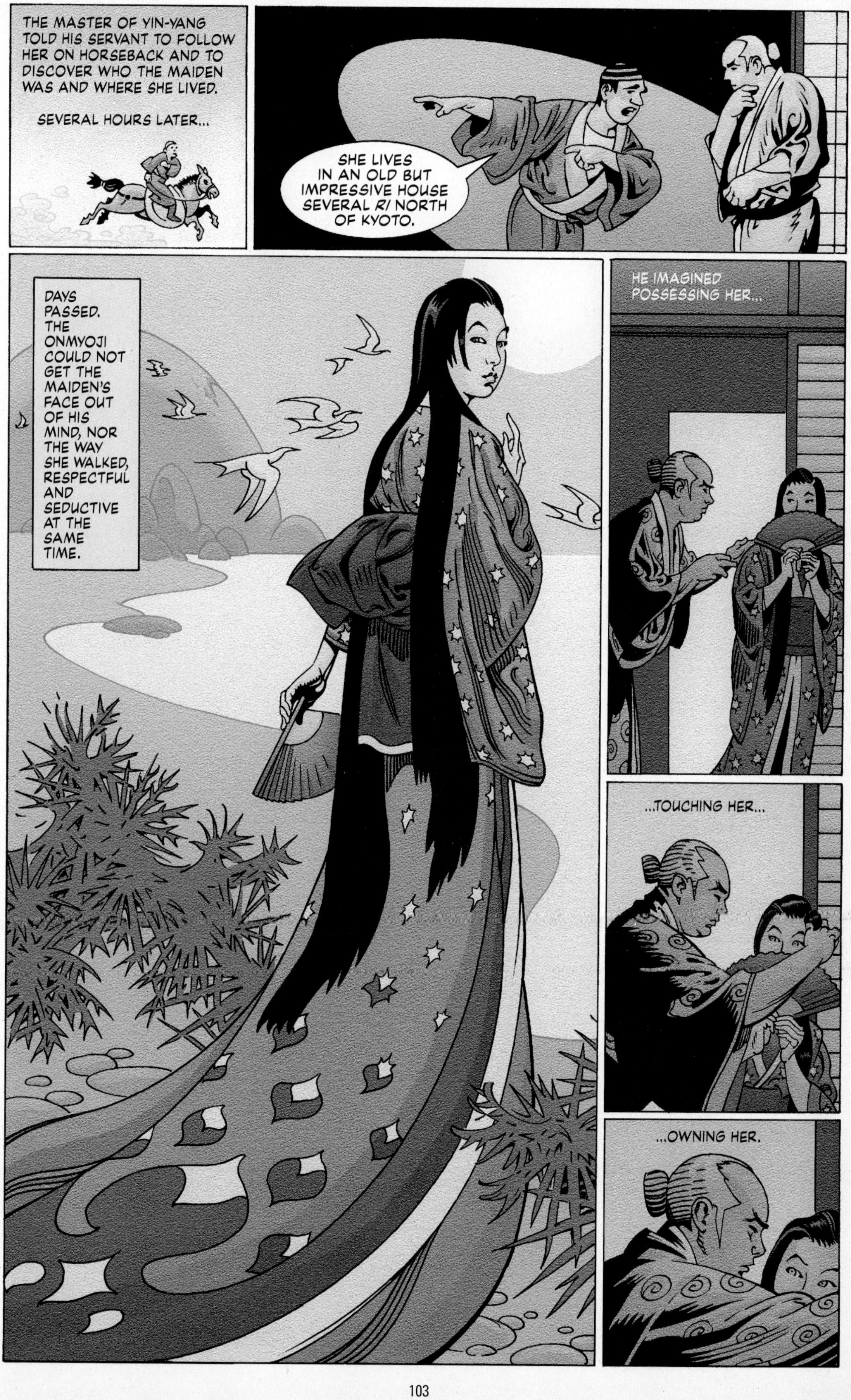
THE MASTER OF YIN-YANG TOLD HIS SERVANT TO FOLLOW HER ON HORSEBACK AND TO DISCOVER WHO THE MAIDEN WAS AND WHERE SHE LIVED.
SEVERAL HOURS LATER...
SHE LIVES IN AN OLD BUT IMPRESSIVE HOUSE SEVERAL RI NORTH OF KYOTO.
DAYS PASSED. THE ONMYOJI COULD NOT GET THE MAIDEN'S FACE OUT OF HIS MIND, NOR THE WAY SHE WALKED, RESPECTFUL AND SEDUCTIVE AT THE SAME TIME.
HE IMAGINED POSSESSING HER...
...TOUCHING HER...
...OWNING HER.

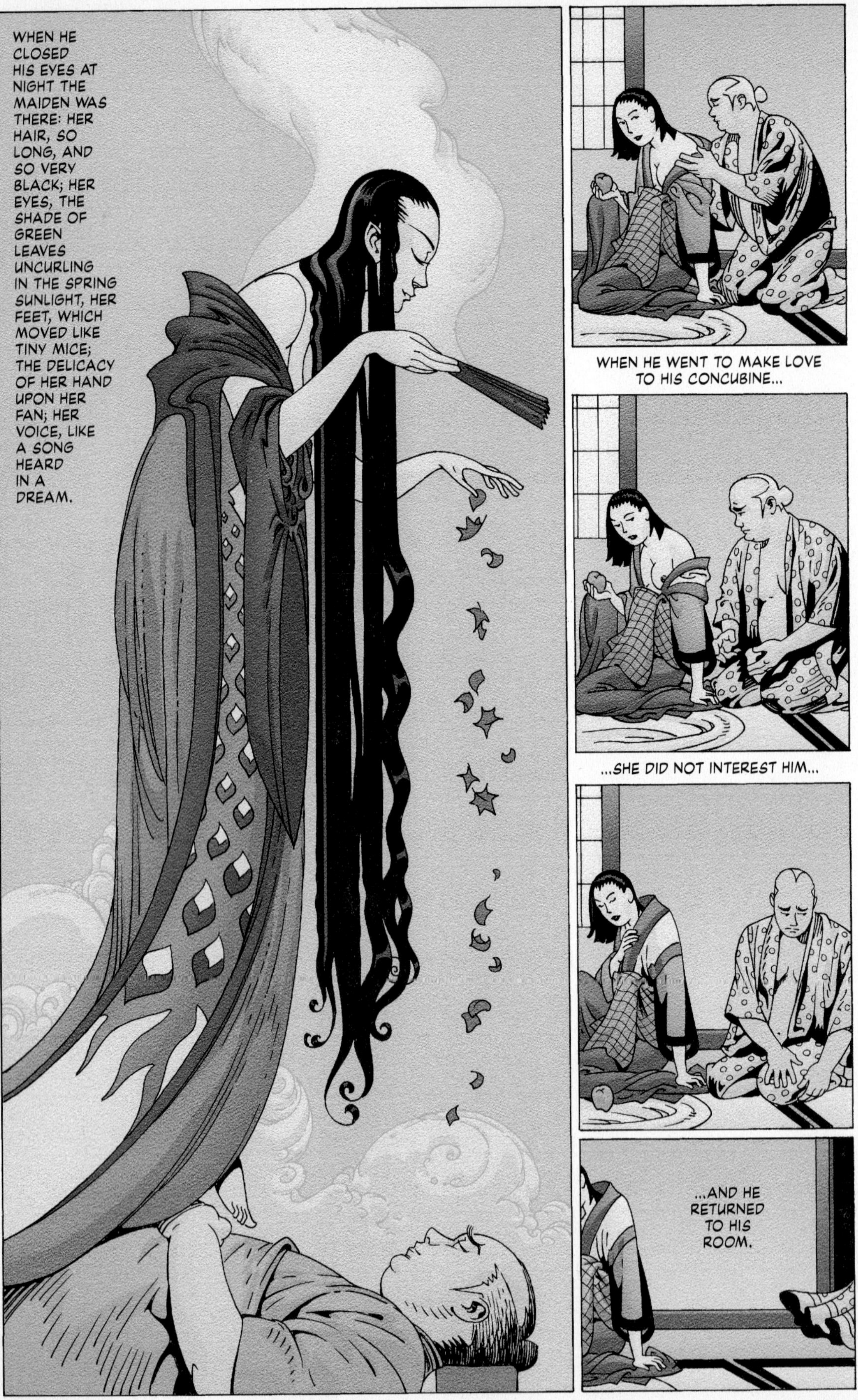
WHEN HE CLOSED HIS EYES AT NIGHT THE MAIDEN WAS THERE: HER HAIR, SO LONG, AND SO VERY BLACK; HER EYES, THE SHADE OF GREEN LEAVES UNCURLING IN THE SPRING SUNLIGHT, HER FEET, WHICH MOVED LIKE TINY MICE; THE DELICACY OF HER HAND UPON HER FAN; HER VOICE, LIKE A SONG HEARD IN A DREAM.
WHEN HE WENT TO MAKE LOVE TO HIS CONCUBINE...
...SHE DID NOT INTEREST HIM...
...AND HE RETURNED TO HIS ROOM.

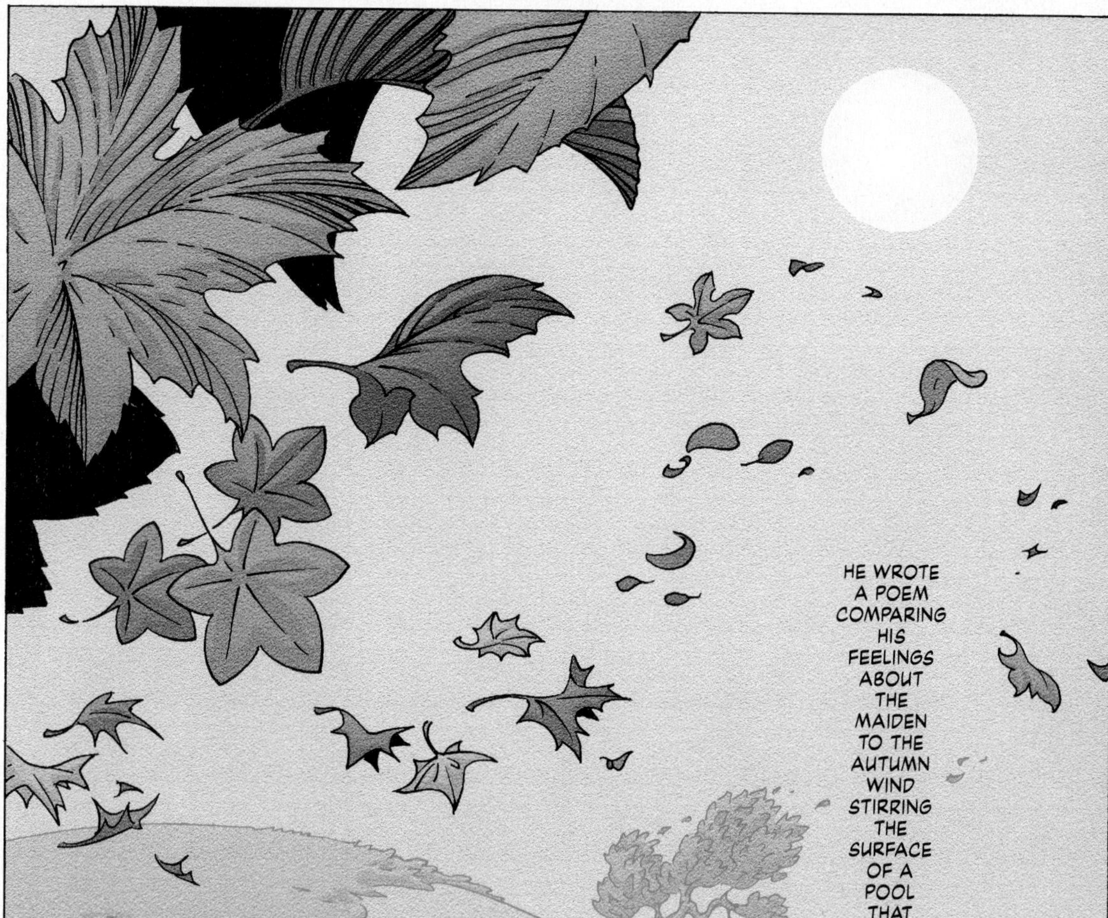
HE WROTE A POEM COMPARING HIS FEELINGS ABOUT THE MAIDEN TO THE AUTUMN WIND STIRRING THE SURFACE OF A POOL THAT HAD, UNTIL NOW, BEEN PLACID.

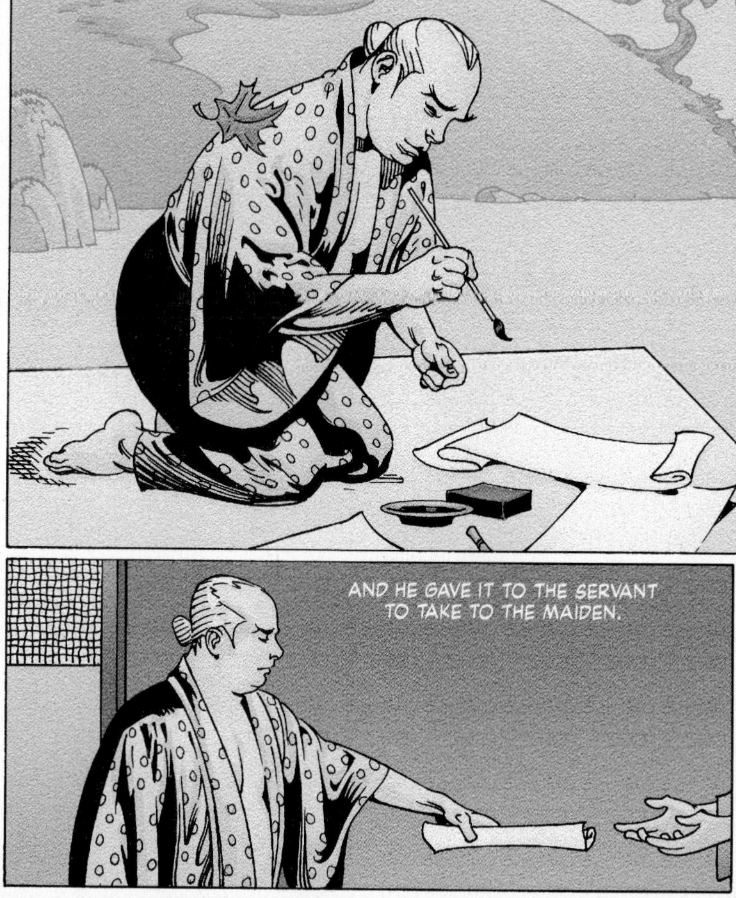
AND HE GAVE IT TO THE SERVANT TO TAKE TO THE MAIDEN.

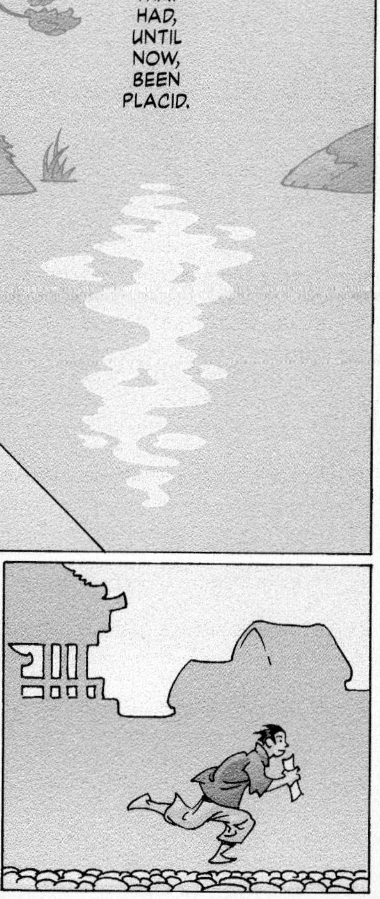

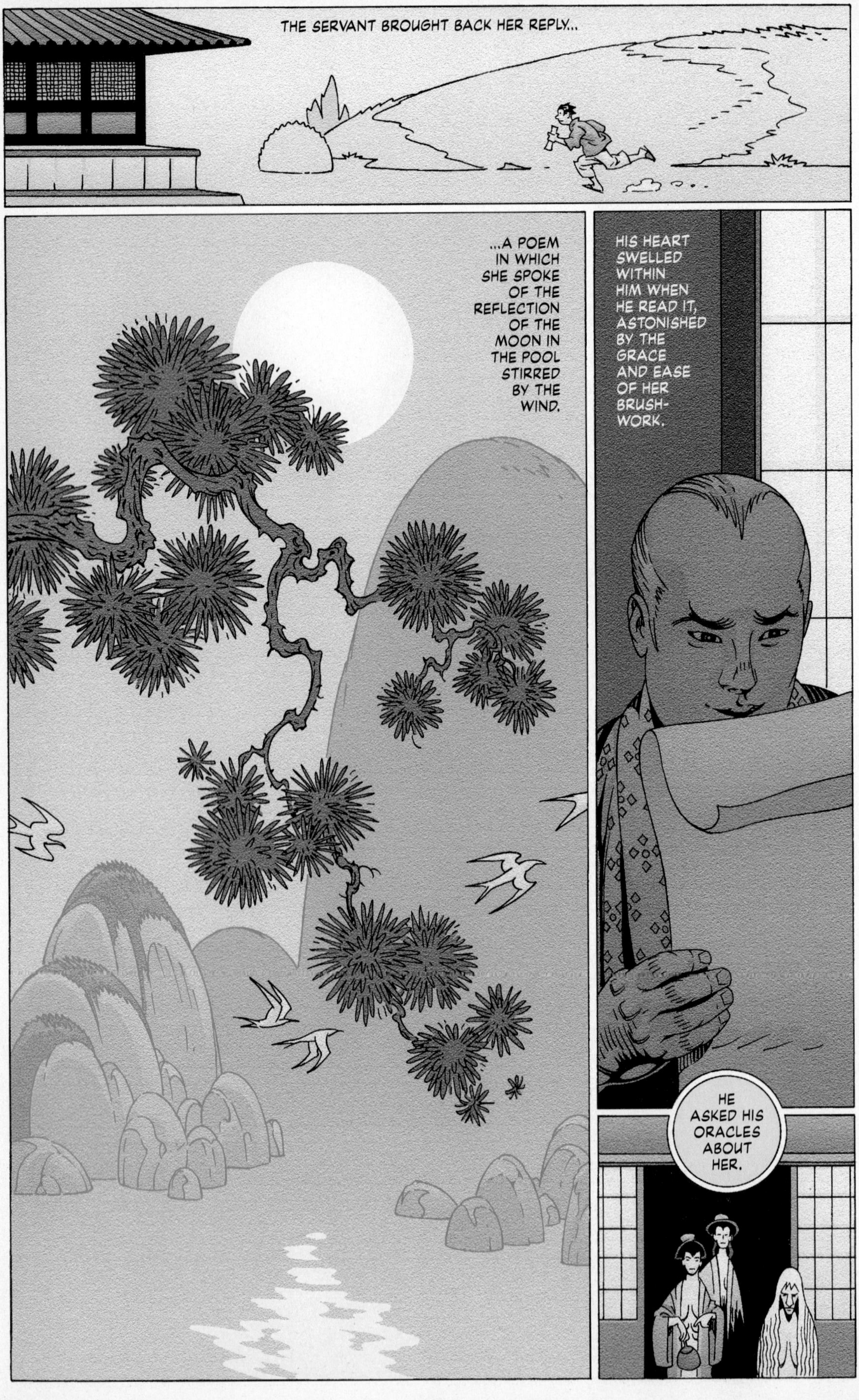
THE SERVANT BROUGHT BACK HER REPLY...
...A POEM IN WHICH SHE SPOKE OF THE REFLECTION OF THE MOON IN THE POOL STIRRED BY THE WIND.
HIS HEART SWELLED WITHIN HIM WHEN HE READ IT, ASTONISHED BY THE GRACE AND EASE OF HER BRUSH-WORK.
HE ASKED HIS ORACLES ABOUT HER.

HEE HEE HEE
HEE HEE HEE
HEE

HEE HEE HEE HEE HEE HEE HEE HEE HEE

THE MAN SHE LOVED IS DEAD.

GOOD. WHEN IS THE MOST PROPITIOUS DAY TO VISIT HER?

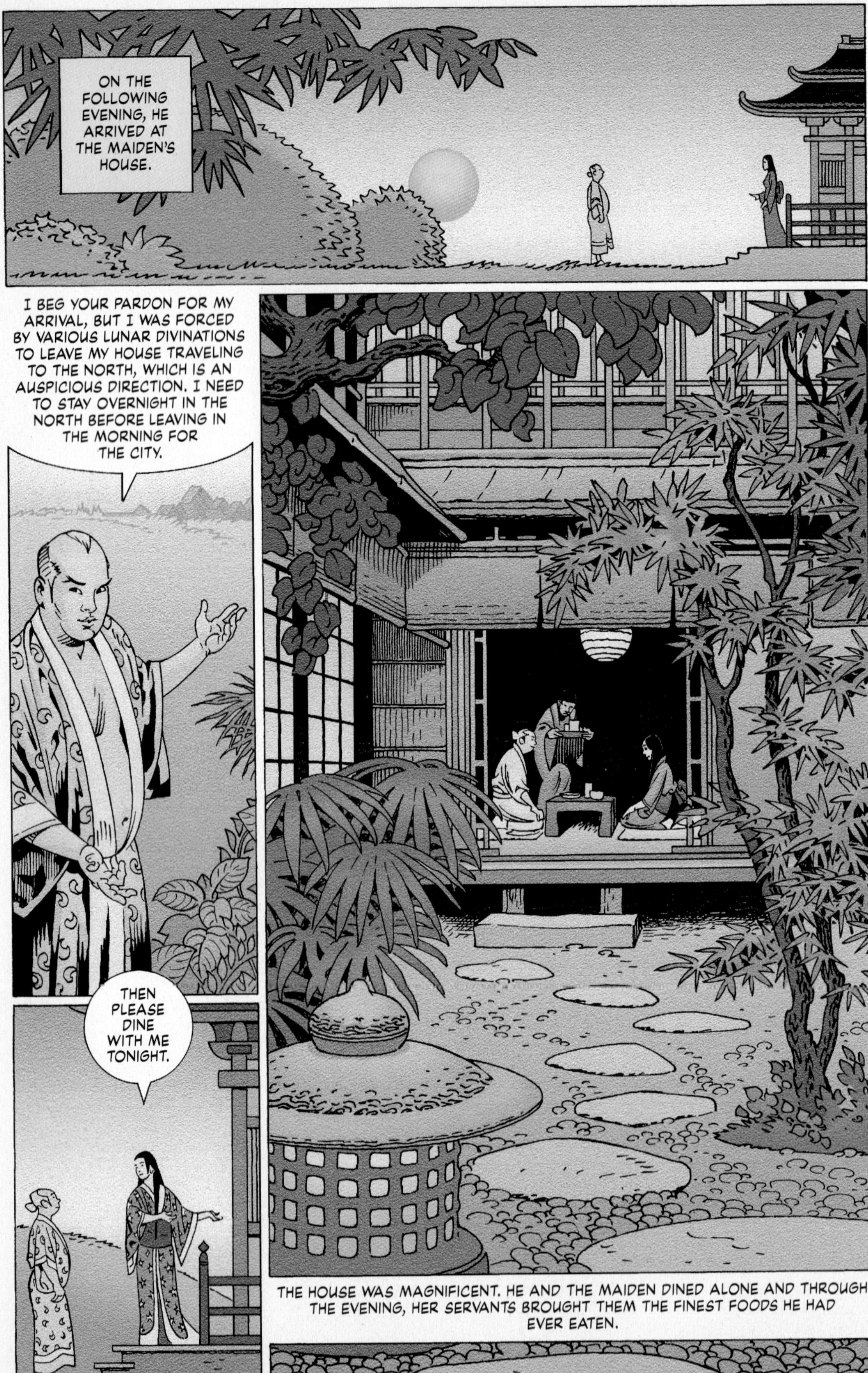
ON THE FOLLOWING EVENING, HE ARRIVED AT THE MAIDEN'S HOUSE.
I BEG YOUR PARDON FOR MY ARRIVAL, BUT I WAS FORCED BY VARIOUS LUNAR DIVINATIONS TO LEAVE MY HOUSE TRAVELING TO THE NORTH, WHICH IS AN AUSPICIOUS DIRECTION. I NEED TO STAY OVERNIGHT IN THE NORTH BEFORE LEAVING IN THE MORNING FOR THE CITY.
THEN PLEASE DINE WITH ME TONIGHT.
THE HOUSE WAS MAGNIFICENT. HE AND THE MAIDEN DINED ALONE AND THROUGH THE EVENING, HER SERVANTS BROUGHT THEM THE FINEST FOODS HE HAD EVER EATEN.

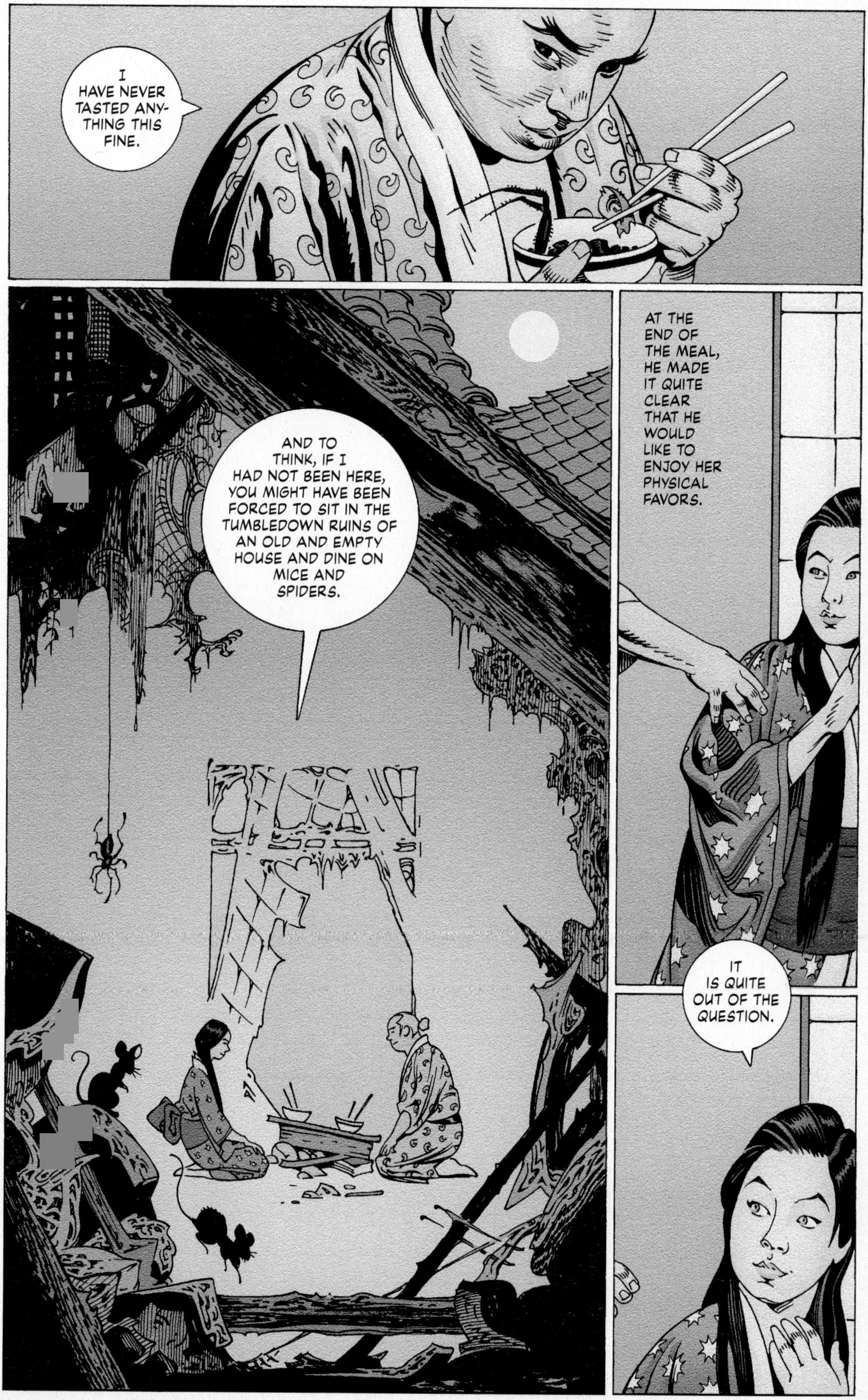
I HAVE NEVER TASTED ANYTHING THIS FINE.
AND TO THINK, IF I HAD NOT BEEN HERE, YOU MIGHT HAVE BEEN FORCED TO SIT IN THE TUMBLEDOWN RUINS OF AN OLD AND EMPTY HOUSE AND DINE ON MICE AND SPIDERS.
AT THE END OF THE MEAL, HE MADE IT QUITE CLEAR THAT HE WOULD LIKE TO ENJOY HER PHYSICAL FAVORS.
IT IS QUITE OUT OF THE QUESTION.

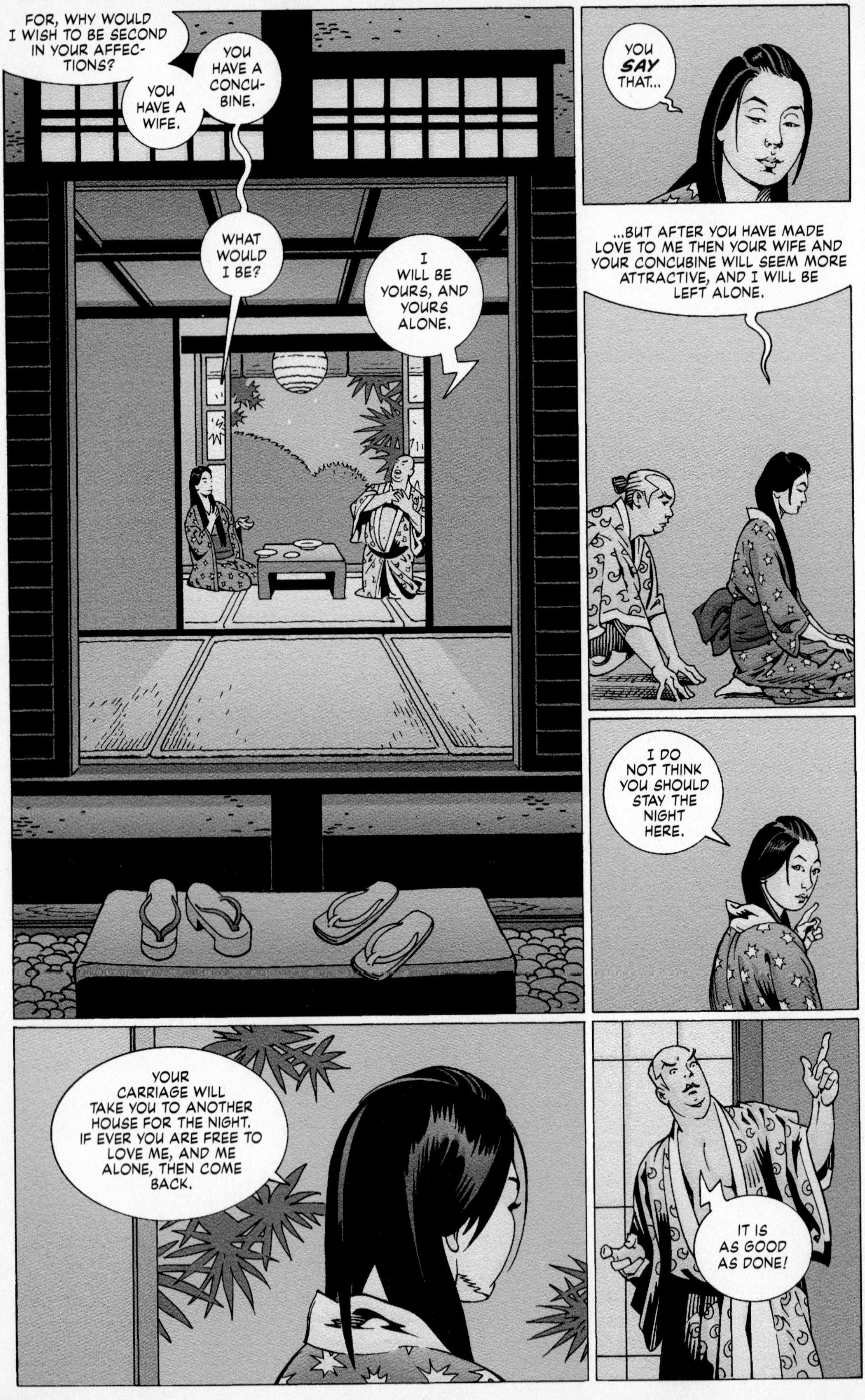
FOR, WHY WOULD I WISH TO BE SECOND IN YOUR AFFECTIONS?
YOU HAVE A WIFE.
YOU HAVE A CONCUBINE.
WHAT WOULD I BE?
I WILL BE YOURS, AND YOURS ALONE.
YOU *SAY* THAT...
...BUT AFTER YOU HAVE MADE LOVE TO ME THEN YOUR WIFE AND YOUR CONCUBINE WILL SEEM MORE ATTRACTIVE, AND I WILL BE LEFT ALONE.
I DO NOT THINK YOU SHOULD STAY THE NIGHT HERE.
YOUR CARRIAGE WILL TAKE YOU TO ANOTHER HOUSE FOR THE NIGHT. IF EVER YOU ARE FREE TO LOVE ME, AND ME ALONE, THEN COME BACK.
IT IS AS GOOD AS DONE!

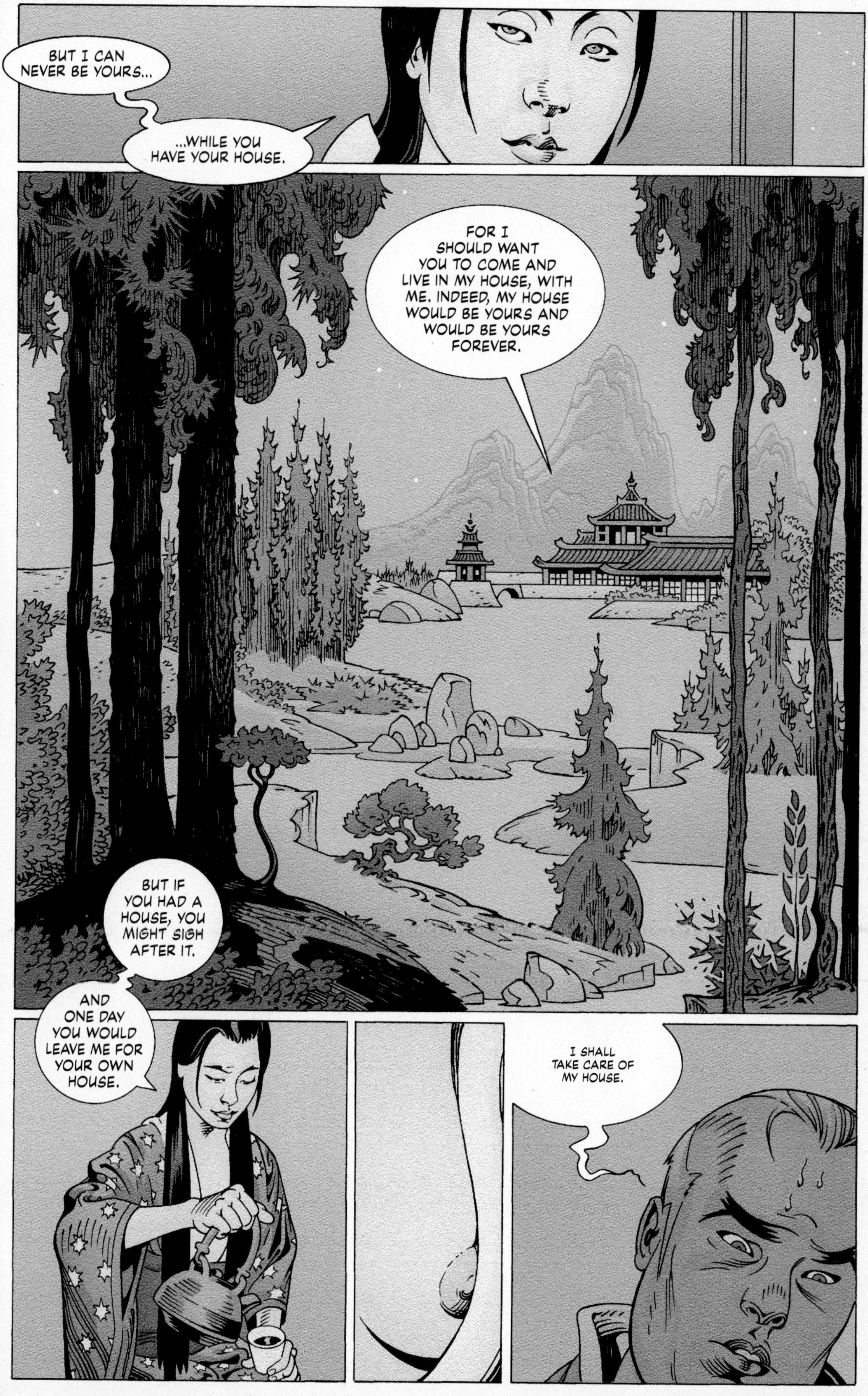
BUT I CAN NEVER BE YOURS...
...WHILE YOU HAVE YOUR HOUSE.
FOR I SHOULD WANT YOU TO COME AND LIVE IN MY HOUSE, WITH ME. INDEED, MY HOUSE WOULD BE YOURS AND WOULD BE YOURS FOREVER.
BUT IF YOU HAD A HOUSE, YOU MIGHT SIGH AFTER IT.
AND ONE DAY YOU WOULD LEAVE ME FOR YOUR OWN HOUSE.
I SHALL TAKE CARE OF MY HOUSE.

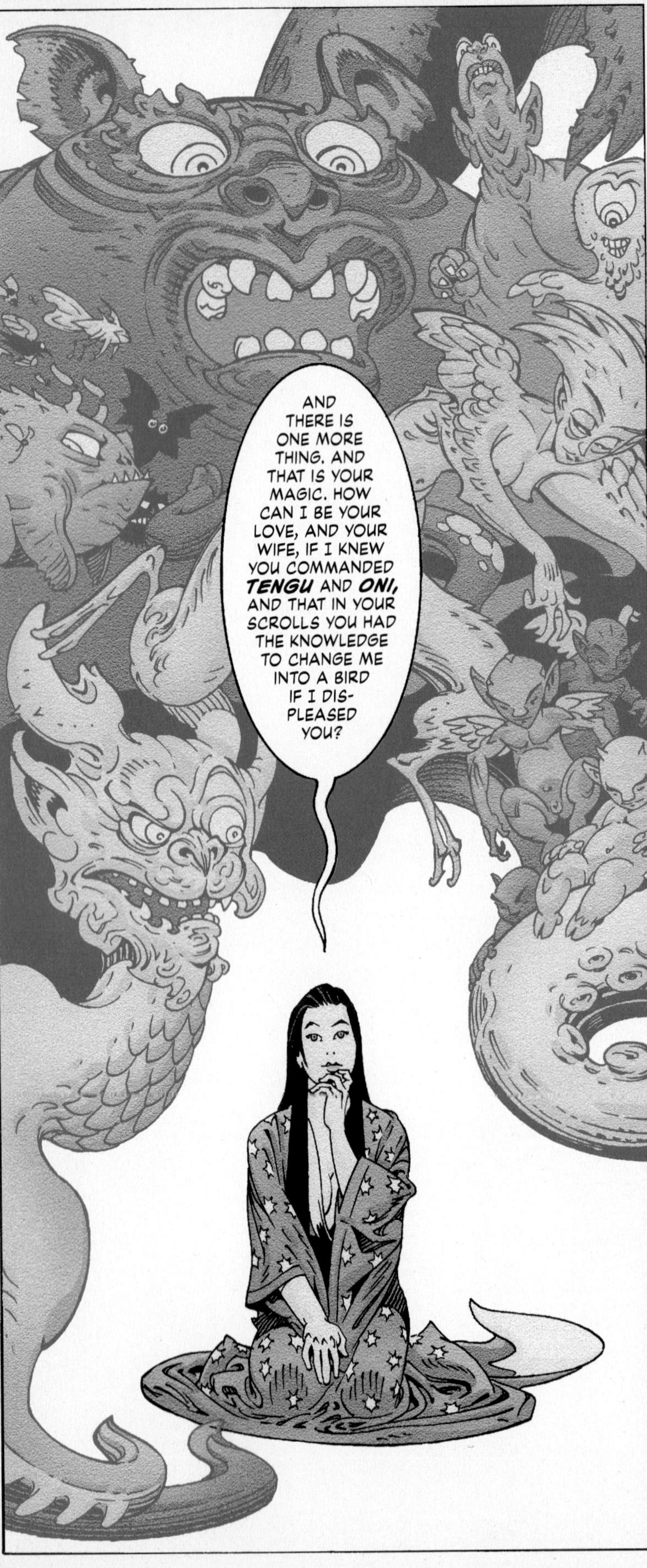

AND THERE IS ONE MORE THING. AND THAT IS YOUR MAGIC. HOW CAN I BE YOUR LOVE, AND YOUR WIFE, IF I KNEW YOU COMMANDED **TENGU** AND **ONI,** AND THAT IN YOUR SCROLLS YOU HAD THE KNOWLEDGE TO CHANGE ME INTO A BIRD IF I DIS-PLEASED YOU?

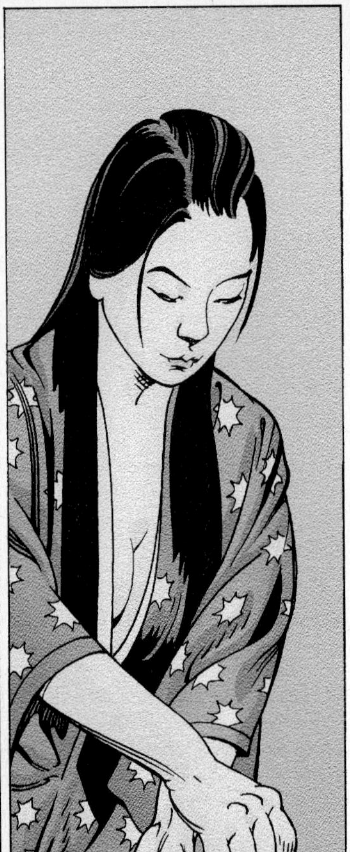

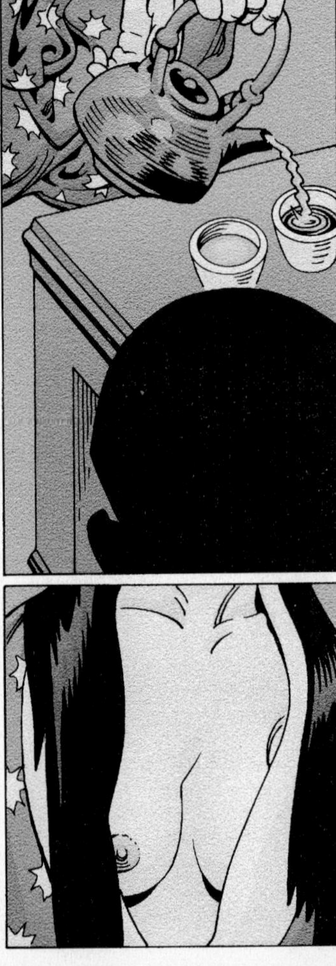

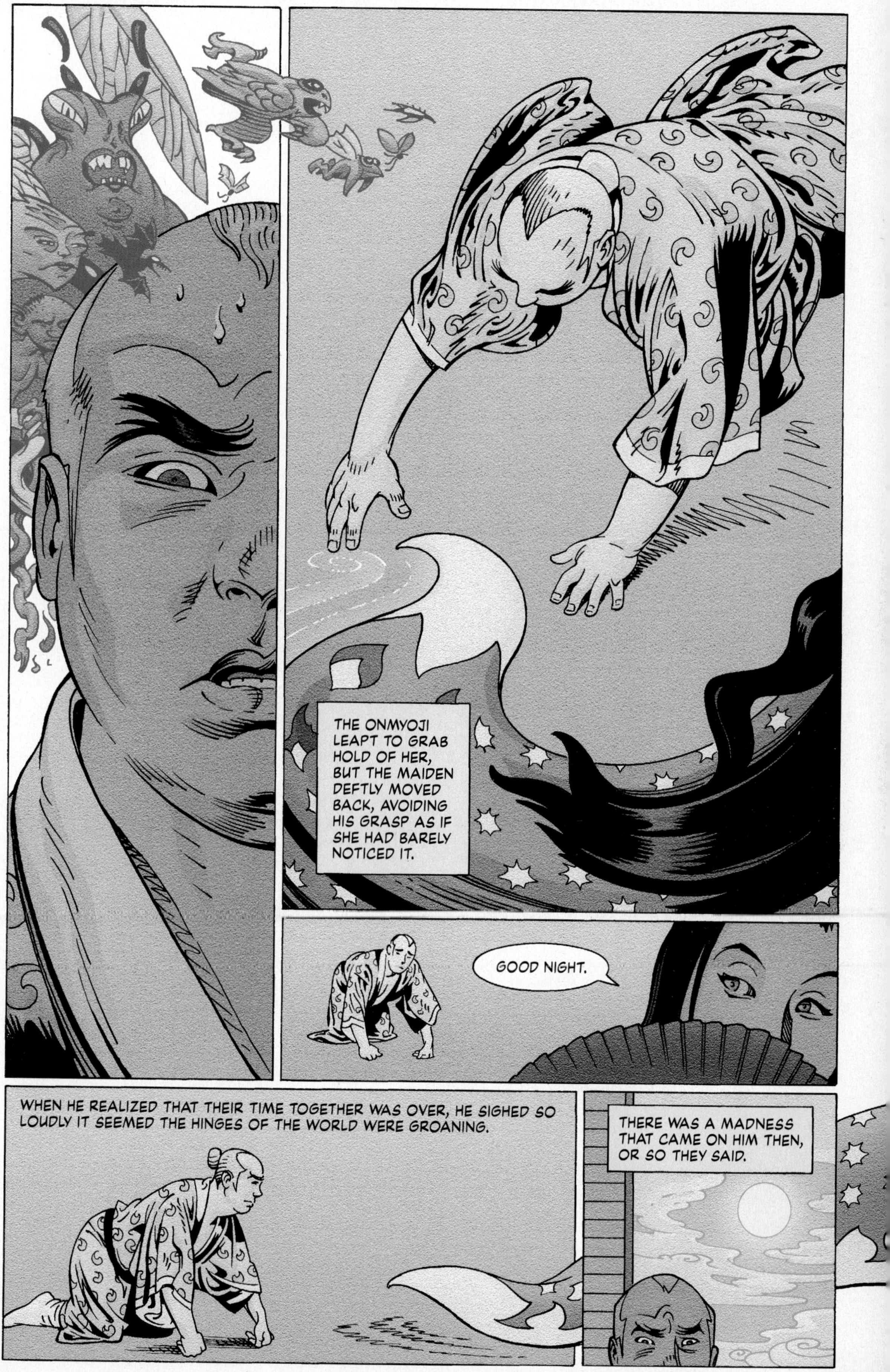
THE ONMYOJI LEAPT TO GRAB HOLD OF HER, BUT THE MAIDEN DEFTLY MOVED BACK, AVOIDING HIS GRASP AS IF SHE HAD BARELY NOTICED IT.
GOOD NIGHT.
WHEN HE REALIZED THAT THEIR TIME TOGETHER WAS OVER, HE SIGHED SO LOUDLY IT SEEMED THE HINGES OF THE WORLD WERE GROANING.
THERE WAS A MADNESS THAT CAME ON HIM THEN, OR SO THEY SAID.

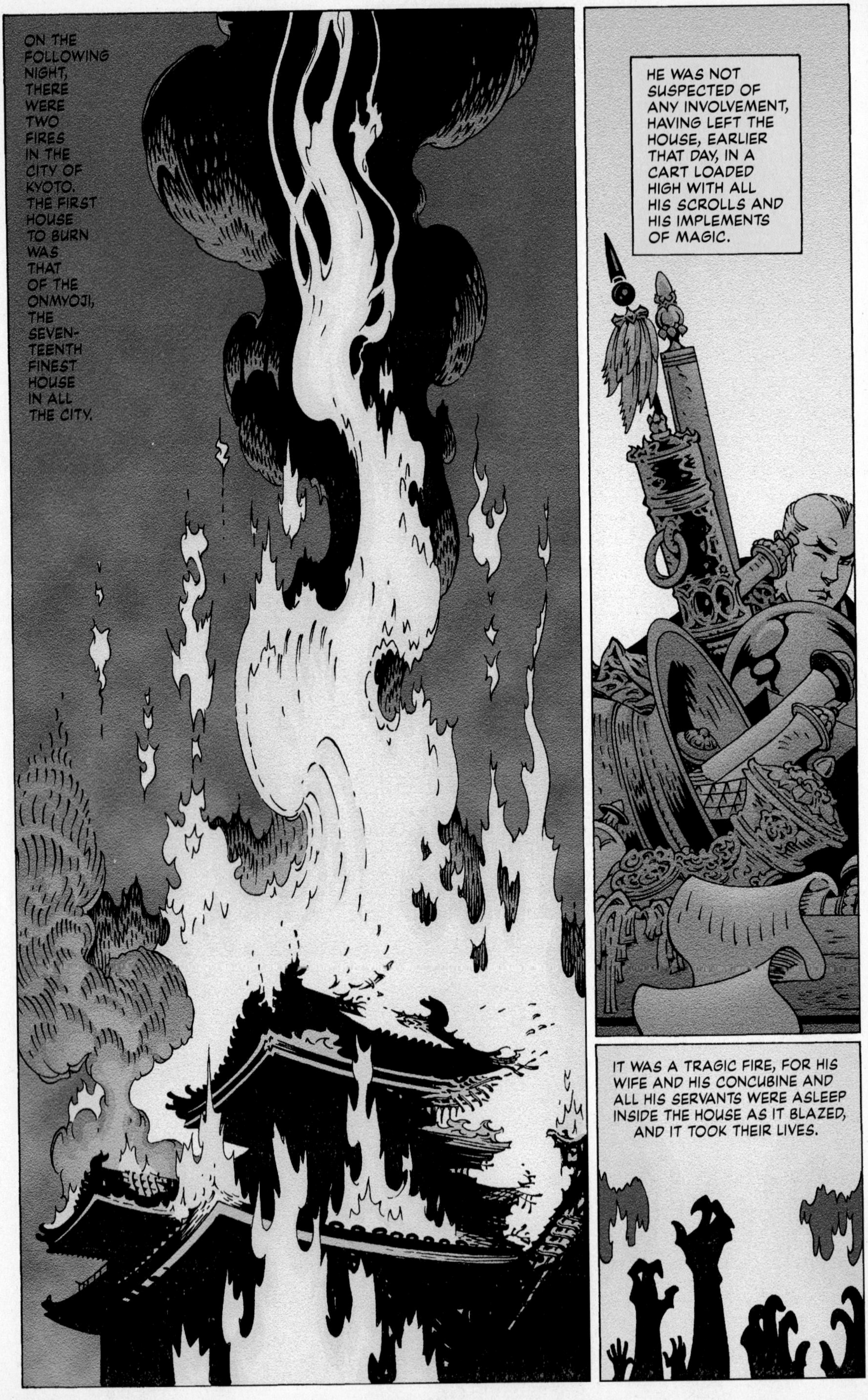
ON THE FOLLOWING NIGHT, THERE WERE TWO FIRES IN THE CITY OF KYOTO. THE FIRST HOUSE TO BURN WAS THAT OF THE ONMYOJI, THE SEVENTEENTH FINEST HOUSE IN ALL THE CITY.
HE WAS NOT SUSPECTED OF ANY INVOLVEMENT, HAVING LEFT THE HOUSE, EARLIER THAT DAY, IN A CART LOADED HIGH WITH ALL HIS SCROLLS AND HIS IMPLEMENTS OF MAGIC.
IT WAS A TRAGIC FIRE, FOR HIS WIFE AND HIS CONCUBINE AND ALL HIS SERVANTS WERE ASLEEP INSIDE THE HOUSE AS IT BLAZED, AND IT TOOK THEIR LIVES.

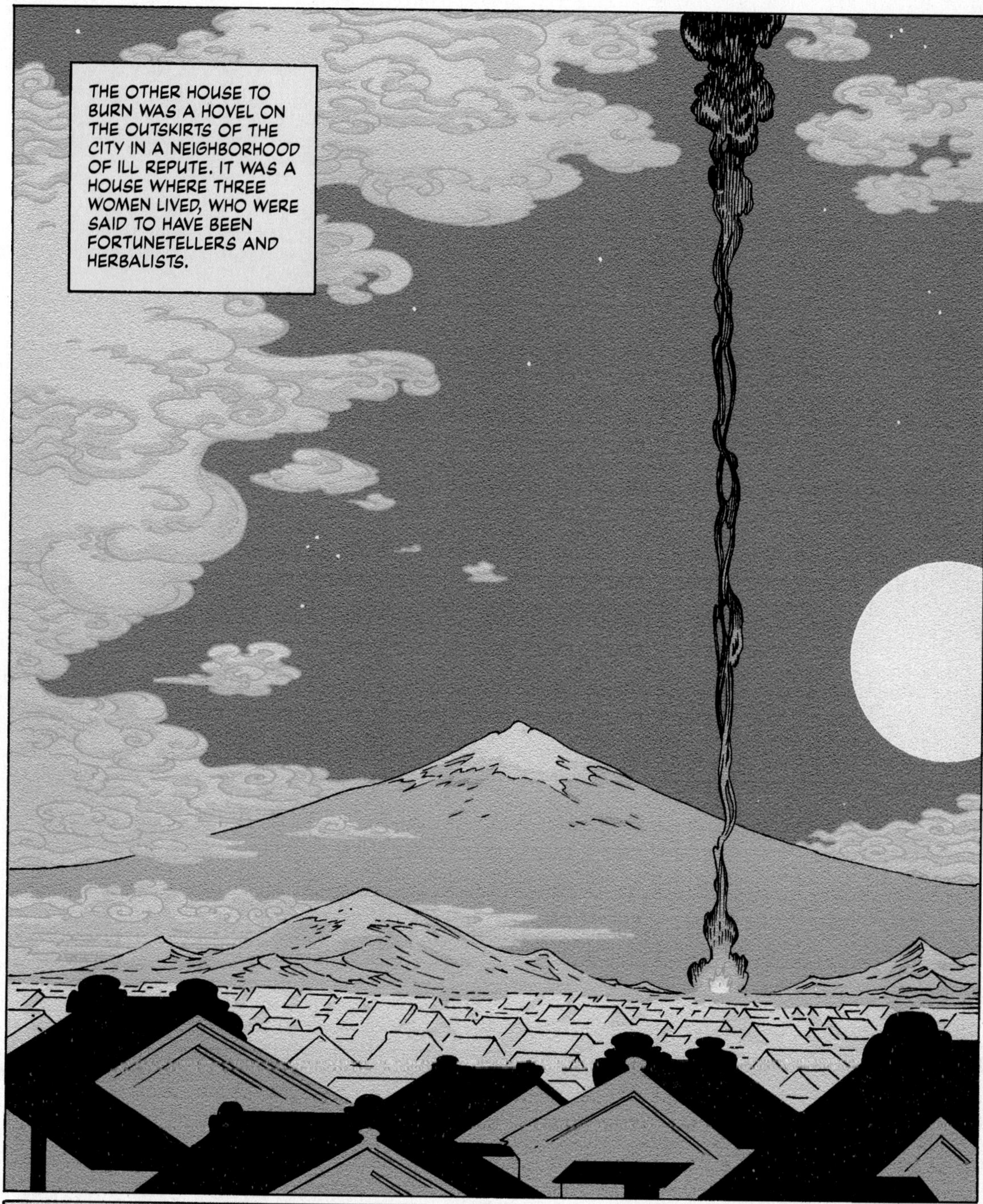
THE OTHER HOUSE TO BURN WAS A HOVEL ON THE OUTSKIRTS OF THE CITY IN A NEIGHBORHOOD OF ILL REPUTE. IT WAS A HOUSE WHERE THREE WOMEN LIVED, WHO WERE SAID TO HAVE BEEN FORTUNETELLERS AND HERBALISTS.

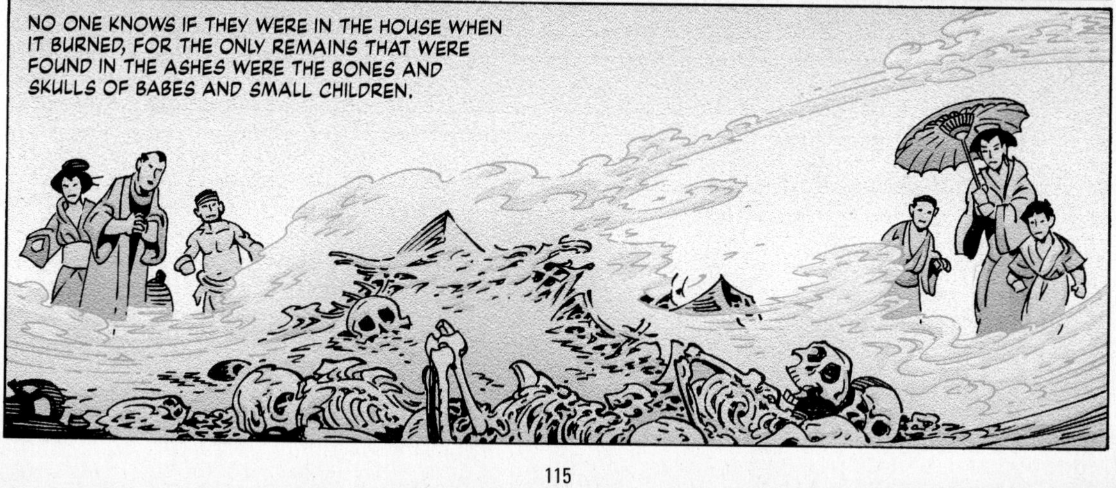
NO ONE KNOWS IF THEY WERE IN THE HOUSE WHEN IT BURNED, FOR THE ONLY REMAINS THAT WERE FOUND IN THE ASHES WERE THE BONES AND SKULLS OF BABES AND SMALL CHILDREN.

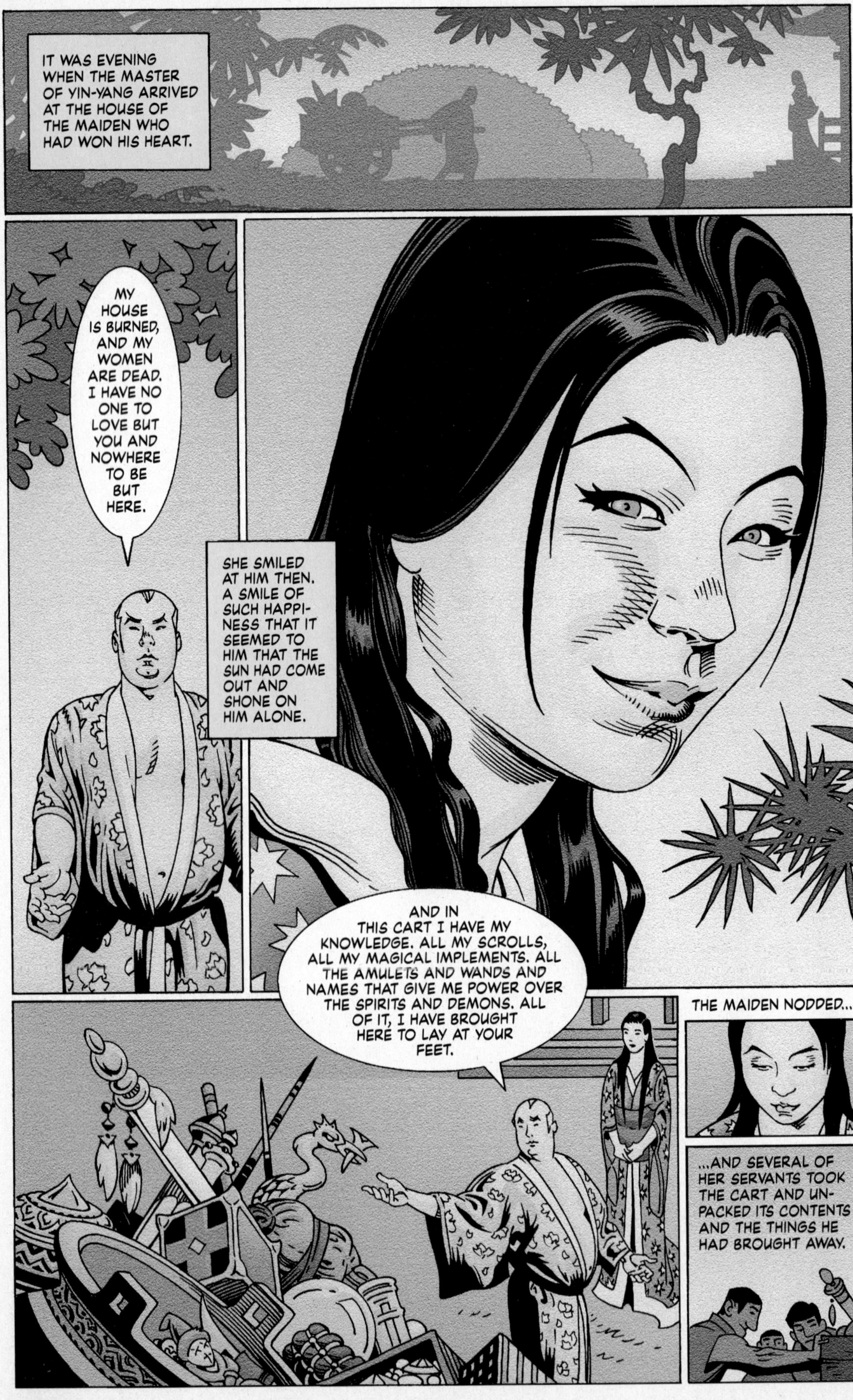
IT WAS EVENING WHEN THE MASTER OF YIN-YANG ARRIVED AT THE HOUSE OF THE MAIDEN WHO HAD WON HIS HEART.
MY HOUSE IS BURNED, AND MY WOMEN ARE DEAD. I HAVE NO ONE TO LOVE BUT YOU AND NOWHERE TO BE BUT HERE.
SHE SMILED AT HIM THEN. A SMILE OF SUCH HAPPINESS THAT IT SEEMED TO HIM THAT THE SUN HAD COME OUT AND SHONE ON HIM ALONE.
AND IN THIS CART I HAVE MY KNOWLEDGE. ALL MY SCROLLS, ALL MY MAGICAL IMPLEMENTS. ALL THE AMULETS AND WANDS AND NAMES THAT GIVE ME POWER OVER THE SPIRITS AND DEMONS. ALL OF IT, I HAVE BROUGHT HERE TO LAY AT YOUR FEET.
THE MAIDEN NODDED...
...AND SEVERAL OF HER SERVANTS TOOK THE CART AND UNPACKED ITS CONTENTS AND THE THINGS HE HAD BROUGHT AWAY.

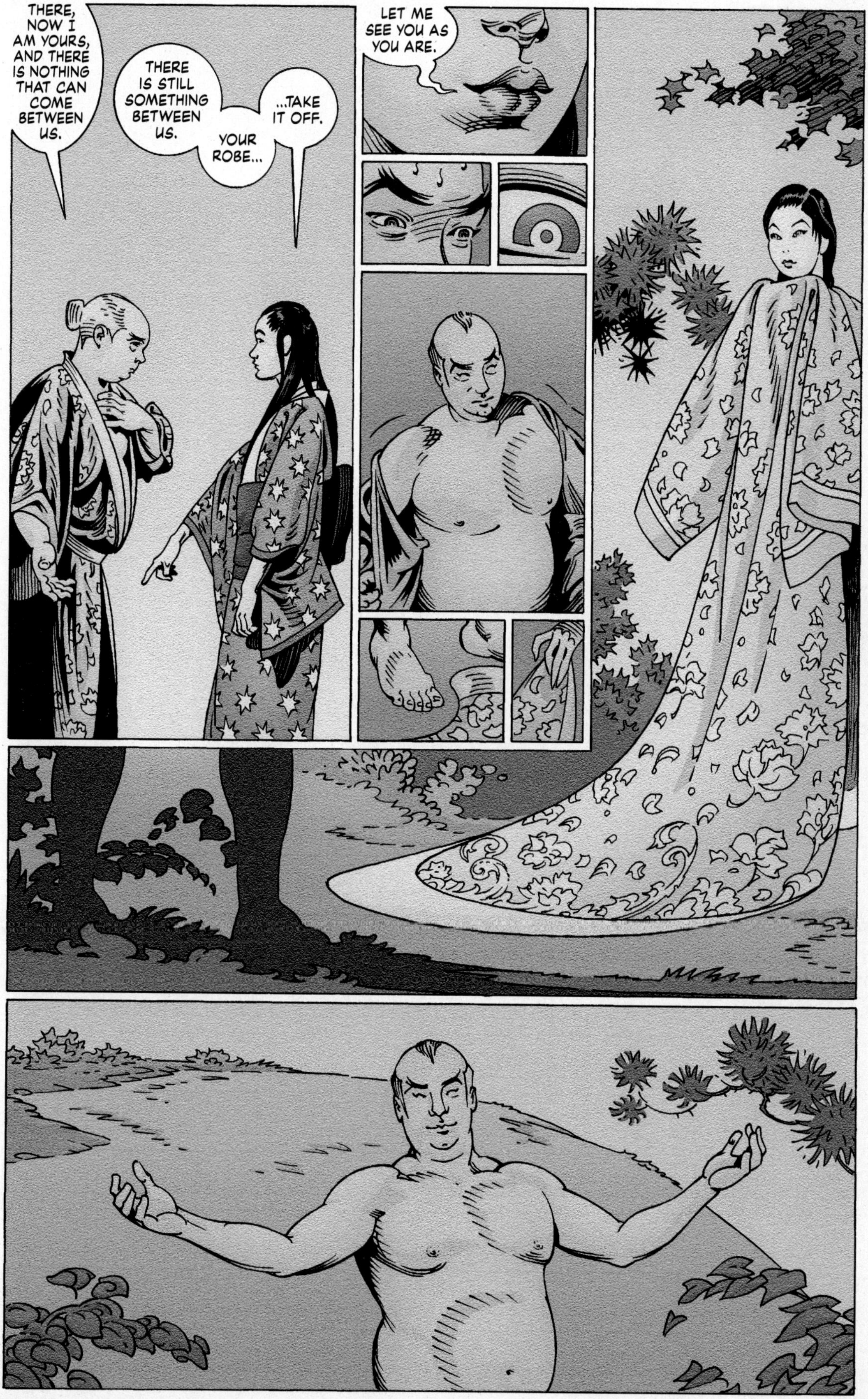
THERE, NOW I AM YOURS, AND THERE IS NOTHING THAT CAN COME BETWEEN US.
THERE IS STILL SOMETHING BETWEEN US.
YOUR ROBE...
...TAKE IT OFF.
LET ME SEE YOU AS YOU ARE.

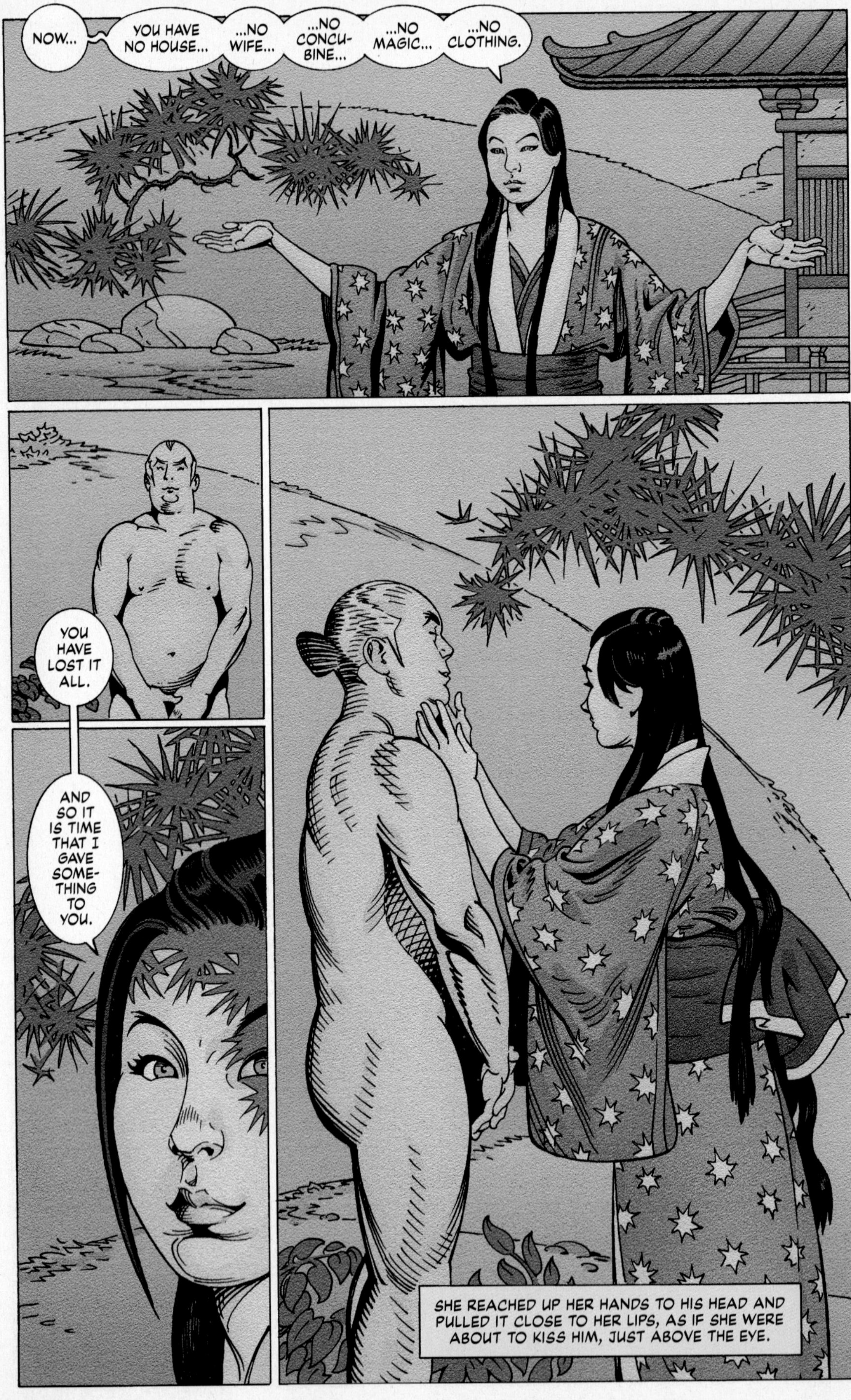
NOW...
YOU HAVE NO HOUSE...
...NO WIFE...
...NO CONCUBINE...
...NO MAGIC...
...NO CLOTHING.
YOU HAVE LOST IT ALL.
AND SO IT IS TIME THAT I GAVE SOMETHING TO YOU.
SHE REACHED UP HER HANDS TO HIS HEAD AND PULLED IT CLOSE TO HER LIPS, AS IF SHE WERE ABOUT TO KISS HIM, JUST ABOVE THE EYE.

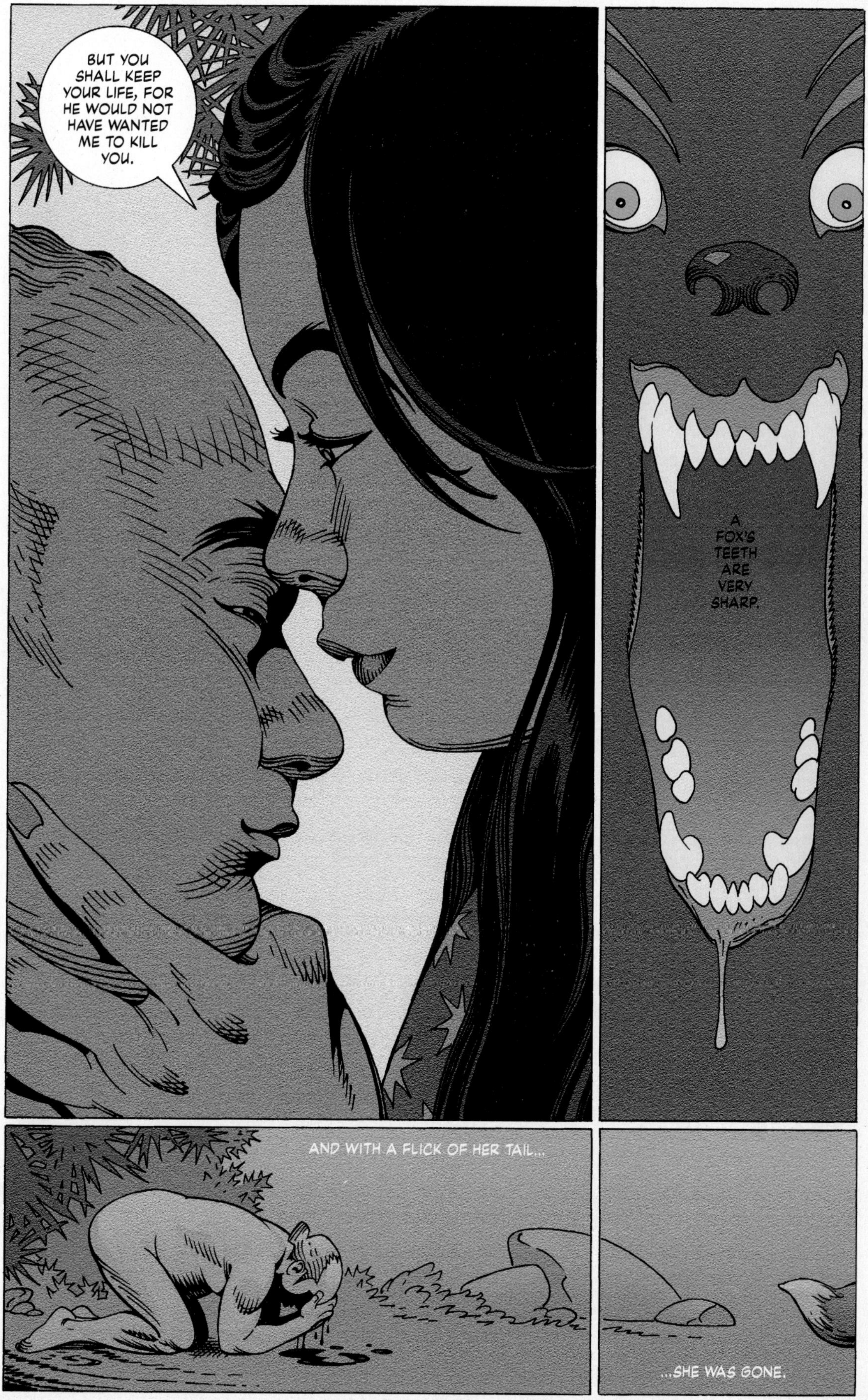
BUT YOU SHALL KEEP YOUR LIFE, FOR HE WOULD NOT HAVE WANTED ME TO KILL YOU.
A FOX'S TEETH ARE VERY SHARP.
AND WITH A FLICK OF HER TAIL...
...SHE WAS GONE.

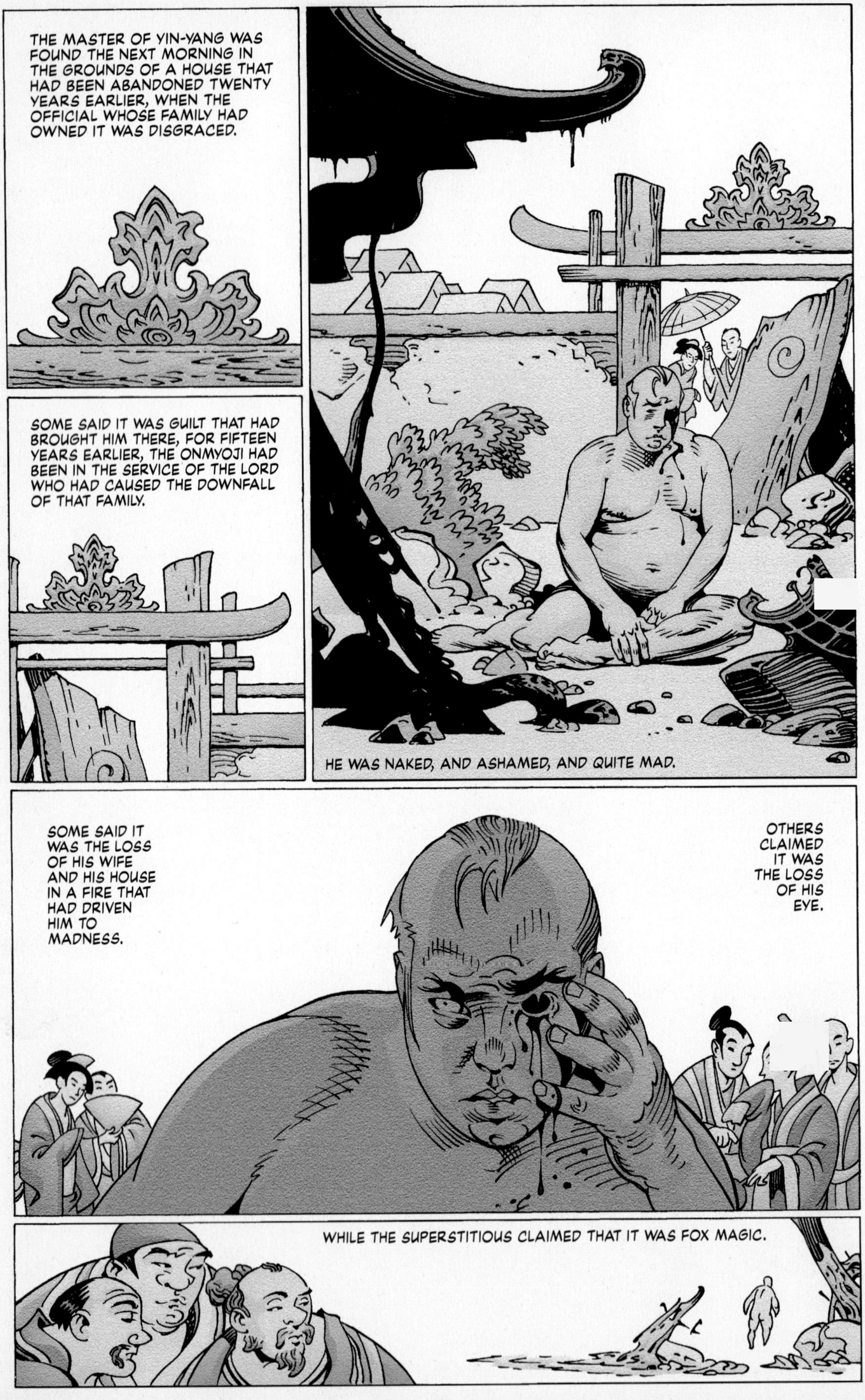
THE MASTER OF YIN-YANG WAS FOUND THE NEXT MORNING IN THE GROUNDS OF A HOUSE THAT HAD BEEN ABANDONED TWENTY YEARS EARLIER, WHEN THE OFFICIAL WHOSE FAMILY HAD OWNED IT WAS DISGRACED.
SOME SAID IT WAS GUILT THAT HAD BROUGHT HIM THERE, FOR FIFTEEN YEARS EARLIER, THE ONMYOJI HAD BEEN IN THE SERVICE OF THE LORD WHO HAD CAUSED THE DOWNFALL OF THAT FAMILY.
HE WAS NAKED, AND ASHAMED, AND QUITE MAD.
SOME SAID IT WAS THE LOSS OF HIS WIFE AND HIS HOUSE IN A FIRE THAT HAD DRIVEN HIM TO MADNESS.
OTHERS CLAIMED IT WAS THE LOSS OF HIS EYE.
WHILE THE SUPERSTITIOUS CLAIMED THAT IT WAS FOX MAGIC.

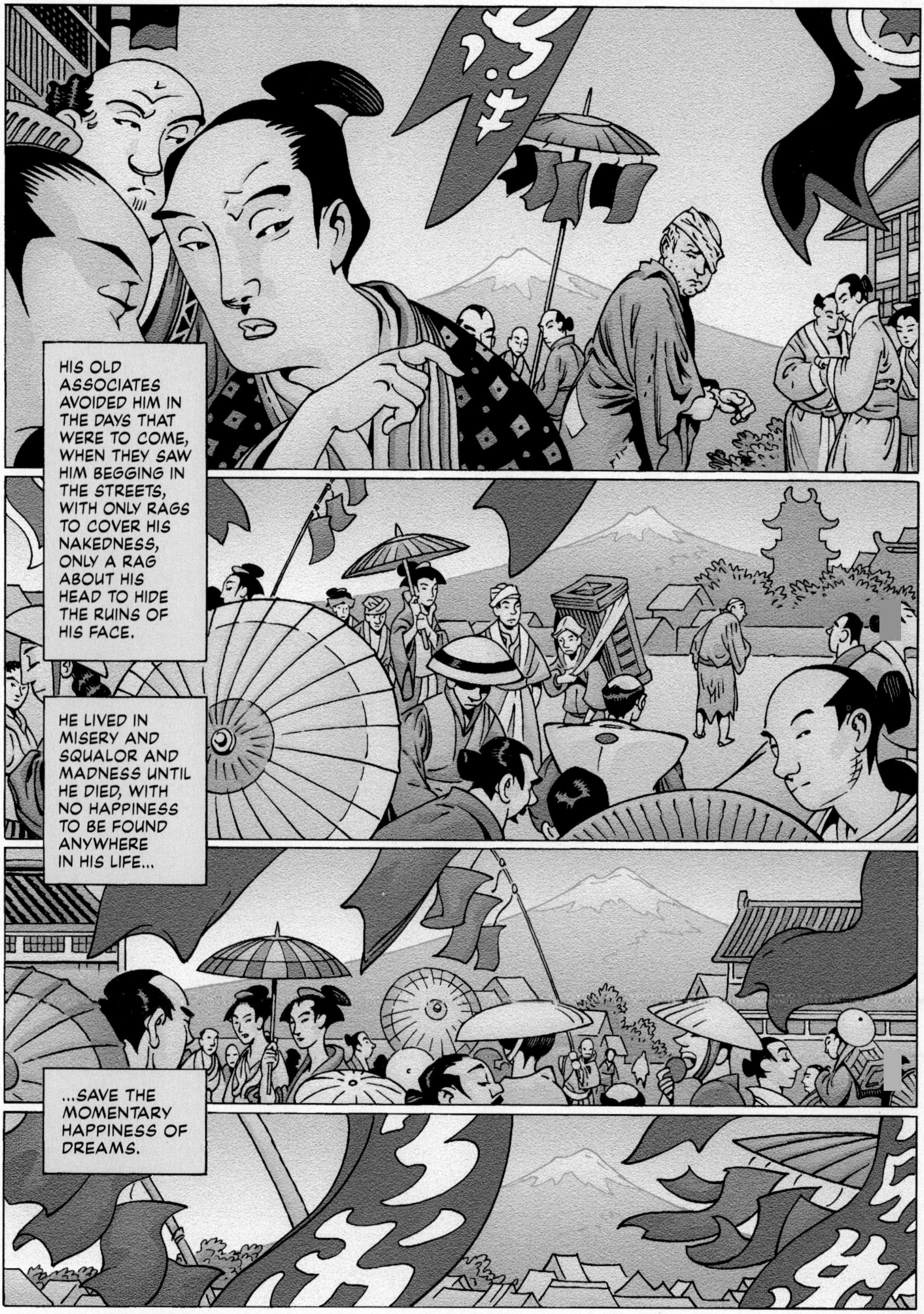
HIS OLD ASSOCIATES AVOIDED HIM IN THE DAYS THAT WERE TO COME, WHEN THEY SAW HIM BEGGING IN THE STREETS, WITH ONLY RAGS TO COVER HIS NAKEDNESS, ONLY A RAG ABOUT HIS HEAD TO HIDE THE RUINS OF HIS FACE.
HE LIVED IN MISERY AND SQUALOR AND MADNESS UNTIL HE DIED, WITH NO HAPPINESS TO BE FOUND ANYWHERE IN HIS LIFE...
...SAVE THE MOMENTARY HAPPINESS OF DREAMS.

BUT OF HOW HE LIVED, BEYOND THIS POINT, AND OF HOW HE DIED...

...ALL THE TALES ARE SILENT.

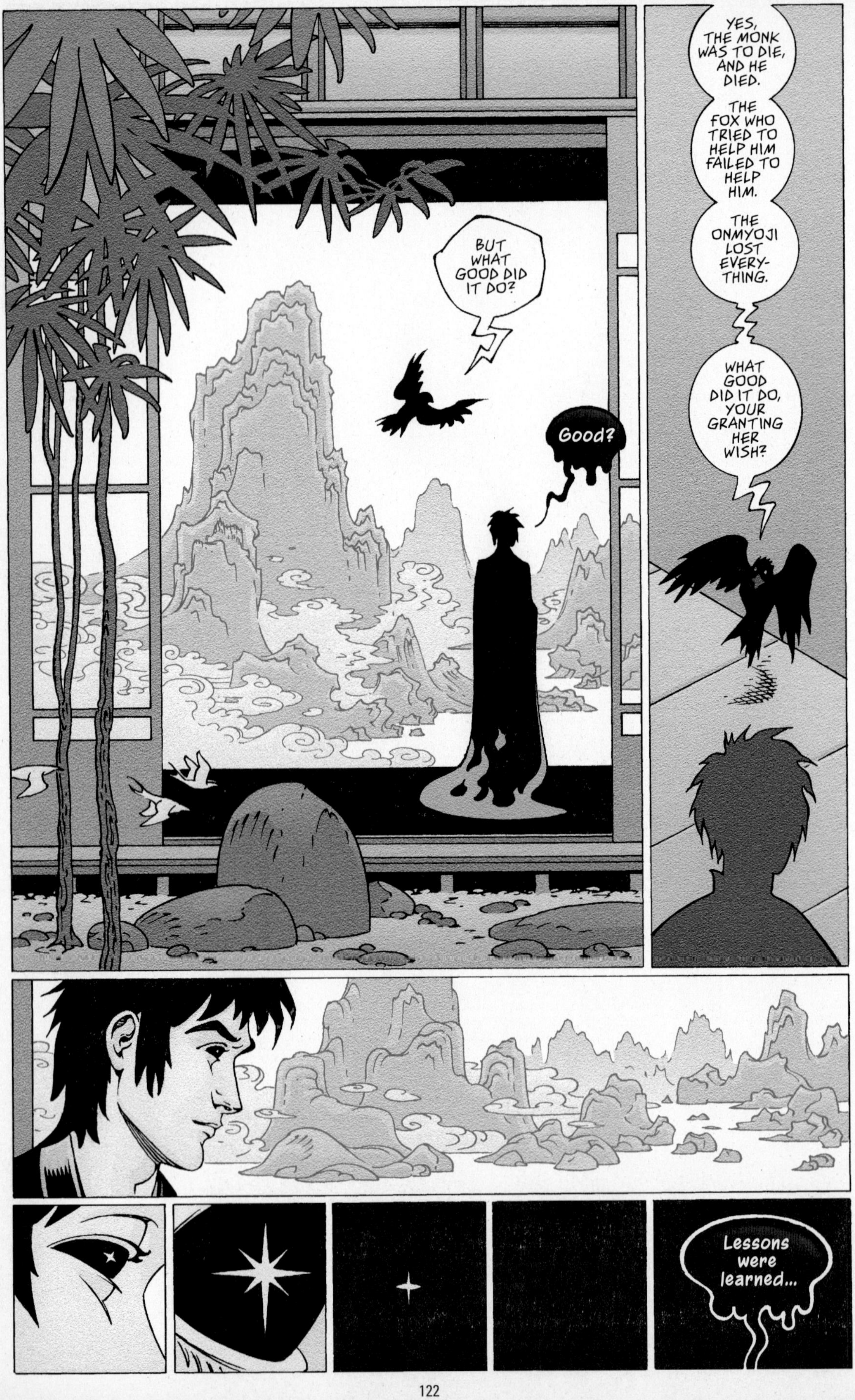
BUT WHAT GOOD DID IT DO?
Good?
YES, THE MONK WAS TO DIE, AND HE DIED.
THE FOX WHO TRIED TO HELP HIM FAILED TO HELP HIM.
THE ONMYOJI LOST EVERY-THING.
WHAT GOOD DID IT DO, YOUR GRANTING HER WISH?
Lessons were learned...

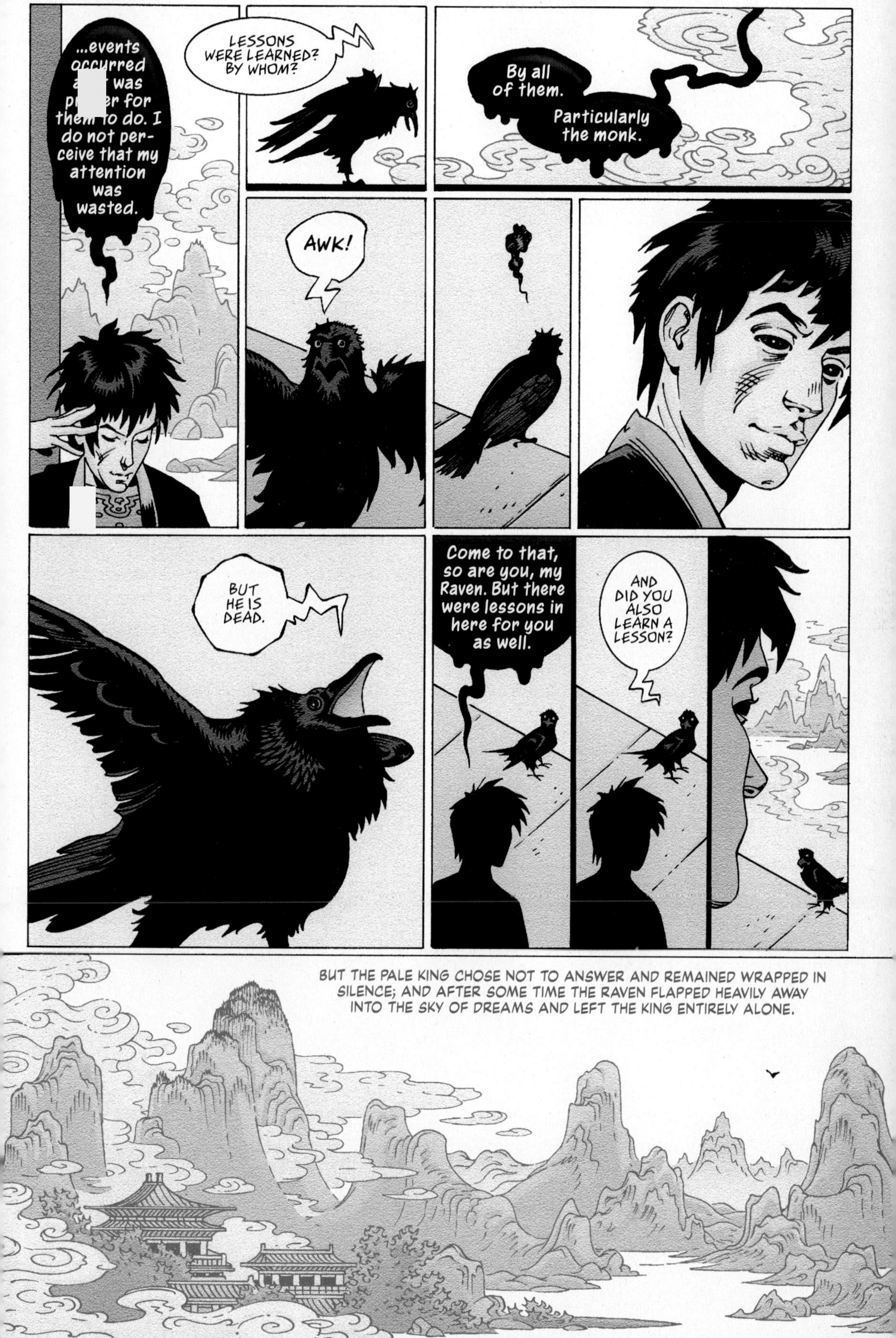
...events occurred a was pr er for them to do. I do not perceive that my attention was wasted.
LESSONS WERE LEARNED? BY WHOM?
By all of them.
Particularly the monk.
AWK!
BUT HE IS DEAD.
Come to that, so are you, my Raven. But there were lessons in here for you as well.
AND DID YOU ALSO LEARN A LESSON?
BUT THE PALE KING CHOSE NOT TO ANSWER AND REMAINED WRAPPED IN SILENCE; AND AFTER SOME TIME THE RAVEN FLAPPED HEAVILY AWAY INTO THE SKY OF DREAMS AND LEFT THE KING ENTIRELY ALONE.

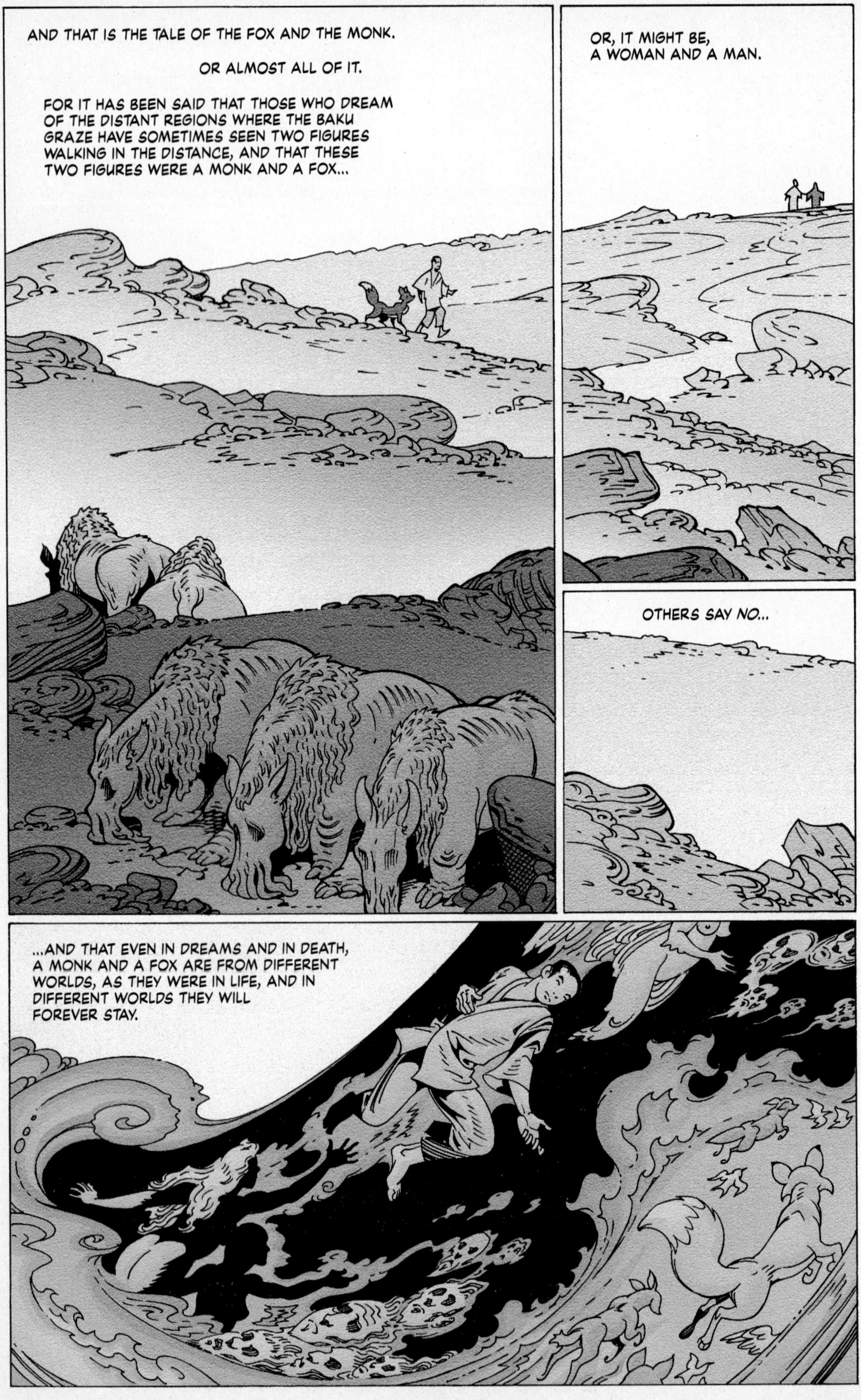
AND THAT IS THE TALE OF THE FOX AND THE MONK.
OR ALMOST ALL OF IT.
FOR IT HAS BEEN SAID THAT THOSE WHO DREAM OF THE DISTANT REGIONS WHERE THE BAKU GRAZE HAVE SOMETIMES SEEN TWO FIGURES WALKING IN THE DISTANCE, AND THAT THESE TWO FIGURES WERE A MONK AND A FOX...
OR, IT MIGHT BE, A WOMAN AND A MAN.
OTHERS SAY NO...
...AND THAT EVEN IN DREAMS AND IN DEATH, A MONK AND A FOX ARE FROM DIFFERENT WORLDS, AS THEY WERE IN LIFE, AND IN DIFFERENT WORLDS THEY WILL FOREVER STAY.

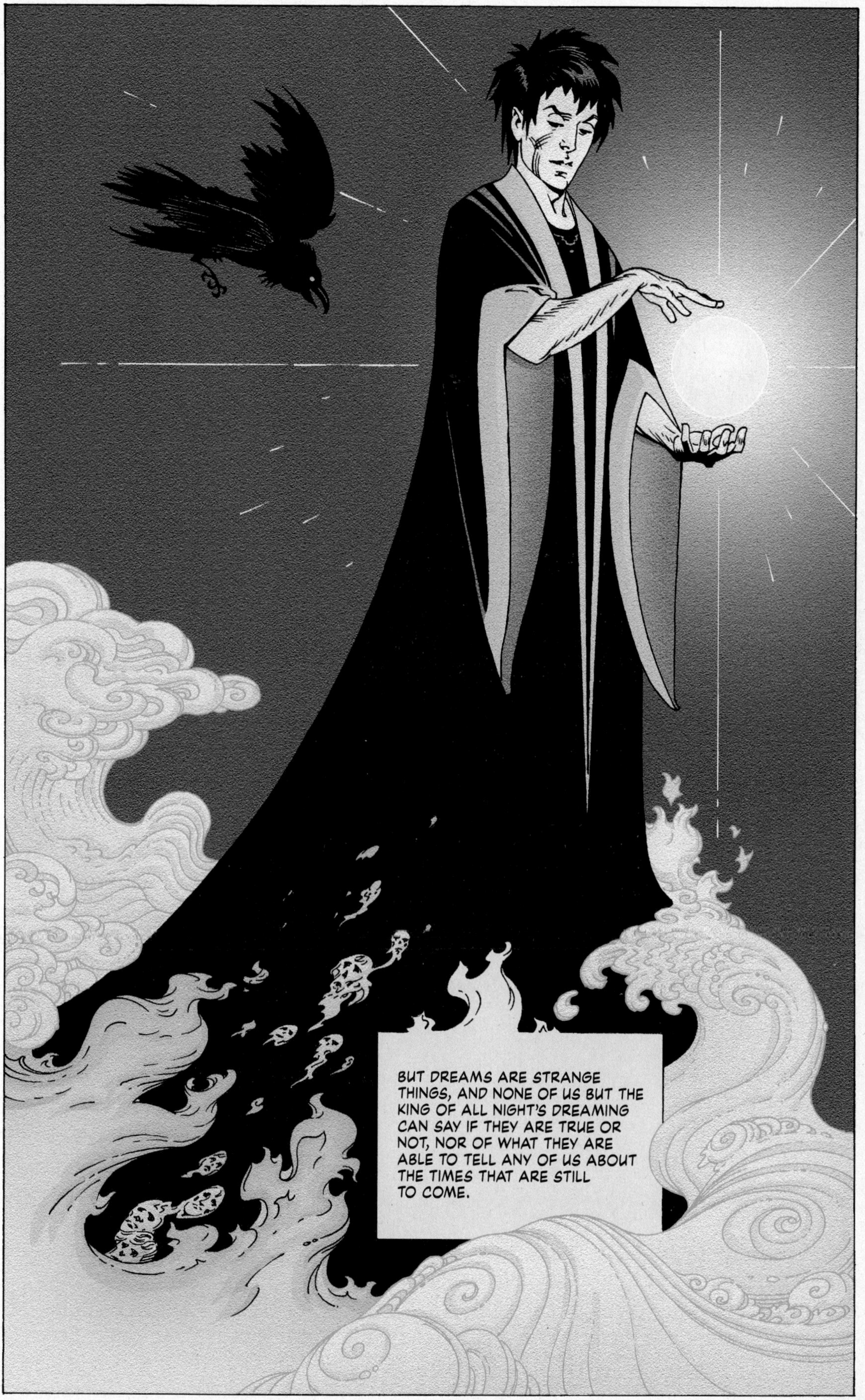
BUT DREAMS ARE STRANGE THINGS, AND NONE OF US BUT THE KING OF ALL NIGHT'S DREAMING CAN SAY IF THEY ARE TRUE OR NOT, NOR OF WHAT THEY ARE ABLE TO TELL ANY OF US ABOUT THE TIMES THAT ARE STILL TO COME.

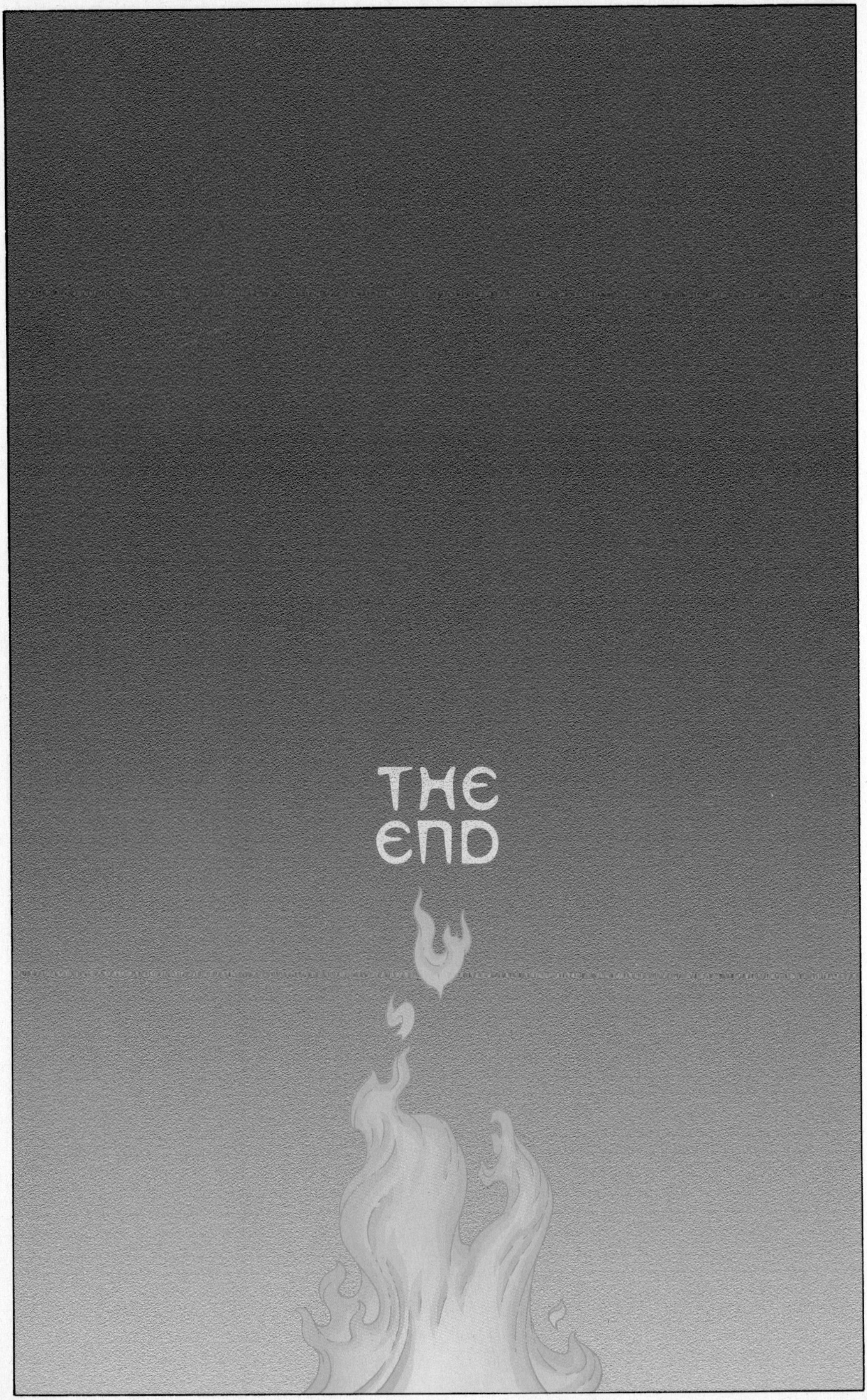
THE END

AFTERWORD BY NEIL GAIMAN

Although I meant to do many things with *The Dream Hunters*, I did not intend to upset, baffle and confuse academics and book-lovers. The book came about because, at the request of editor Jenny Lee, Yoshitaka Amano made a poster for Sandman's tenth anniversary, and I loved it. When VERTIGO supremo Karen Berger asked if I would like to write something new for the anniversary year, I asked if I could work with Mr. Amano. He loved the idea, but requested that it be an illustrated book, not a comic.

I loved the idea. Mr. Amano, and his assistant Maia, sent me reference material on the time and the place I planned to set the story, suggested I might want to include Baku, and I began to write, chapter by chapter, and to send the story to Mr. Amano as each chapter was finished.

A call from Jenny Lee: it was thought that the book might be too short. Could I write something more?

I wrote an afterword, intended to fill several pages, giving a perfectly spurious account of the history of the story I had just written. It was not expected to be convincing: This was a *Sandman* story, after all—nobody would believe that Cain and Abel, or the Three Witches, or even the Dream Lord himself, had been described in a Japanese story written hundreds of years ago.

Mr. Amano had drawn and painted twice as many pictures as we had expected, and all but one of them were included in the book, leaving only one page for the afterword. We printed it in very small type and forgot about it.

Somewhere in there, I was on the phone to P. Craig Russell. Getting Craig on the phone is never easy—when he is on a long project he wakes and sleeps according to his own mysterious circadian rhythms, and is diurnal or nocturnal depending on the project, which means you never know when to call, and you never know when not to call, and mostly when you do call he's fast asleep, and when you do get hold of him you count yourself lucky and talk for hours.

Craig asked what I was working on, and I read him the first two chapters of *Dream Hunters*. "Oh," he said. "I want to do that as a comic. I can see it in my head." Craig loves adapting prose into comics. His opera comics and his Kipling and Wilde adaptations are remarkable and fine.

I told him that it would be a prose book, that Mr. Amano would be doing paintings for it, and, a little wistfully, Craig agreed that he wasn't going to get to draw it as a comic.

Time passed. *Sandman: The Dream Hunters* was published, and I learned that if you put things in small type at the back of a book they are believed, unquestioningly, as the first of a stream of requests came in from people and from universities who found themselves unable to obtain the source texts I had claimed to have drawn from. I explained to each of them that I had made them up, and I apologized.

Sandman's twentieth anniversary approached. P. Craig Russell and I were working together on the comics adaptation of my novel *Coraline*. We were on the phone. "You know," said Craig, out of the blue, "I still want to adapt *The Dream Hunters*."

Ten years had passed. I pondered. Something that would not replace the Amano book but complement it...and a new Craig Russell Sandman comic, at that. "I don't know," I said. "I'll ask Karen."

I expected many things from Craig's *Dream Hunters*. What I did not expect was the strange feeling that came from reading a new *Sandman* comic. While I wrote *Sandman* for the better part of a decade, I never got to read it. And now I was. It was magical.

I hope you enjoy it as much as I did.

And I would like to apologize to anyone who has spent time trying to find the stories that *Sandman: The Dream Hunters* was based upon. They exist in Lucien's library, not in any of our own.

18 Sept 2008
Somewhere above the Pacific

AFTERWORD BY P. CRAIG RUSSELL

Well, he had *me* fooled.

For the past year when friends asked me what project I was working on, I would say I'm adapting Neil Gaiman's *The Dream Hunters*, an ancient Japanese fairy tale that Neil adapted from the original into the *Sandman* universe and very cleverly too, the way he wove Cain and Abel and the three witches into the fabric of his "retold" tale. A seamless transition, I said. It was only a few weeks ago I learned, along with practically everyone else, that Neil's story was entirely of his own invention, its faux pedigree a whimsical part of the whole.

This is a project that has felt charmed to me from the start. From the time I first read Neil's first rough draft of the story ten years ago, I knew immediately I wanted to make this story "mine." At that time Neil and I had only collaborated on two projects: *Sandman #50* and his short story "One Life; Furnished in Early Moorcock." I've spent much of my career doing adaptations of classic literature (Kipling, Oscar Wilde, etc.) and operas (*The Magic Flute, The Ring of the Nibelung, Salome*) but have always said, particularly on being given the original script to *Sandman 50*, that if I was offered scripts of this caliber every day I'd never need to do another adaptation. True, since Neil had already written *The Dream Hunters* as a short story, what I was doing was *technically* an adaptation, but it was an adaptation of a *living* writer. A different situation. A little more nerve-racking, though Neil has never been anything but an encouraging and enthusiastic partner. A Dream (ouch) to work with.

In its settings – an ancient and imaginary Japan complete with talking animals, demons and spirits both pleasant and malign amid natural settings that ranged from the loveliest gardens to the wildest of supernatural thunderstorms – *The Dream Hunters* played to all my three major influences: Asian art (particularly Japanese woodblock prints), European Art Nouveau (especially the graphics of Alphonse Mucha), and reaching all the way back to my childhood, the lush linearity of the earliest Disney masterpieces. Though that may sound contradictory – "lush and linear" – it represents image-making that is at once visually rich, even profligate, in its settings and effects combined with animation's stringent demand that every line serve a purpose. Nothing wasted. That economy of line is the common denominator of all three of these influences and an important part of the visual heritage of cartooning. For me, at least.

One of the happiest aspects of this experience, though, was the daily pleasure of receiving Lovern Kindzierski's e-mailed jpegs of the coloring. Early on, we decided to approximate the color palette of Japanese woodblock prints of the 17th, 18th, and 19th centuries – colorful yet muted – using the frequently overexploited possibilities of computer coloring to produce effects no more extreme than those that might have been used on the original woodblock prints. As he has on every project we've collaborated on for the past seventeen years, Lovern's sensitive coloring hit all the right notes.

It's been almost exactly one year since I began *The Dream Hunters,* and it's been one of the happiest experiences of my working life. And it seems somehow fitting, given the nature of Sandman / Morpheus / Dream that what I thought I was adapting, an authentic ancient Japanese fairy tale, was in fact an illusion entirely created by a modern western writer. So what have I been doing the past year?

"Dream or reality – let others decide."

P. CRAIG RUSSELL

AFTERWORD BY KAREN BERGER

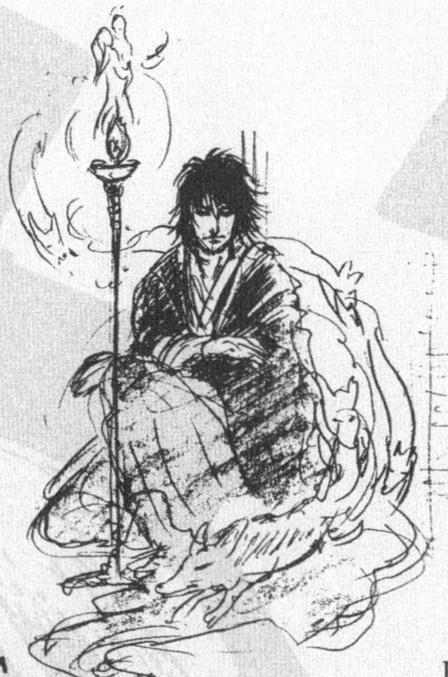

Issue #1

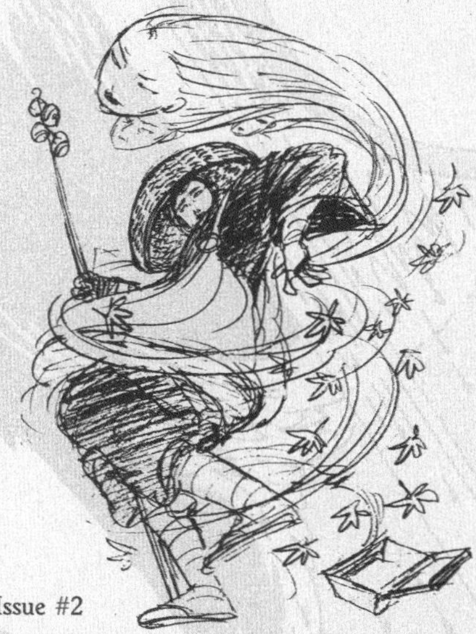

Issue #2

From the time that Vertigo first started, we always prided ourselves on being creatively daring and unexpected in both story and art. And we've always made a pointed effort to really experiment with the covers, from the range of art styles and mediums, to overall concepts and designs to attracting talent from inside and outside the comics industry. With *The Sandman: The Dream Hunters*, we're proud to introduce the wonderfully gifted Yuko Shimizu.

An award-winning illustrator and fine artist, Yuko did a beautiful drawing of Neil to accompany an article he had written in *The New York Times* a couple of years ago, and after meeting her and seeing the wealth and beauty of her work, we knew that we were destined to work together someday. Our stars aligned on *The Dream Hunters*. Yuko's bold, yet lyrical art style fit perfectly with the themes of the story, fusing an inimitable style of modern illustration and classical Japanese art into some unforgettable cover images.

This is only the first you'll be seeing of Yuko Shimizu at Vertigo. She's currently the cover artist for *The Unwritten*, a new monthly series that will forever change the boundaries between fiction and reality. And one of these days, we'll hopefully talk her into doing some interior work as well.

Yuko's covers for the original miniseries follow, accompanied by the variant covers by some of comics' greatest artists. And on this page, treat yourselves to Yuko's alternate sketches for each issue. Think of them as covers that could have been . . .

Issue #3

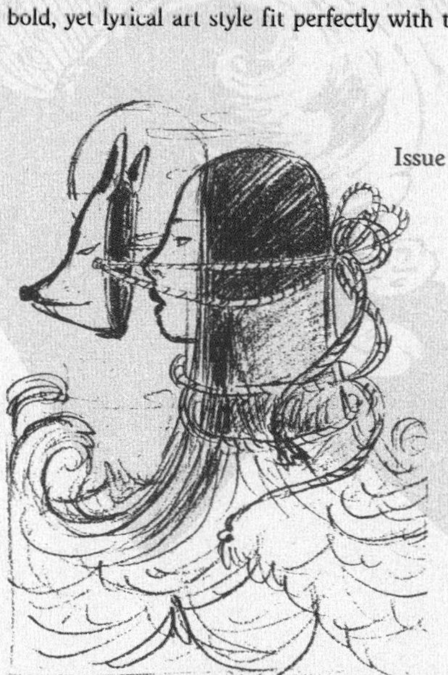

Issue #4

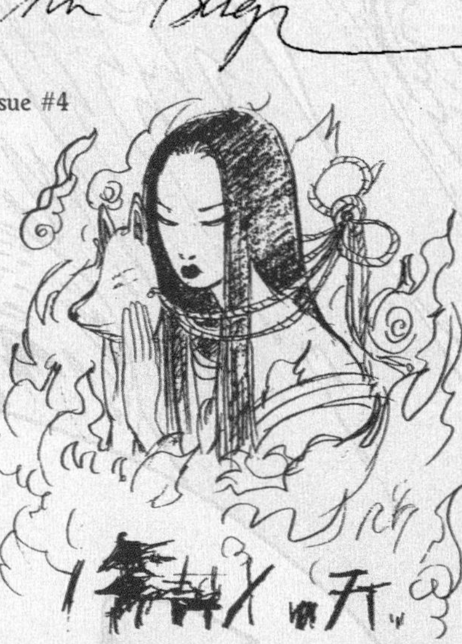

THE DREAM HUNTERS #1 cover by Yuko Shimizu

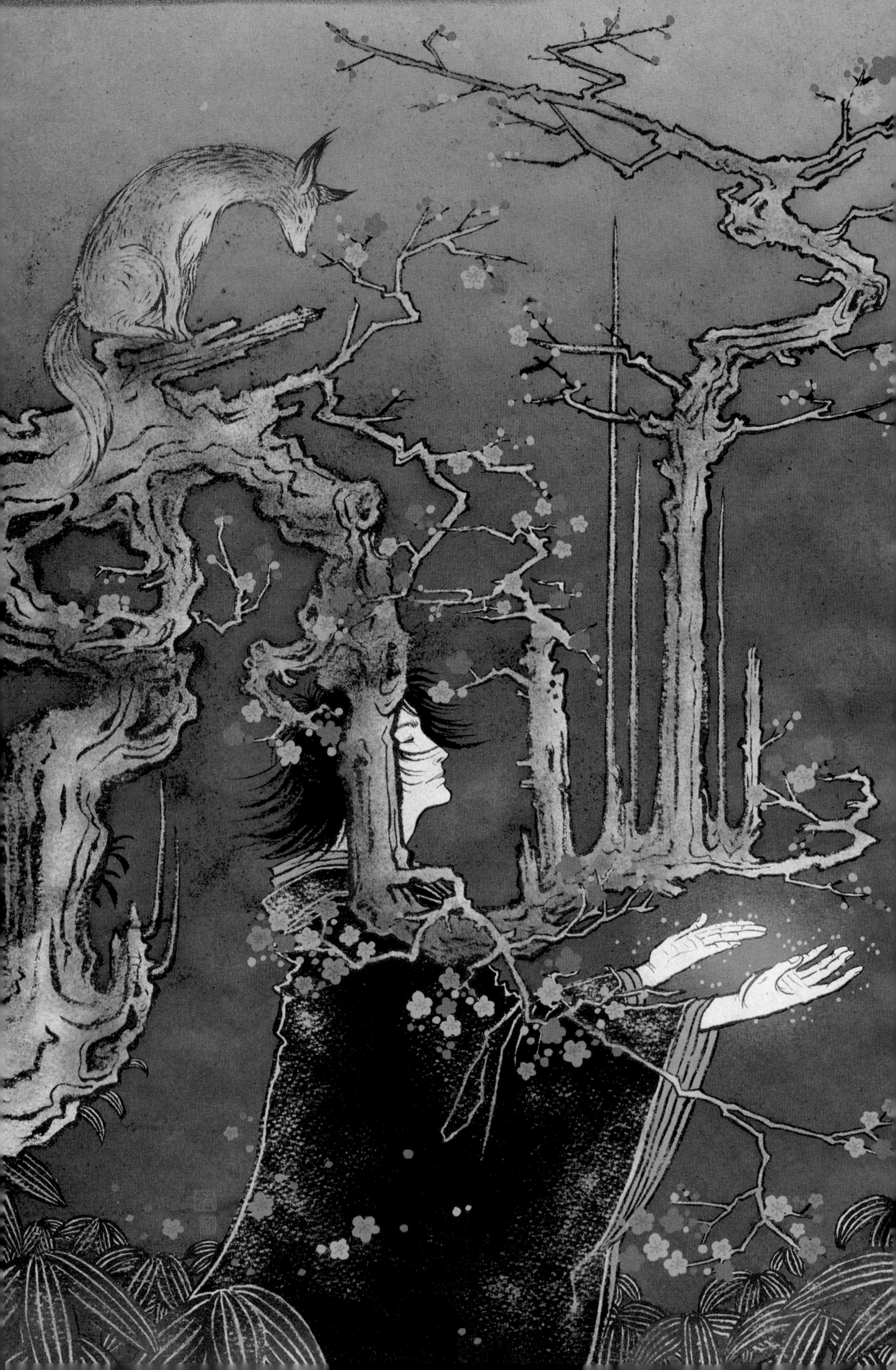

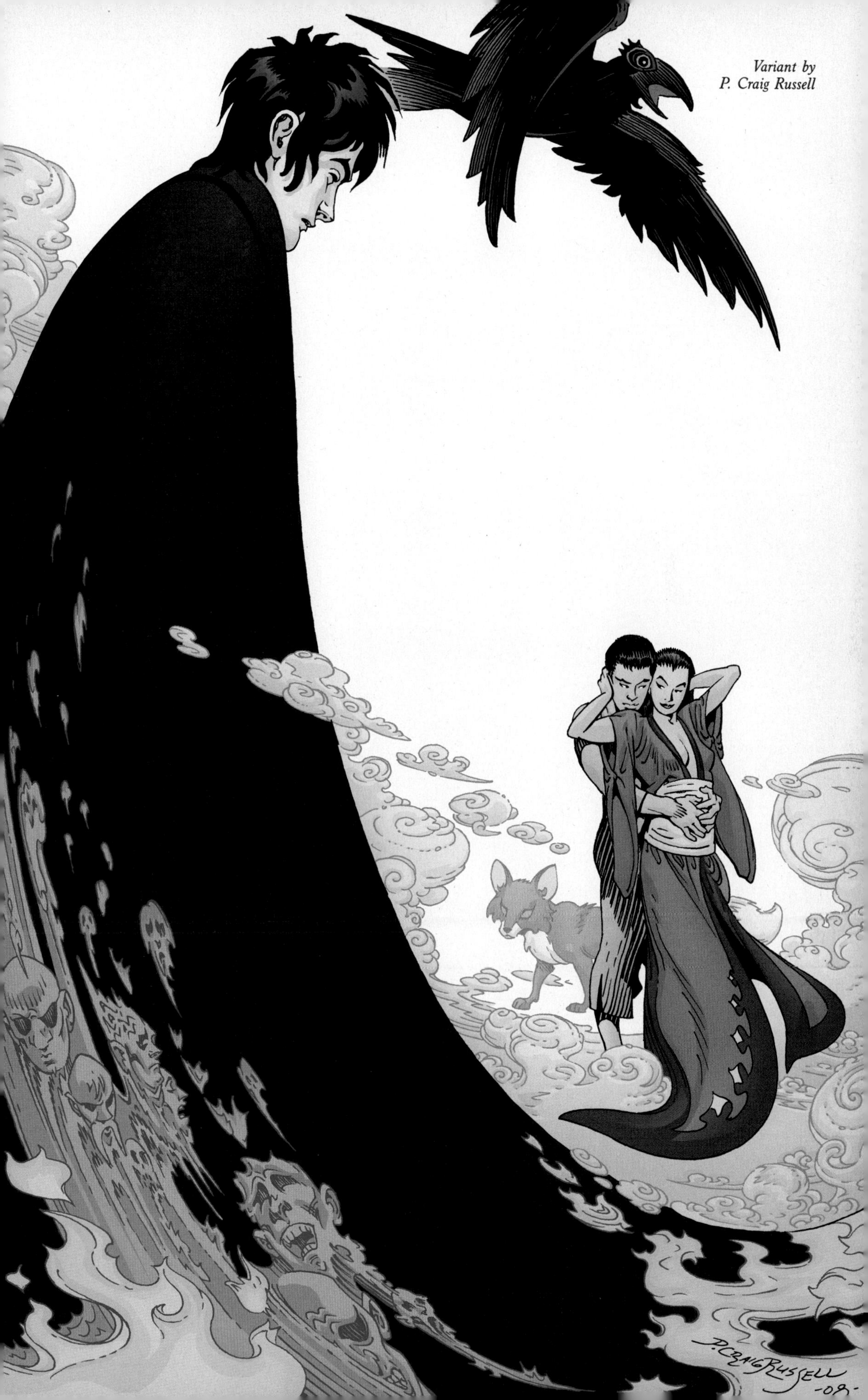
P. CRAIG RUSSELL
-09-

Variant by
P. Craig Russell

THE DREAM HUNTERS #2 cover by Yuko Shimizu

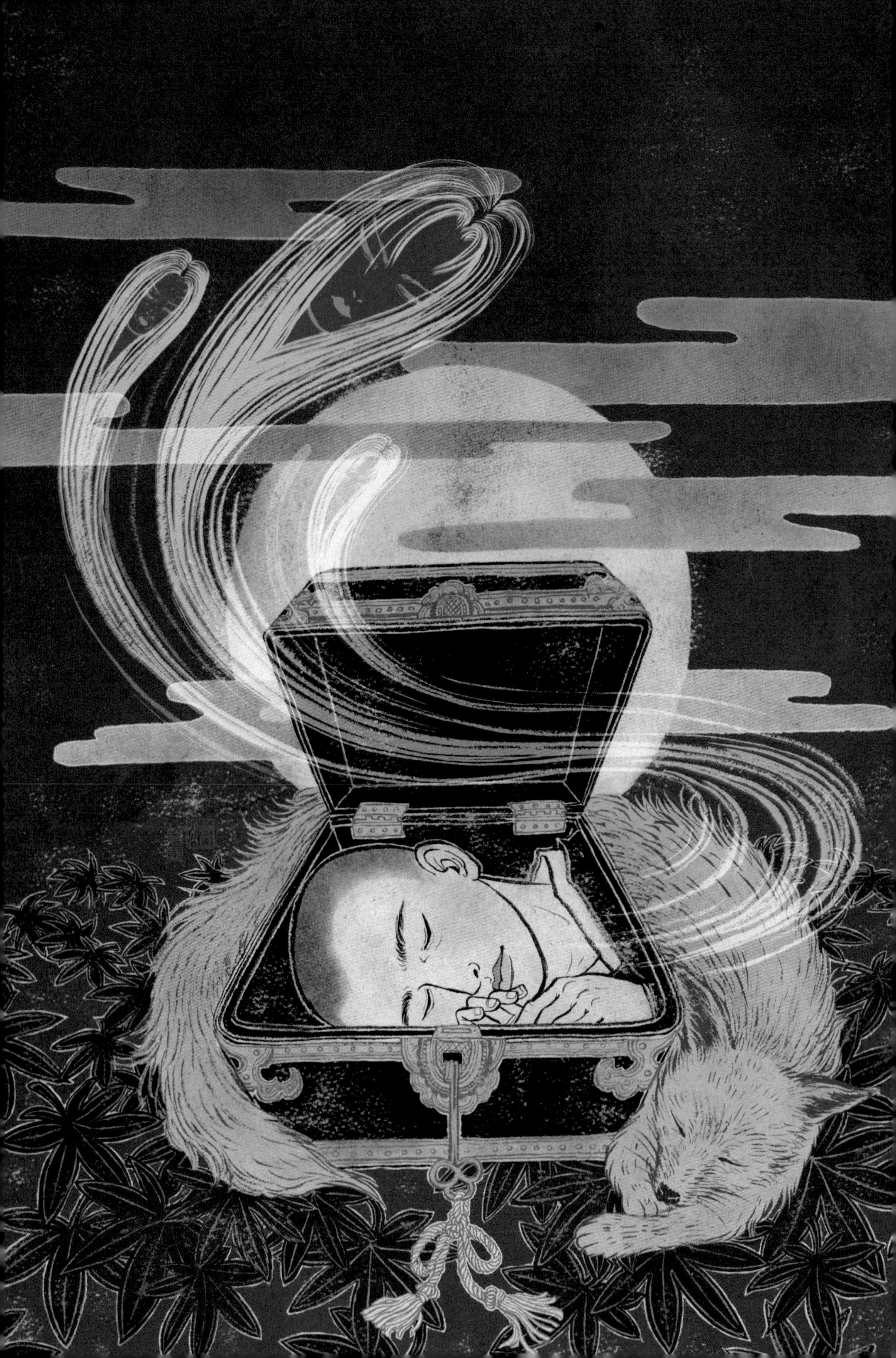

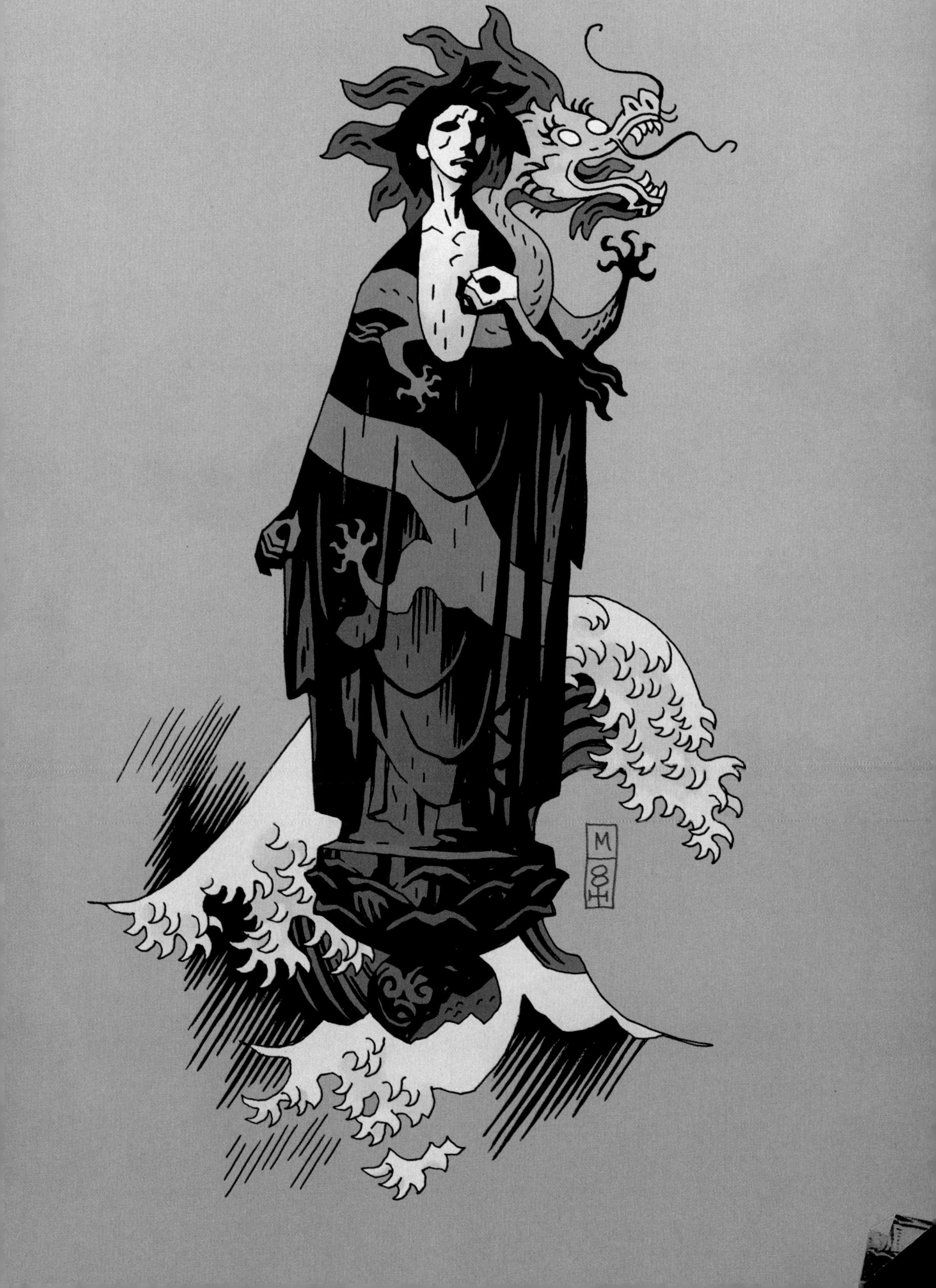

Variant by Mike Mignola

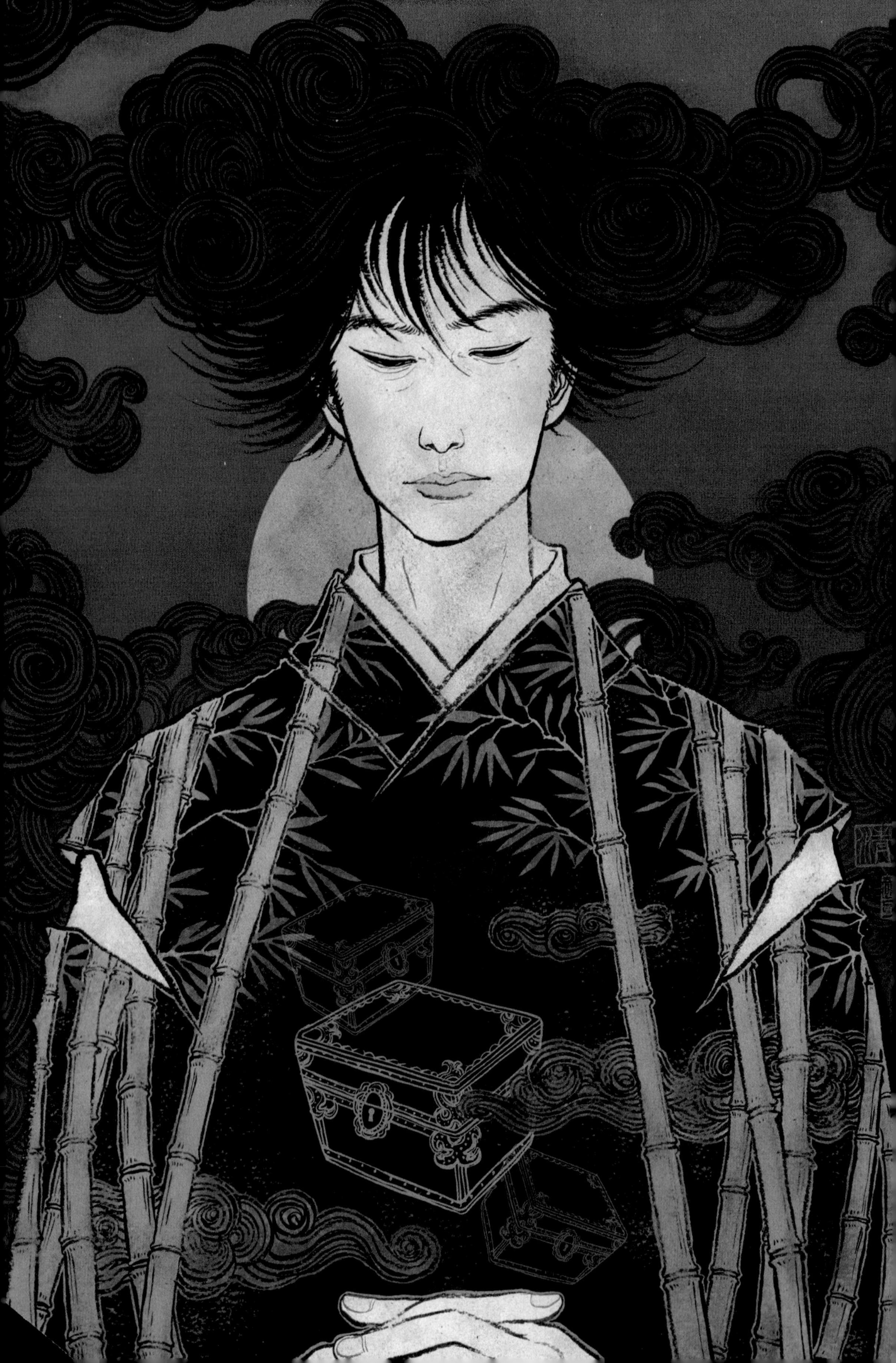

THE DREAM HUNTERS #3 cover by Yuko Shimizu

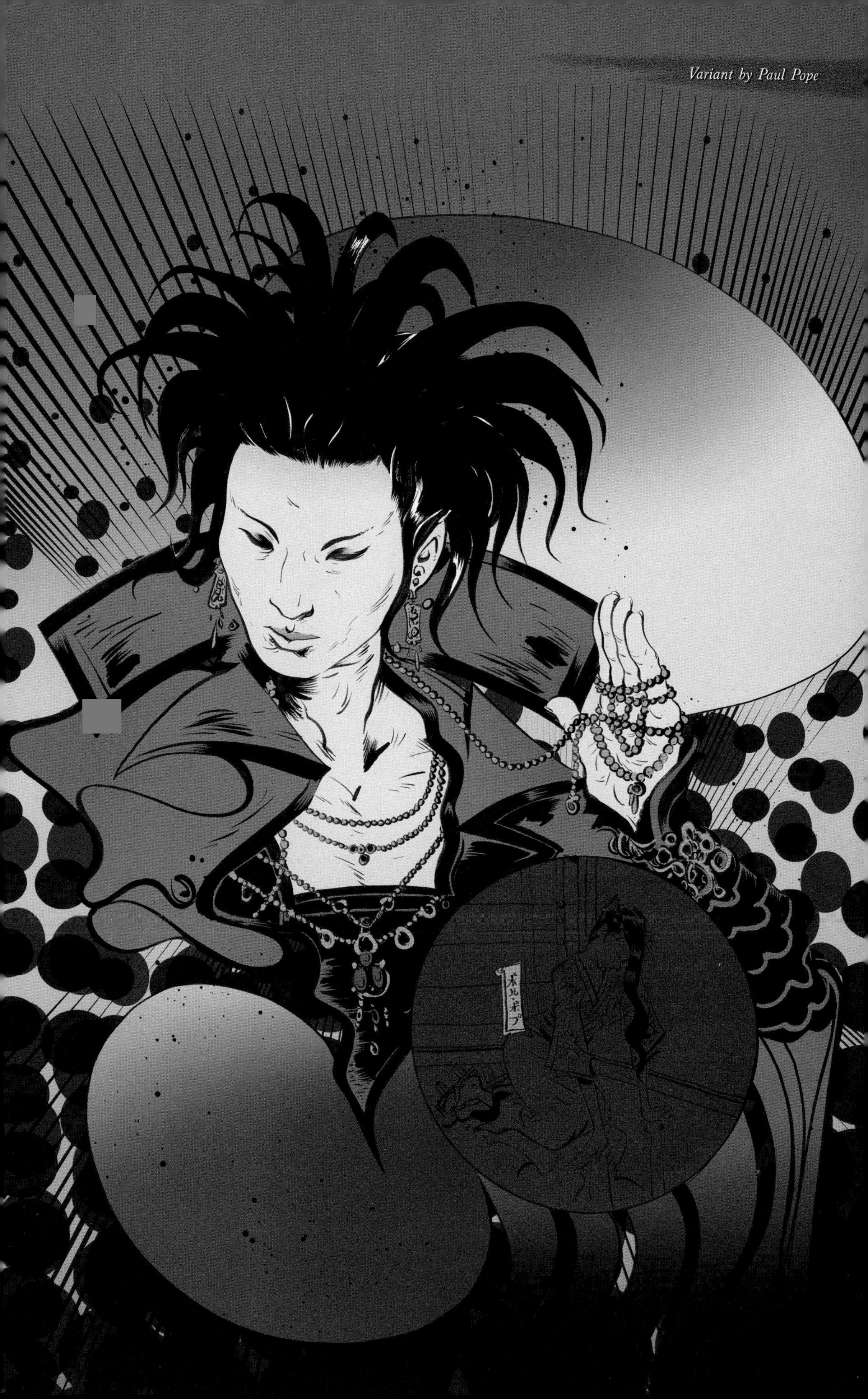
ポル・ポプ

Variant by Paul Pope

THE DREAM HUNTERS #4 cover by Yuko Shimizu

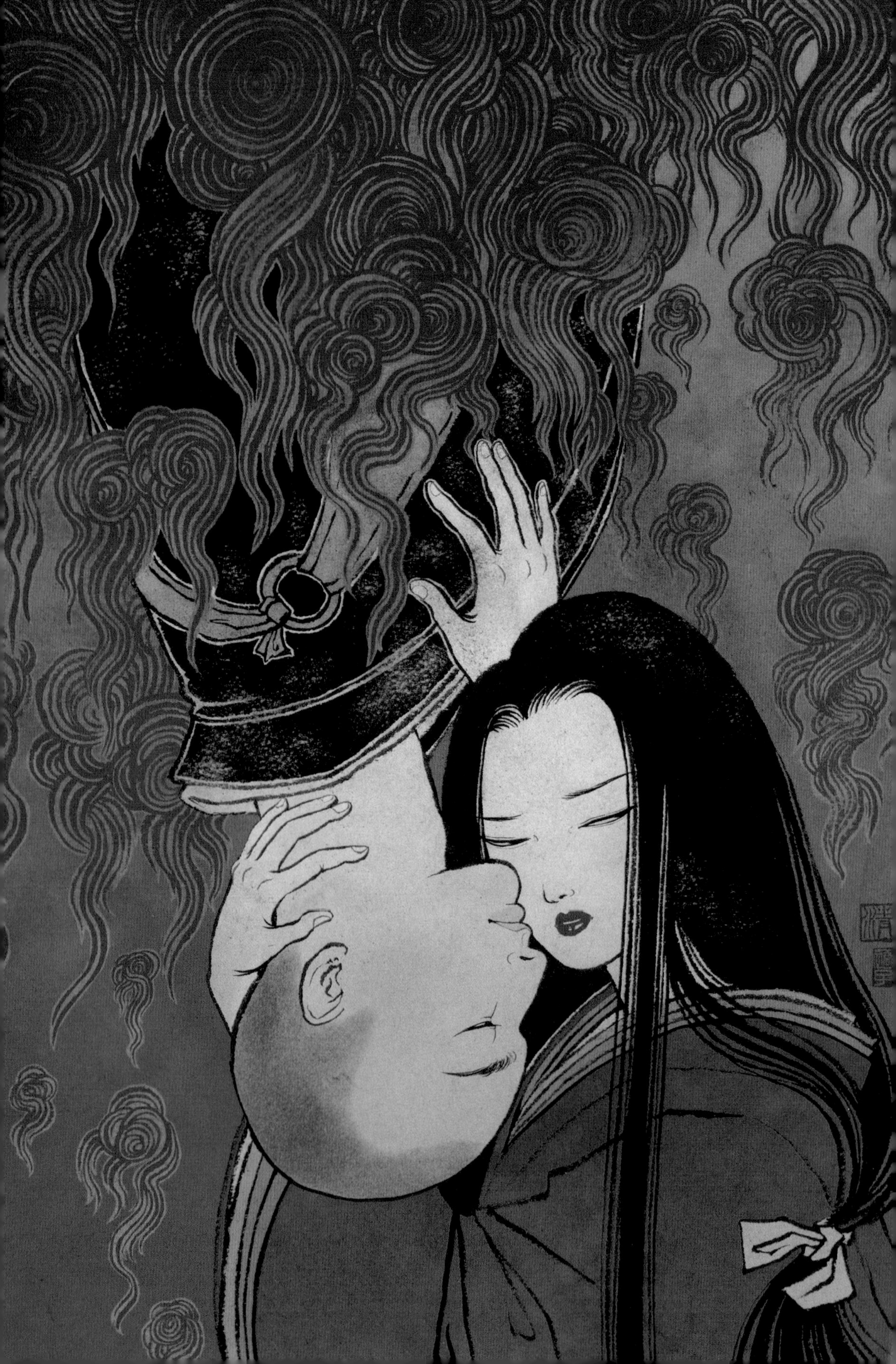

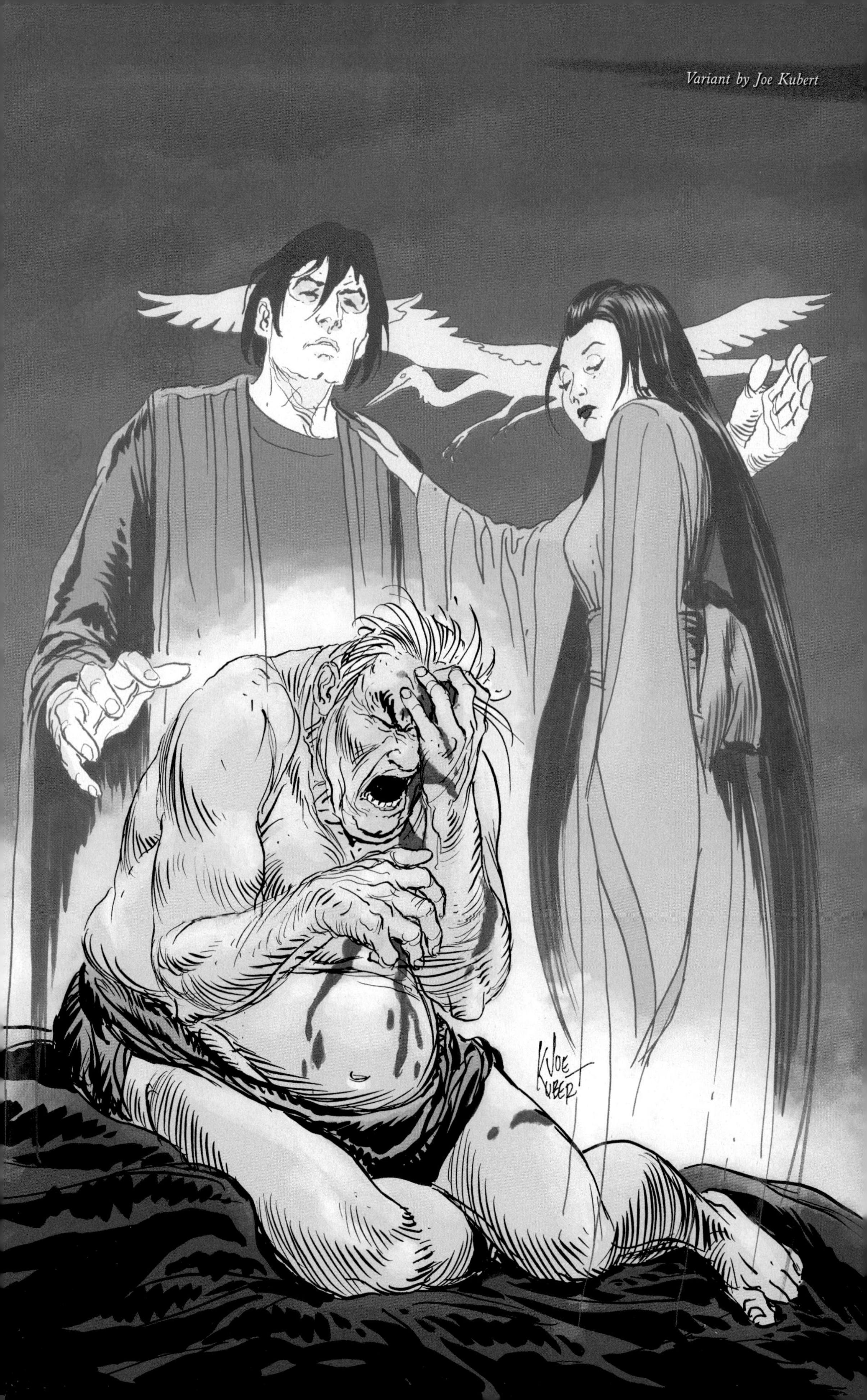

Variant by Joe Kubert

THE DREAM HUNTERS #2 title page by P. Craig Russell

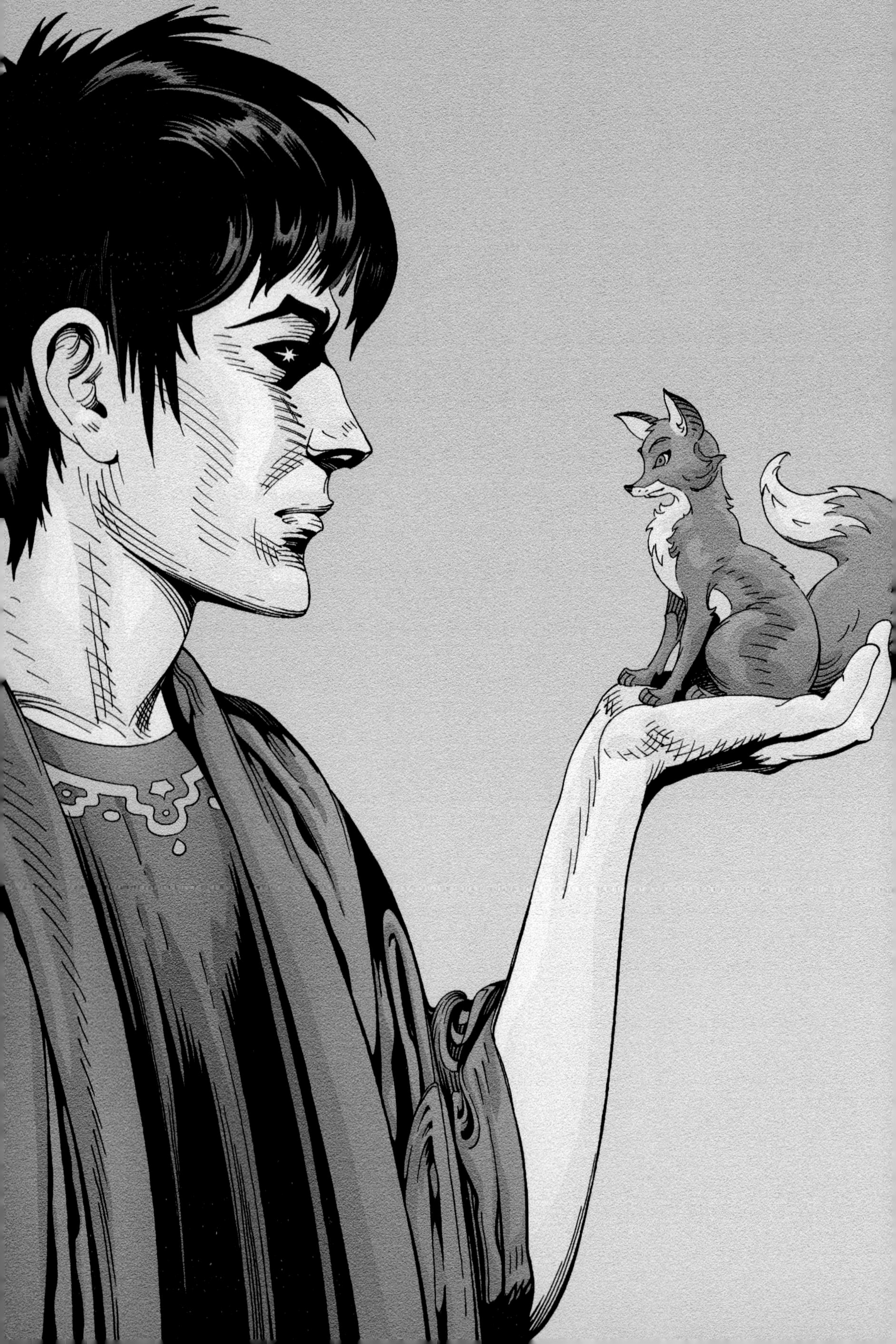

THE DREAM HUNTERS #3 title page by P. Craig Russell

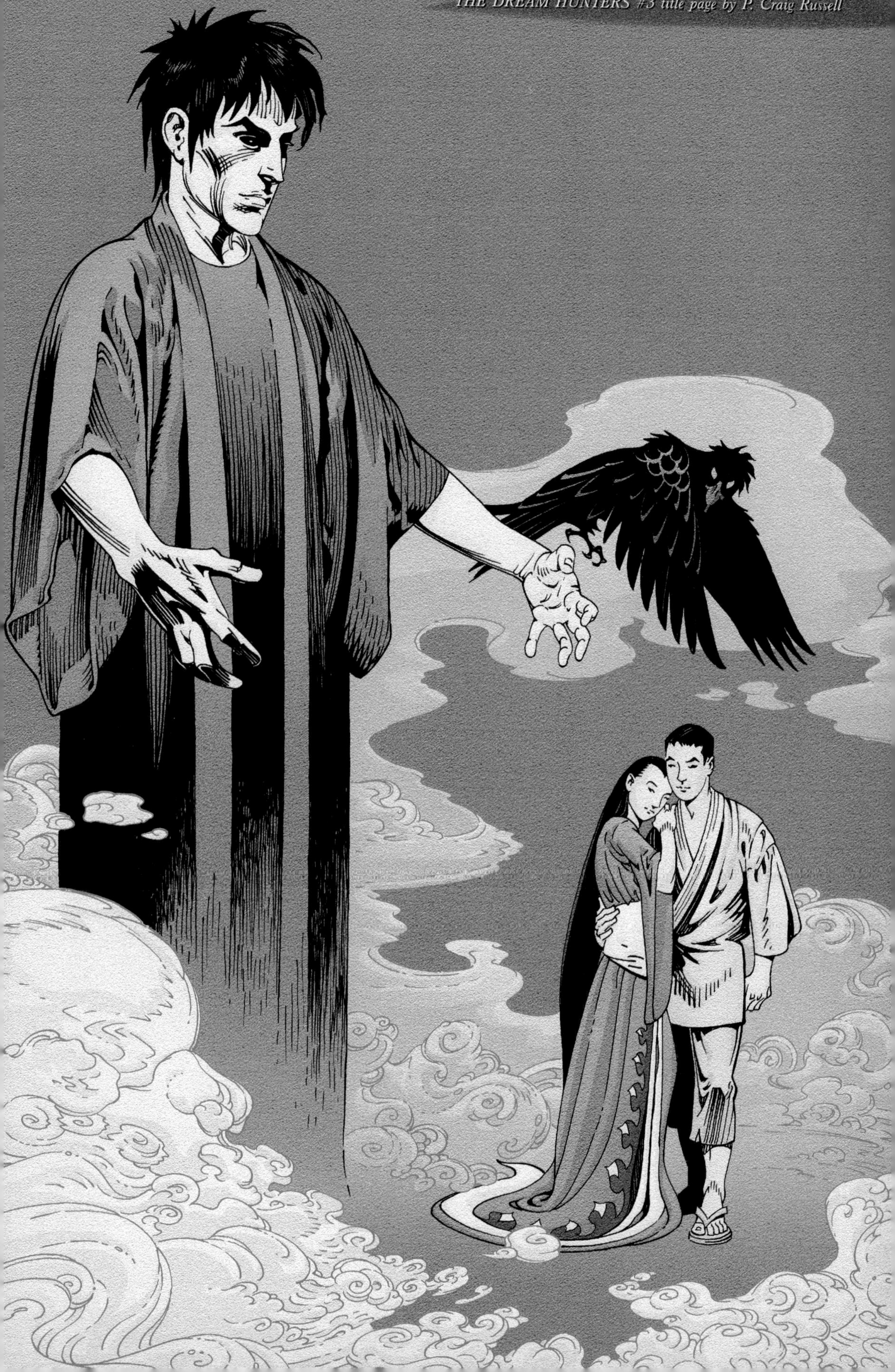

THE DREAM HUNTERS #4 title page by P. Craig Russell

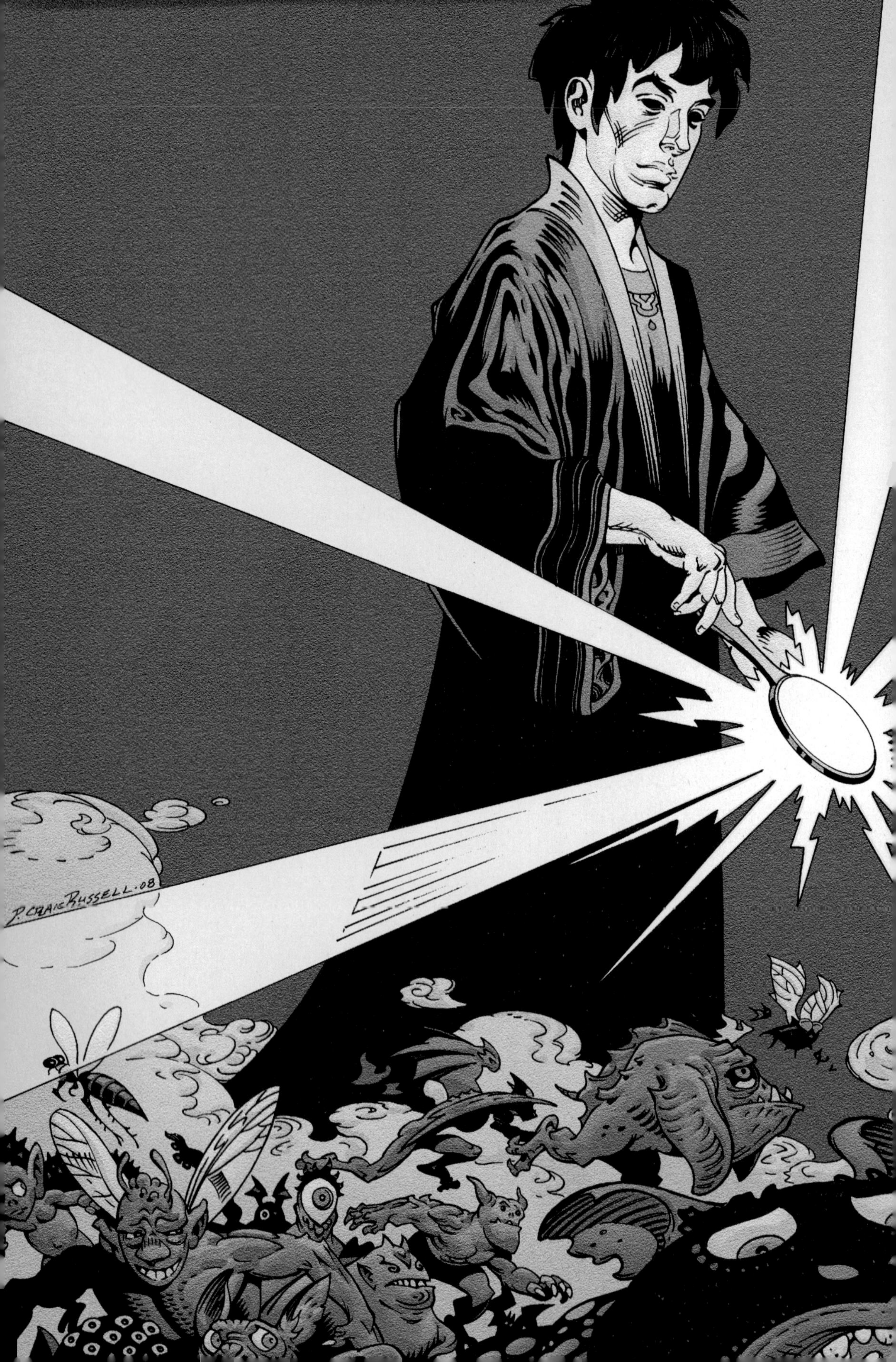
P. CRAIG RUSSELL · 08

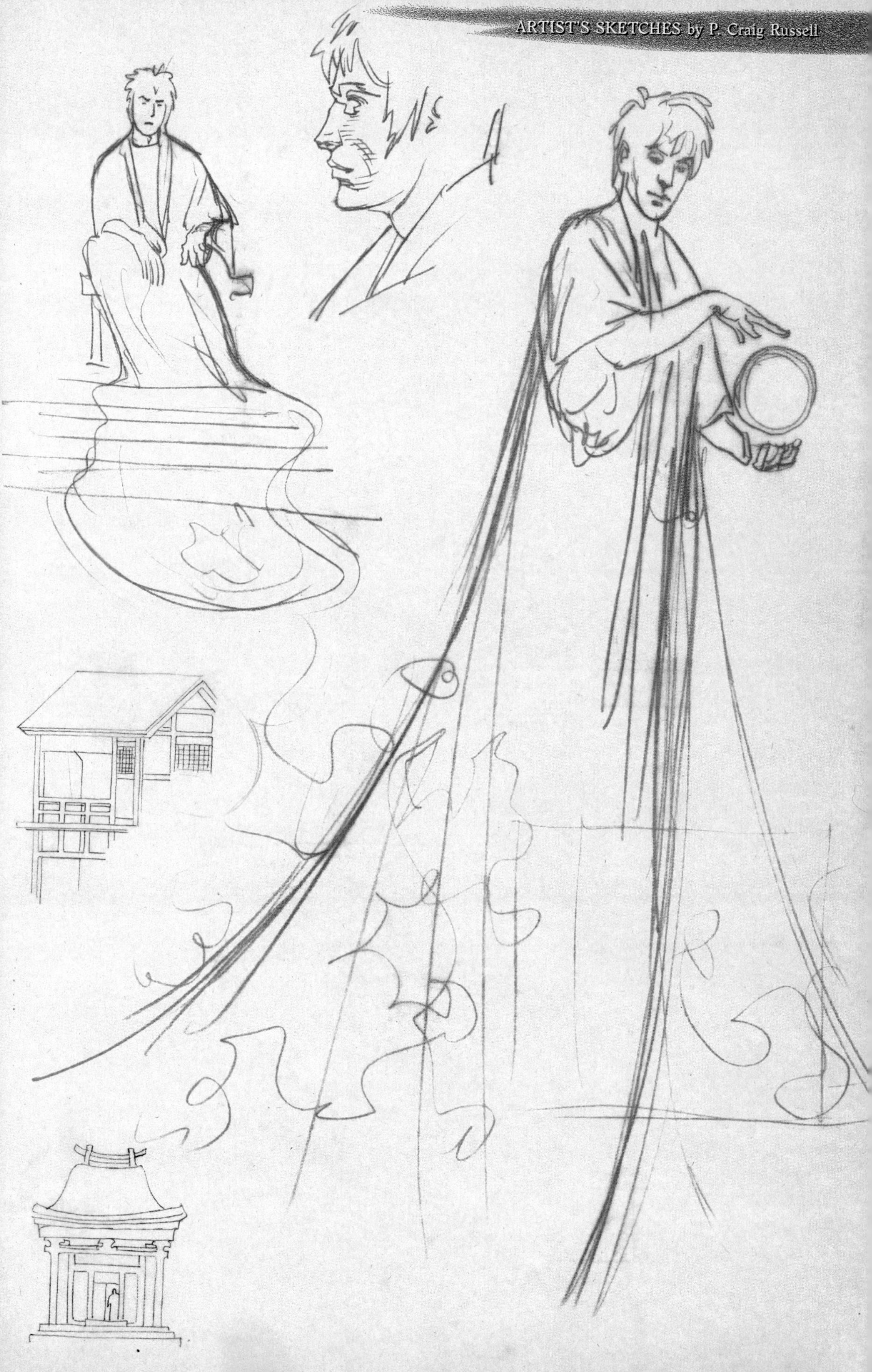

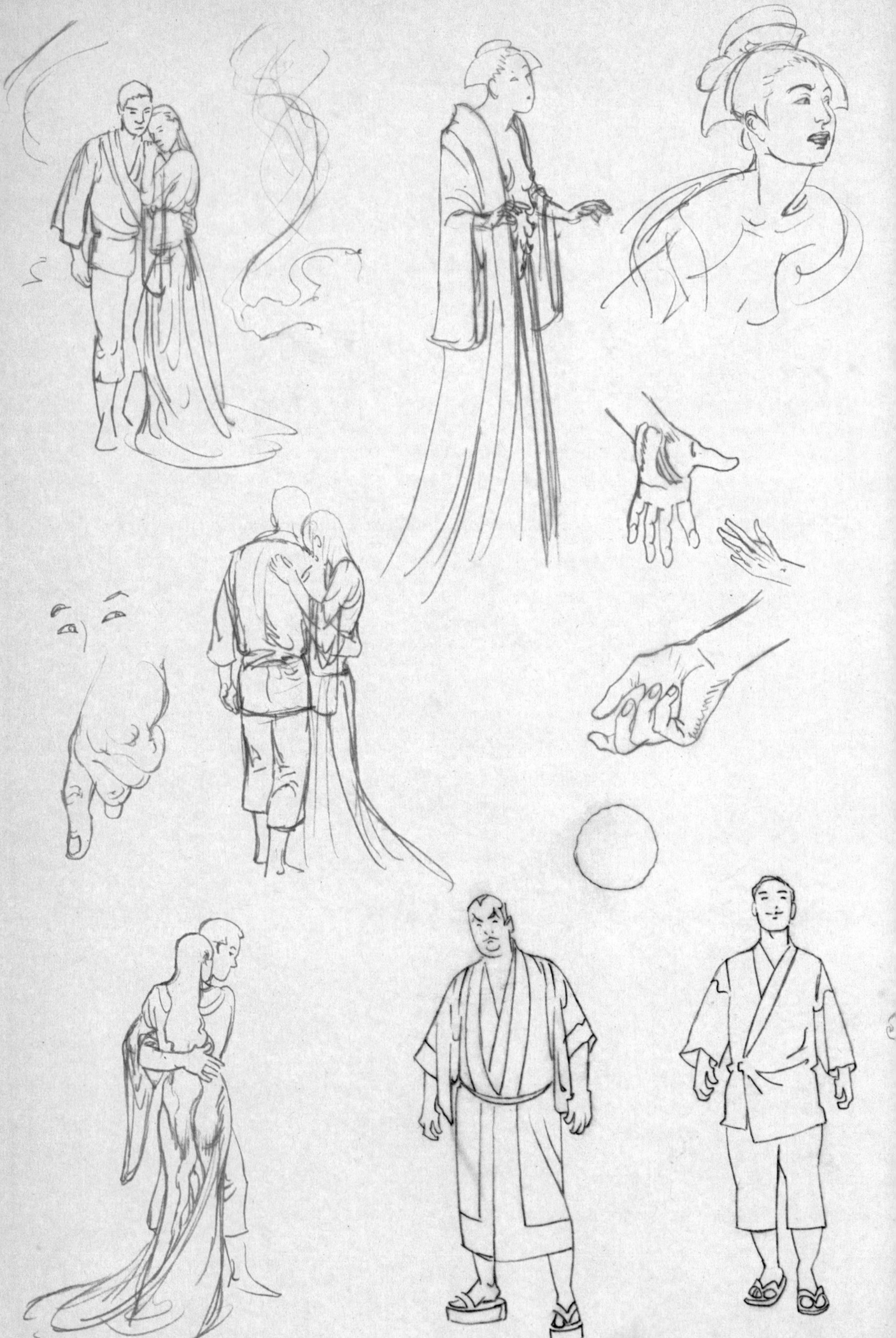

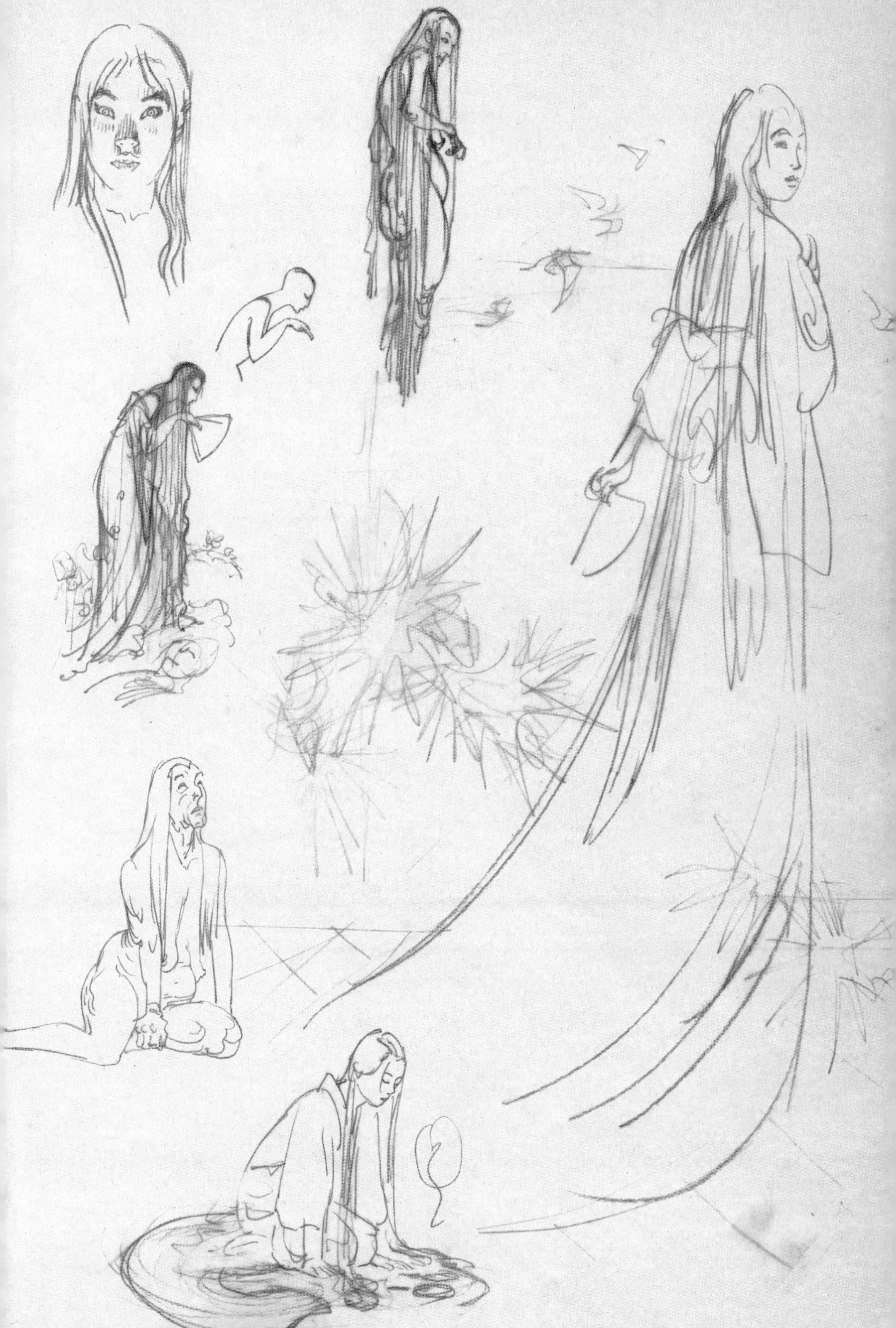

NEIL GAIMAN is the *New York Times* best-selling author of the Newbery Medal-winning *The Graveyard Book* and *Coraline*, the basis for the hit movie. His other books include *Anansi Boys*, *Neverwhere*, *American Gods* and *Stardust* (winner of the American Library Association's Alex Award as one of 2000's top novels for young adults) and the short story collections *M Is for Magic* and *Smoke and Mirrors*. He is also the author of *The Wolves in the Walls* and *The Day I Traded My Dad for Two Goldfish*, both written for children. Among his many awards are the Eisner, Hugo, Nebula, World Fantasy and the Bram Stoker. Originally from England, he now lives in the United States.

P. CRAIG RUSSELL lives in Kent, Ohio, and has been producing comic books, illustrations and graphic novels for 35 years. His work ranges from mainstream titles such as BATMAN, *Star Wars* and *Conan* to a series of adaptations of classic operas (*The Magic Flute, Salome, I Pagliacci, The Ring of the Nibelung*), a series of Jungle Book stories, and an ongoing series adapting the complete fairy tales of Oscar Wilde. He has collaborated with Neil Gaiman on five projects, including THE SANDMAN #50 and *Coraline*.

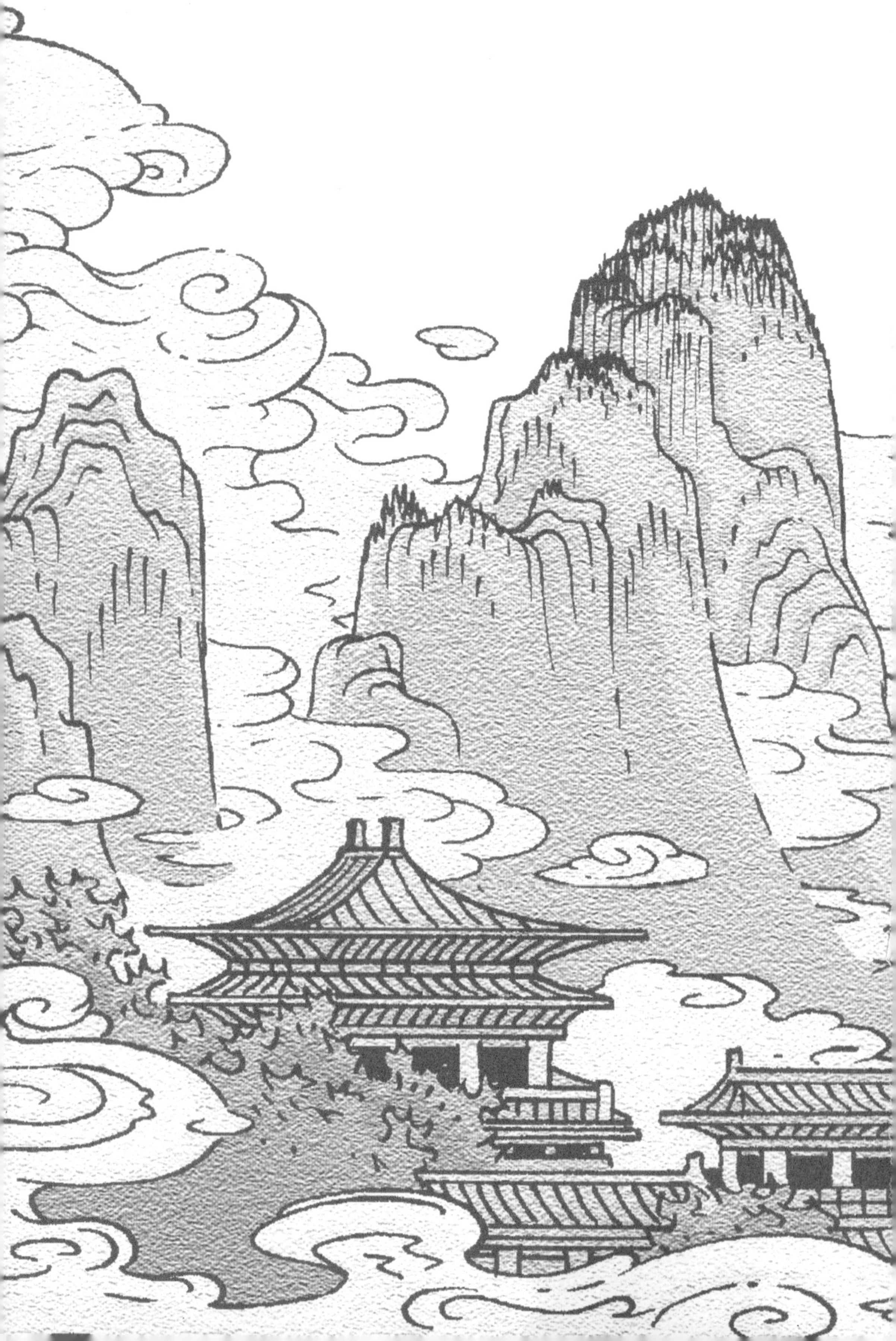